M

A Season

DAN GABLE AND
THE PURSUIT OF
PERFECTION

Simon & Schuster

on the Mat

Nolan Zavoral

 **SIMON & SCHUSTER**
Rockefeller Center
1230 Avenue of the Americas
New York, NY 10020

10 9 8 7 6 5 4 3 2 1

Library of Congress Cataloging-in-Publication Data

Zavoral, Nolan.
    A season on the mat : Dan Gable and the pursuit of
perfection / Nolan Zavoral.
        p.   cm.
    Includes index.
    1. Gable, Dan.   2. Wrestling coaches—United
States—Biography.   3. Iowa Hawkeyes (Wrestling
team)   I. Title.
GV1196.G33Z39   1998
796.812'092—dc21
[B]   97-51494   CIP
ISBN 0-684-84787-6

Photo Credits:
1,2,3: Photos courtesy of the Iowa State University
men's sports information office
4,6,8,11,12,14,15,17: The Des Moines Register
5,7,9,10,16,18: The Cedar Rapids Gazette
13: Charlie Neibergall

Acknowledgments

THIS BOOK could not have been written without the incredible access and cooperation that Dan Gable provided, and I thank him. Time always went quickly in his presence.

The University of Iowa wrestlers almost without exception opened themselves and their sport to me, even during the trying times of practice and weight cutting. Trainers Kristen Payne and Jerod Gayer welcomed me into the circle of the team and were both personable and professional.

Thanks, too, to these people, champions all: Annie Breitenbucher, for her unshakable belief that I was meant to write this book; Ira Berkow, for serving as midwife to the book and generously allowing me to tap his talent; Kathy Vinge, for her diligence and wonderful good humor in meeting transcription deadlines; Toni Mendez and Jeannette Smith, for leading me through the maze of publishing and giving agents a good name; Jeff Neuman, for his editor's eye, heart, and backbone.

Others: Archbishop Harry Flynn and publicist Tim Anderson of the Archdiocese of St. Paul and Minneapolis; the monks of St. John's Abbey, Collegeville, Minnesota, and the school's wrestling coach, John Elton; filmmakers David Gould, Bryan Less, and Kevin Kelley; and journalist Randy Brubaker.

I found helpful, and nearly indispensable, Russ Smith's

5

book, *Dan Gable: "The" Wrestler,* as well as Mike Chapman's *From Gotch to Gable.*

Finally, F.A.B. and C.A.Z. won't expect thanks but are getting it anyway.

For Pal (1914–92)

chapter 1

THE TEAM BUS shouldered through spitting snow, heading north and west out of Iowa City, up two-lane highways empty of traffic. It was Thanksgiving Day, 1996, and in farmhouses glowing with lights it wasn't difficult to imagine the smell of roasting turkey and the garbled chorus of family voices. A different kind of family was riding in the bus, a fraternity of athletes with Popeye arms and Olive Oyl waists: the University of Iowa wrestling team, two-time defending NCAA champions, coached by Dan Gable.

The team had already spent six weeks in the wrestling room, drilling and fighting for starting berths, and now the Hawkeyes were ready to open the 1996–97 season in a double-dual meet against South Dakota State and Buena Vista University on Friday night in Spencer, Iowa. Last year's team had given Gable his fourteenth national title in his twenty years at Iowa, and while two individual champions had graduated, the cupboard was hardly bare: *Amateur Wrestling News*, the Oklahoma-based monthly that is the bible of the sport, ranked the Hawkeyes No. 1 in its preseason poll. Gable anticipated another strong season—if he could get through it. If he could *last*.

When he got off the bus after the five-and-a-half-hour

trip, Gable was stiff and sore. Arthritis had padlocked his joints, made movement such a chore that he needed help tying his shoes. At age forty-eight—bespectacled and balding, standing five-foot-eight, unremarkable in appearance—Gable walks like an old man, a listing, creaking ship with leaks. He had long contemplated a life outside of coaching, and he was thinking about it now more than ever.

Wrestling had done this to him, but it also had given him an Olympic gold medal to encase behind glass and display on his mantle. It had allowed him the chance to visit the Carter White House (after turning down Nixon's invitation because Gable preferred to use the time to train). It conferred upon him a measure of fame and status, and he was known and admired in the unlikeliest circles. In the November 1996 *GQ* cover story, actor Tom Cruise spoke reverentially about Gable's fighting spirit and dedication.

In his prime, in the late 1960s and early '70s, Danny Mack Gable was a fierce *sumbitch*. Nobody trained harder. Dislocated fingers were popped back so he could resume practice. It was rumored that he sometimes pushed himself to such limits in the Iowa State wrestling room that he had to be taken out on a stretcher. Not true, Gable said, almost wistfully. "At the time, my goal was to not be able to get back to my feet to get out of there," he later recalled. "A couple of times I was so exhausted that I would start crawling towards the door. Then I'd be good enough to get to my feet. So I never really did do it, but that was my goal." He mowed the lawn in double layers of sweats during sweltering Iowa summers, half-running, to keep in shape. The day after winning a gold medal in Munich, he ran four miles.

For most of his career, Gable was unconquerable up to 150 pounds. As a scrawny, nerdy-looking 95-to-112-pound wrestler at Waterloo (Iowa) West High, he won sixty-four straight matches and three state championships. He won another 117 straight at Iowa State University and two NCAA titles before the national championships of his senior year on a snowy night in March 1970, in Evanston, Illinois. ("TITLE TO CYCLONES—GABLE FAILS!" screamed the headline in the state newspaper, the *Des Moines Register.*) For the next two years, Gable worked out three times a day, eight hours of running and lifting and hard wrestling, striving for Olympic perfection. He got it; in the 1972 Summer Olympics in Munich—before the Black September slaying of Israeli athletes—Gable went undefeated in his six matches, pinning three opponents and shutting out three. No one scored on him, even though he competed on a damaged left knee that required surgery a year later. The feat towers in Olympic wrestling history. "If he were in the World Series, it would be the equivalent of pitching two no-hitters," Iowa State coach Bobby Douglas said. "You just don't do that."

Gable jumped from competing to coaching with barely a twitch, becoming one of the most successful coaches in the history of college athletics. Under Gable, Iowa has never lost a Big Ten title, winning twenty in a row entering the 1996–97 season, but that hardly mattered to him. "The one that matters is at the end of the season—the nationals," he said. "That's what you work the whole year toward. The rest just gets you ready."

His teams had amassed a 340–20–5 dual meet record and had not lost in more than two years. Gable coached the 1984 U.S. Olympic freestyle team that won seven of ten gold medals in Los Angeles in the absence of the powerful Russians. Three American gold medalists—Randy Lewis and the Banach brothers, Ed and Lou—had wrestled for Gable at Iowa; a silver medalist, Barry Davis, returned in the fall for his senior year at Iowa and won his third national title.

Iowa teams were molded in Gable's image: tough and relentless, attacking constantly. The coach made sure of that. He once barricaded the 1995–96 team in the locker-room sauna until they figured out that they should wrestle hard for the team as well as for personal glory. Six weeks later, the Hawkeyes won another national title.

On the Thanksgiving night, Gable and his team ate at Maxwell's, on West Okoboji Lake. In summer, the area serves as the Iowa Riviera—deep glacial lakes spread over pool-table prairie. Now, as winter set in, the lakes had frozen and the tourists were gone. Riding around the lake, Gable guessed at the cost of expensive homes; his father, a hard-drinking realtor many years ago, before his stroke, would know better.

Gable sat at a candle-lit table with his wife, Kathy, and their four daughters, who ranged in age from eight to nineteen. Christmas lights framed the windows that faced the lake. From a buffet, the athletes and the coaches and their families wolfed down turkey and dressing, mashed and baked potatoes, cranberry sauce, and bread and biscuits and pies. Gable looked up when one of his assistant coaches, Tom Brands, a 1996 Olympic gold medalist, rose, shrugged into his jacket, and announced, "I'm going for a walk on the lake. Who's coming?"

A couple of wrestlers followed him into the eerie glow of snow under moonlight, the lake vast and frozen. One of Gable's daughters asked her father if it was all right, Brands and the others walking out onto the lake at night. What if something happened?

Gable smirked. "It's OK," he said. "He's only a coach."

Gable didn't eat much. He'd had an upset stomach, and it was hanging on. He drank water. He loved the smell of coffee, but never drank it because he couldn't abide its taste. When the Brands party returned, everyone filed to the door. A waitress thanked Gable, who was last in line.

"Good luck," she said, which caused him to square his shoulder to her and deliver his standard riposte.

"Luck? Ah, we don't want luck," he said. "Luck is when you win the lottery. Attitude: That's how you win."

Outside, the best amateur wrestling talent in the country was packing and firing snowballs. There was Jessie Whitmer, 118 pounds; he had waited four years for his chance to start and now here it was, less than twenty-four hours away. Tomorrow night, the Hawkeyes would meet Division II South Dakota State and then Buena Vista, a Division III school from Storm Lake, Iowa. Whitmer, a small-town Iowan like many on the team, had worked hard and lifted weights and built himself into a toy Schwarzenegger. Gable pecked at Whitmer through his varsity career, which consisted of forty matches, none of them in the crucible of NCAA championship competition, believing one day he would be a starter. In team meetings and practices, Gable hyped Whitmer's thickly muscled arms and chest ("Jessie Whitmer, strongest man in the world!"), although Gable also teased Whitmer that he needed lifts to make himself five feet tall and court his girlfriend. Gable liked Whitmer, who had absorbed four years of punishment with only a letter jacket that he wore all winter to show for it. "[Quitting] never crossed my mind," Whitmer said. "In my family, we just don't quit anything. Once you start, you're in it for good."

Whitmer took over at 118 after another fifth-year senior, Mike Mena, moved up to 126—though Mena was flirting with dropping back down. Gable, with his powerful presence and position, would try to convince him that his best weight was 126, but ultimately the decision would be Mena's. It was one of many ways in which Gable allowed his wrestlers to function as individuals in a team setting. Over the years, he had permitted wrestlers to skip practices and work out at times more in sync with either their biorhythms or their biology labs. Others he could push to the brink of their physical and emotional limits, until, like Barry Davis, they screamed their anguish at him—and then did what he said. With some wrestlers, in certain situations, Gable had chosen to become their worst enemy and their best friend. He once put 118-pound Tim Riley through such a grueling weight-cutting session that Riley retreated to his room and lay on his bed exhausted. Meanwhile, Gable went out and returned with a cardboard box and fed Riley small wedges of pizza.

Mena offered a different sort of challenge. He could scramble Iowa's lineup plans if he insisted on returning to 118 and won a "wrestle-off" against Whitmer. But Mena had had a hard enough time last season making the lower weight, and Gable thought that he was as formidable at 126 as he was at 118. For his part, Whitmer possessed uncommon strength for a 118-pounder, leading Gable to believe that he could surprise everyone and win the national title.

Mena needed to harness his hair-trigger emotions to capture the national title that had so far escaped him. He finished seventh and third in the 1994 and '95 NCAA championships, respectively, and after being ranked No. 1 at 118 all of last season, he placed fifth in 1996. "Right now I like where I'm at," he said early in the 1996–97 season. "I've honed my skills really well. I've got confidence. Winning [a national title] is a challenge; it's not [something I] fear anymore. Some people are scared. They're like, 'man, I'm not good enough.' Me, I think I'm good enough."

Around Mena, several teammates were throwing snowballs at one another or at the bus, making the metal thump like an electric bass. Mena pulled his stocking cap low over his head of curly, jet-black hair, and watched. Gable, limping and listing toward the bus, warned that he didn't want anyone getting hurt before the team even wrestled its first match.

"But this is just starting to get fun," one of the snowball-throwers said.

Mena perked up. He was the unmarried father of a three-year-old daughter, and he could mimic any parent.

"Oh, sure, it's always fun—until somebody gets hurt," he said.

"Shuddup, Mena," somebody said, and Mena bent to pack a snowball of his own.

In the middle of their lineup, the Hawkeyes offered college wrestling's version of Murderers' Row: Mark Ironside at 134 pounds, Lincoln McIlravy at 150, and Joe Williams at 158. Combined, they had a collegiate record of 217–21 and three NCAA titles—two for McIlravy and one for Williams.

Ironside, a junior from Cedar Rapids, Iowa, placed sixth in the 1995 NCAA championships in '96. He was a bulldog on the mat, his unceasing aggression stamping him as a Gable clone. "I grew up knowing who Dan Gable was and watching the Iowa teams on TV," Ironside said. "I *loved* watching that stuff. I'd tape all those matches and hit replay, and my brother and I would watch them snowball the tournament. Just domination. That's all it was. Domination. No looking back. Just a straight line. Wanting to win—that's the main thing—and going for it. And I knew if I wanted to be a national champion

—and I'm *going* to be a national champion—this was where I was going to do it."

Ironside, his expression forever locked between pensiveness and a scowl, hung out on the road with Williams, an African American and the only wrestler of color among the starting ten. Sculpted by gyms and genetics, with a twenty-nine-inch waist, Williams possessed a Greek god's body. He won the NCAA's 158-pound title in 1996 and lost only once in thirty-seven matches. He had lapses in concentration that worried Gable, times when he cruised in matches and didn't win as convincingly as he should have. He was a four-time state high-school champion in Illinois, each year at a different weight, 135 to 160. "Lost a match my freshman year, the only time in high school," Williams remembered. "I was winning, 12–1, and I slammed the kid, and I was disqualified. [Unnecessary roughness is grounds for disqualification.] That kind of sucked, but I think that the loss in the long run helped me, got me focused a little bit more."

McIlravy, prone to facial cuts and concussions, was a fifth-year senior who took off last season to train for an Olympic team he failed to make. Sometimes in the heat and clamor of the Iowa wrestling room McIlravy would stare at the framed black-and-white photographs of past Iowa national champions, and he would fasten on Ed Banach, a two-time winner at 177 before finishing second in 1982 and winning the 190-pound title in 1983. "I looked at it as a freshman, and I thought, How could you possibly be on top twice, and then not be on top?" But it had happened to McIlravy. He won national titles in 1993 and '94, then finished second in '95—in Iowa City, no less. Gable left the day after for a Hawaiian vacation, but was consumed by McIlravy's defeat. "I got on the plane, and I pulled a cap down over my eyes, 'cause I was bawling like a baby," Gable said. "I was leaving the city, and we'd won, yeah, but I felt for my athletes. I felt for Lincoln. If you'd seen the look on McIlravy's face on the [medal] stand, you'd know what I mean. I thought he was gonna die."

McIlravy—a South Dakotan with burnt blond hair, a wife, and a baby due in April—already had lodged himself in Gable's mind as a contender for the title of greatest wrestler in University of Iowa history. It would depend on how McIlravy did this season, and how he would fare in subsequent Olympic attempts. McIlravy was a smooth, intuitive wrestler, probing the length of an opponent's body for a weakness like a man eating an ear of corn. His three-year collegiate record was 74–3–9. "McIlravy and Ironside are a lot alike, mentally," Gable observed. "When they smell blood, they don't let up. Williams might."

Mike Uker, a 167-pound senior, and Lee Fullhart, a 190-pound sophomore, both placed in the top eight last season in the NCAA championships, for which they earned All-American honors. Uker finished eighth at 150, but this season he would jump two weights, to 167, because McIlravy was returning at 150 and Williams was immovable at 158. Uker said that adding weight wouldn't be a problem, and his confidence on that point was understandable considering that his girlfriend waited tables at Joensy's, a corner restaurant in Solon, near Iowa City—an establishment advertising "Iowa's biggest and best tenderloins." Uker, smiling and amiable, a native of Osage, Iowa, wrote reminders to himself in black pen and taped them to his locker. One read:

> Bend knees
> Big Ten champion
> NCAA champion

"If I bend my knees, it's a way for me not to be taken down. It's a way for me to take other guys down," Uker said. "It's a way to win nationals."

Fullhart, from Decorah, Iowa, had expressive dark eyes that seemed to speak before he did. He missed six weeks last season because of knee surgery, but returned to help Iowa win the national title. "Actually, I should have done better [than fourth]," he said. "I didn't perform that well. Part of it was an unusual situation, me just being there, and I didn't have it together in the semifinals." Fullhart was worn out, Gable said, as McIlravy had been when he lost in the NCAA championships in Iowa City. Gable vowed that Fullhart would not run out of gas this time.

On Friday night, Fullhart would open the season against his younger brother, Bob, a freshman at South Dakota State. Bob expected to lose. "I'm not as intense about it as Lee," he said. "He goes all-out all year all the time. Wrestling is his life. He's pushed himself, doing what he wants to do. In some ways I envy him. He wants to wrestle and go on to be an Olympic champ. I don't. I want to go hunting and fishing when I want to."

Heavyweight Wes Hand and 142-pounder Kasey Gilliss, both freshmen, and Tony Ersland, a 177-pound senior, were uncertain commodities on Gable's squad. None had started previously or gotten closer to NCAA tournament competition than the bleachers. Hand, from Tama, Iowa, spoke in the studied speech that Iowans take from the farm. He sat by himself on the bus, content. "I was recruited by four schools, but it was Iowa all along," he said. "People pushed money—scholarship money—at me, and it was hard to turn down, but not when I thought about wrestling for Gable.

"He's extraordinary. I knew he would be, but it goes way beyond that. It's like he knows what you need to learn before you need it. I don't know—those are just words. You have to be around him to see it."

With his blond bangs and natural insouciance, Gilliss more resembled a surfer from Malibu, California, than a wrestler from Bismarck, North Dakota, where he won three state titles. Gilliss would be expected to fill a major hole created by the graduation of Bill Zadick, a tough Montanan who won the 142-pound national title as a senior last season. Gilliss possessed big scoring moves but still unnerved Gable. "I've got a lot to learn about him," Gable said. "He's been a winner, and we need him to score, but I want him to add basic stuff, like leg tackles." Nevertheless, Gilliss's emergence, coupled with Whitmer moving in at 118 and Mena moving up to 126, freed Gable to give Jeff McGinness a redshirt year to train. McGinness, a four-time state champion from Iowa City, won the NCAA's 126-pound title as a sophomore in 1995, but in 1996 began having trouble making weight and lost his composure in the NCAA championships, where he failed to make the top eight.

As for Ersland, Gable had been urging him throughout the last two weeks of practice to pick up the pace and push his physical limits—"C'mon, Tony, *move!*" Sleepy-eyed and quiet-spoken, Ersland was from Humboldt, the farming community in northwest Iowa that produced Frank Gotch, who made big money in the early 1900s wrestling professionally throughout the country and world. Ersland was well aware of the tradition he sprang from; he also seemed aware of his own shortcomings. When during the 1996–97 season he read an opposing coach's statement in a newspaper about supposed "holes in the Iowa lineup," he stalked into Gable's office and slammed down the paper. " 'Holes in the Iowa lineup!' " he thundered. "They mean me. They mean *me!*"

Gable hoped the Ersland would use that outrage as motivation to plug that hole. Gable's goal every year wasn't just to win the NCAA championships, but to have a national champion at every weight. Anything less was too low an aspiration to be worthy of the pursuit.

In the morning, Gable and most of his wrestlers spilled out of their rooms in Okoboji's Village East motel and congregated in the sauna and hot tub. Gable had ordered them to "loosen up a little, get a sweat going." Gable wore black swim trunks and tortoise-shell glasses. Nearing full baldness, he had little more than a monk's tonsure of red hair circling his head. His body was lean and hard.

Nearly twenty-five years after his last match, Gable still kept in shape, working out daily, doing what his body permitted: riding an exercise bike, lifting weights. He peered across the pool at an exercise room that contained, among other apparatuses, a rowing machine. No, Gable said, he couldn't consider rowing. "My hips have got too much calcium buildup," he explained. "They just freeze on me. I can't get my legs up to my chin." Gable's shoulders were rounded mounds of muscle and his arms were pulsing sledgehammers. His upper body tapered to a less imposing torso. "He has no hips," the novelist John Irving, a wrestling aficionado, wrote of his longtime friend. "No ass. His legs are sinewy as a sprinter's. . . . It is not a beautiful body, it has no Greek design and the muscles lack the definition required by beach prima donnas."

Worse, Gable's knees bore the scars of eight surgeries. He looked down at them as he sat on the edge of the hot tub and dangled his legs in the water. "Had 'em opened up wide; this was years ago. They cleaned everything out—cartilage, other stuff in there, everything—when they didn't have to. With all they've learned since then, I would have had arthroscopy today . . . wouldn't have been so bad. It'd be different."

Archie Gilliss, Kasey's father, sat on a slatted plastic chair near Gable. They talked for a few minutes about the team and Kasey's place on it, and then Archie leaned forward and asked if this would be it, Gable's last year. In one form or another, the question would be put to Gable all season, by parents and the media, by strangers on the street: Would this be it?

"When I get up, I think this will be my last year," Gable said. "I'm hurtin' a little then. But when I go to bed I want to coach next season."

The question seemed to lift Gable to his feet, send him padding toward his room, a towel thrown over his right shoulder. Gilliss watched his exit. "Gable is what we all want to be," he said. "He's a success."

A few on the team stayed behind. Uker, in tight red briefs, emerged from the sauna, his face flushed and sweaty. He walked behind Gilliss to a sliding glass door and opened it and jumped into the snow at the base of a ridge in back of the motel. He lay there for a minute, steam rising from his body, and then came back in, slid the door shut, and shook himself all over like a dog who has just been given a bath. He took a towel and shivered and smiled and joined several teammates on the pool deck.

After a while, the entire squad reassembled in the motel lobby to board the bus to go to lunch. Hawkeye fans had festooned the lobby with black-and-gold ribbons, placing pillows with needlepoint of the school mascot—an angry-looking bird with a steam-shovel beak—on the chairs and sofas. "GO HAWKS!" and "GO GABLE!" read hand-lettered signs that sat on the registration desk. The entourage of thirty rode in bright, cold sunlight to Tweeter's, a restaurant-bar whose walls were plastered with University of Iowa sports posters and pictures. Owner Craig Tvedte, (pronounced "Tweet"), remembered when Danny Mack Gable was training for the 1972 Olympics, how Gable and a couple of his former Iowa State teammates drifted into Okoboji to run a two-week wrestling camp for kids out of a local Presbyterian church. Gable always sat in back and drank grapefruit juice and kept to himself. He sat in back now, with his team, while they ordered. Mena and a couple of his teammates made moves on a waitress in tight jeans, but, in wrestling parlance, she earned escape points. Ben Uker, a sophomore and Mike's younger brother, fidgeted as he waited for his food. He wouldn't wrestle tonight, but he was ready. He had suffered myriad injuries, including a knee injury that required surgery. "It was cartilage," he said. "It kept me behind two and a half months. Finally, I'm back."

The starters ate as much as they pleased. For the only time in the season, making weight would not be a problem: Because of the Thanksgiving holiday, the three coaches involved— Gable, Jason Liles of South Dakota State, and Al Baxter of Buena Vista—agreed to hold weigh-ins for their teams well ahead of the matches and to allow a five-pound variance. Back on the bus, the Iowa wrestlers eagerly anticipated naps back at the motel.

Gable, seated in front, rose and lifted the bottom of a hollowed-out Styrofoam cup to his mouth.

"Welcome to flight fourteen forty-one," he announced, turning to his athletes. "To the right is DisneyWorld. Over there, that's the bar where Alger [Royce Alger, the Hawkeyes' strength and conditioning coach and a two-time national champion] got into a fight and got kicked in the side of the head."

Laughter rolled like a wave from the back of the bus. Kathy Gable, at forty-one seven years younger than her husband, stared straight ahead. She was the youngest of nine children, raised Catholic in Waterloo, Dan's hometown, and she had never seen the hilarity of Alger's misadventures. Her husband pointed out through his makeshift megaphone where a couple of other Iowa wrestlers had been arrested and charged with disorderly conduct.

More laughter.

Kathy Gable opened a magazine and started reading.

It was 4:15 P.M. when the Hawkeyes arrived at Spencer High School. "Get a good workout and shower," Gable told his team as he leaned over the top of his seat. "We've been partying a little. Now it's time to put on a little show." From the side of the bus, wrestlers pulled soft black gym bags lumpy with equipment: flat-soled shoes and headgear, socks and sweatsuits and T-shirts, plus black singlets with spaghetti straps edged in gold and worn for competition.

A crowd of 200 had gathered in the bleachers for a wrestling clinic put on by the Iowa staff. Gable, the narrator, wore a green ribbed sweater and beige slacks. He looked oddly clumsy holding a microphone and working his way through the twenty-five-minute presentation. The Brands twins, Tom and Terry, demonstrated techniques in their sweatclothes. Of all the brother combinations that have flowed through the Iowa wrestling room—Ed and Lou Banach, Troy and Terry Steiner, among others—the Brands might be the most celebrated. Built like fire hydrants with arms, they combined for five national titles—Tom won three from 1990 to 1992 before earning his Olympic gold medal in Atlanta, while Terry with two titles, missed making the Olympic team, but was already working toward the next one. They typified what has become known as the Iowa style of wrestling: pressing the attack, pushing, mauling, wearing down the opponent with superior conditioning, and picking his bones in the last period. It was the domination principle: Gable-coached wrestlers crushed their opponents, humiliated them on the mat and on the scoreboard. It not only pumped testosterone levels to new highs, it also produced the kind of team bonus points totals that carried the Hawkeyes to the NCAA championship. In the national meet, a wrestler earns two points for his team with a pin; one-and-a-half points for a technical fall (winning by fifteen or more points), with a near-fall; one for a technical fall alone, and one for a major decision (winning by eight to fourteen points). He receives one point for advancing in the championship bracket, and a half-point for winning in the consolations. Dual-meet bonus points, applicable in Iowa's victories over South Dakota State and Buena Vista, are higher in each case: a pin gives a team six points, technical falls five, major decisions four, and a simple decision three.

Gable stood at the edge of the mat as the Brands walked to the center circle. "We stress leg tackles—driving and penetrating," Gable said. Tom picked up Terry's leg and drove his shoulder into him and dumped him to the mat with a thud, a takedown worth two points. It was called "shooting," and no team did it more fiercely or more frequently than Iowa. Then Tom showed how to kick a man's leg out from under him and send him crashing to the mat like a tree in a tornado. "The outside sweep single," Gable said. "My main move in the Olympics. Also the Brands'."

Gable also touched on hand-fighting, in which a wrestler on his feet tries to gain an advantage by grabbing the other wrestler's wrist. When his opponent attempts to fend off the move and grab a wrist himself, the wrestler in charge can launch a takedown move. The Brands began pawing at each other. "One tries to push the other out of the circle. If you get dropped before that happens, you lose," Gable explained. Tom and Terry often parried this way, and occasionally the pushing led to punching. Even here, demonstrating, they stared with dead eyes at each other and fought for position. Terry pressed and took a lead. "Uh, Tom," Gable chirped into the microphone, "didn't you win the Olympics?"

The Brands grabbed and pushed each other, circled and collided, showing several other drills from the Iowa wresting room, before Gable added an editorial comment. "Oklahoma State likes to back up and shoot low," he said, mentioning the Hawkeyes' archrival, located in Stillwater, Oklahoma. "We like to *stalk*." His voice took an edge. "I should let them [the

Brands] get on the edge of the mat, and get out of bounds, and do that ten times to get out of trouble—that's really an Oklahoma State drill."

The crowd laughed and jeered and booed the Cowboys. Gable had hit upon not only a sore point but a relevant one as well. The top two college wrestling teams in the country, in this season and in seasons past, differed mightily in style, in their basic approaches to wrestling. Oklahoma State wrestlers liked to keep in motion and on their feet, forever changing direction, going clockwise, now counterclockwise, waiting for an opening, a crack they could slip through and score. Iowa wrestlers, in contrast, knew only one direction: straight ahead. They bore in low, forcing mistakes, seldom reaching, their hips solidly under them. John Smith, the Oklahoma State coach, had wrestled at the school in the 1980s, and taught the Cowboys to wrestle the way he was taught. Gable, however, implemented the Iowa style himself, refining and personalizing the aggressive pinning style that he had learned under Harold Nichols at Iowa State.

When the demonstration ended, the bleachers began filling for the meet's first match, Iowa versus South Dakota State. Jennifer Gable, nineteen, the coach's oldest daughter, sat with her boyfriend, Brian Mitchell, a third baseman on the Iowa baseball team. Both sophomores at Iowa, they had been dating for two years, and Mitchell—with the clean-cut good looks that a father looks for in his daughter's suitor—had become as close to the team as the trainers. He and Gable traded information about the wrestling and baseball teams, and sometimes Gable took Mitchell fishing. ("I don't know what I'm doing, but he takes care of me," Mitchell said.) Brian and Jennifer's relationship also spurred a friendship between the parents. Bob Mitchell was a builder in Iowa City, and his wife, Diane, was a nurse.

In the wrestling room adjacent to the gym, the Iowa wrestlers stretched and warmed up with the sort of hand-fighting and pummeling that the Brands had demonstrated earlier. Iowa's head wrestling trainer, Kristen Payne, taped Gable's left hand—his slapping hand. Gable wanted to protect the hand when he slapped certain wrestlers, like Mena, across the face before a match to fire them up. (Gable doesn't slap a wrestler unless the wrestler requests it and his parents agree to it.) Payne, a tall, slim, athletic-looking woman of twenty-seven, was beginning her second season of tending to the sick and injured on the country's top-ranked wrestling team. She was accorded respect in her exclusively male world, she said, although she knew she had to tread lightly through the minefield of macho.

As match time approached, the Iowa wrestlers filtered back to their locker room, their conversations echoing off the walls. A shower hissed. Payne leaned through the door and asked if everyone was dressed so she could enter. All clear, she was told. But just as she stepped into the room, where most of the team had quieted on wooden benches awaiting Gable's instructions, Terry Brands stepped from the shower wearing nothing but an anxious look.

"Kristen! Hey! I didn't know. Sorry. I didn't know . . . But nothin' here you didn't know about, right?"

"No problem. Don't worry about it," she said. "The season doesn't start until that happens. I got my indoctrination early this season is all. I didn't see my first naked wrestler until later last season."

Referee Del Hughes, a former Upper Iowa University wrestler, stopped by to ask if anyone had questions. McIlravy, returning to college competition after a year of wrestling under international rules, wondered if or how soon Hughes would break a hold that look extremely punishing.

"I wouldn't break it right away if it were executed in a legal manner," Hughes responded, as McIlvary studied him. "I'm a firm believer that there is a certain amount of discomfort in wrestling, especially at the college level."

Gable addressed his team next. "We've been on the town a little, been in a real promotion up to now," the coach said. "We ate at nice places, signed autographs. Now it's time to *turn all that off!* If there're too many people around you, just come back in here.

"This is our first competition of the year. It's important

for me to analyze where you're at, considering we've got Penn State and Lock Haven next week.

"These guys have two arms, two legs, they can pin you," Gable continued. "South Dakota State is a good wrestling team —not great. We are, but we have to wrestle up to our abilities. . . . Put your game face on. If someone starts something, keep cool. The easy way to beat a Hawkeye is to get [him] disqualified."

At the end, Gable glanced at Fullhart, whose bullish shoulders filled his black warm-up jacket. "And don't get shown up by your brother," Gable added, smiling.

Whitmer started the 38–6 rout by shooting on Chad Wickman in the first thirty seconds and taking him down. Gable leaped excitedly from his folding chair along the sidelines, the keys to the locker room jingling around his neck. After Whitmer's 10–3 victory at 118 pounds, Mena—the emblem of a Hawkeye tattooed on his lower left leg—defeated Adam Feldman 7–2. Before the 126-pound match was over, Mena's three year old, Elisia, had meandered from the bleachers to a place near the mat to watch her father at work.

Murderers' Row—Ironside (134), McIlravy (150), and Williams (158)—all pinned their opponents, as did Uker. Ersland, won easily at 177, 10–1, and Fullhart showed little sibling mercy in defeating Bob 18–2. Gable seemed elated that Lee had not let up against his brother. "Why should he?" Gable asked. "Once you step on that mat, your reputation is there. Mine, too."

Gilliss and Hand were the only Hawkeyes who lost. In Travis King, South Dakota State's 142-pound wrestler, Gilliss faced a more experienced opponent who had finished fourth in the weight class in last season's NCAA Division II championships. Stocky, quick, and agile, King spun Gilliss to the mat in the first period, a takedown giving SDSU its first lead in any match up to that point. Gilliss, chased into a shell, didn't recover and wound up losing 4–2. He left the mat shaking his head and not looking Gable's way.

Hand's face was a mask of anxiety as he shook hands with Ryan Resel to begin the final match of the dual. Hand looked even more tentative than Gilliss, and lost by the same score, 4–2. Not that there was disgrace in losing to Resel: The 230-pound sophomore would go on to win the NCAA Division II heavyweight title in March.

As Hand and his teammates walked to the locker room to await their next match against Buena Vista, Gable tried to assemble his feelings. The Hawkeyes had won their thirty-third straight dual meet over three seasons, but Gable was already looking ahead to the NCAA championships in four months.

"I've got to talk to the team," Gable said. "I'm not real pleased right now."

Back in the locker room, Gable, hands on hips, looked impatiently at Hand, who was sitting on the bench, shifting his eyes from the floor to the coach. No one moved. It was impossible to know which was worse for Hand, losing to Resel without a whiff of domination, or now being caught in Gable's headlights. Gable was not about to lash equally the two freshmen who lost. Gilliss at least showed heart. Hand seemed tentative, almost timorous.

"The only match we lost mentally was heavyweight," Gable began. "I understand his [Gilliss's] loss, but not yours," he said, pointing at Hand. "You were out there seven minutes, and you only shot two or three times. . . . You'd've won by technical fall if you'd really wrestled him.

"But you let the match get close, and let the clock tick down, and . . ."

Gable set his jaw. He had reached a familiar place, taking defeat personally.

"Hell, I feel worse than you do," he told Hand. "That's the problem."

In Buena Vista, the Hawkeyes faced a team that traditionally hung around the top ten in the Division III championships. But as a Division III school, the Beavers were unable to give athletic scholarships to attract wrestlers, as Iowa and other Division I schools did. It was not surprising, then, that the Hawkeyes easily won every match in a 52–0 romp. Hand was one of six Iowa wrestlers who won by pin. Gable unleashed his left hand, slapping Hand across the face as he had not done before Hand's first match. "He told me, 'Will you hit me as hard as you can?'" Gable said. "I hit him as hard as I could. His lips snarled like a dog. I know what'll get him riled.

"Hand looks at himself as a newcomer. Sorry, buddy, you're not a newcomer to me when you step into our starting lineup."

Uker, Gable said, "looked solid," and the extra weight he had to put on "didn't look like a problem." Ersland "held up well."

Gable and his team and the Brands spent an hour after the match signing autographs for the milling fans. The Fullharts, Lee and Bob, found each other and talked for a few minutes and then left with a handshake. Then they all disappeared into a cold, snowy night.

chapter 2

WRESTLING DIDN'T TOTALLY CLAIM Dan
Gable until he was thirteen years old. He had tried baseball and
football and track, and had been an outstanding age-group
swimmer at the Waterloo YMCA, hard by the banks of the
Cedar River. The pool was a cheerless place, twenty yards long,
tucked away in the windowless basement like a family embar-
rassment. The swim team kept him balanced when his home
life threatened to undo him. It introduced him to competition,
a craving that never left. And, in a way, it threw him into
wrestling's lap.

He had regularly beaten a teammate in practice and in
meets, but when the teammate hit a growth spurt and began
beating Gable, Gable realized he would have to wait for his
own hormonal intervention or look to another sport. Wrestling
offered a viable alternative. His father, a former high-school
wrestler, had taken him to meets, and the youngster would
thrash around with friends under the bleachers, imitating what
they saw on the mat. Even before he began winning state titles,
Gable sensed that wrestling was a coat that fit him well.

"When I grabbed ahold of somebody, it was with an ease
that I could control him," Gable said. "It just came so much
easier [than swimming]. I don't know why, exactly."

Even then, Gable possessed a type A athletic personality. He loved to lose himself in a workout. He didn't care what people thought. All he cared was that he had a key in his pocket, given to him by his high-school wrestling coach, Bob Siddens, and the key opened the gym in the morning, and he could work out before anyone else even got to school.

"It's the only sport I've ever competed in that puts you totally in a situation of constant [motion] without breaks," Gable said. "I mean, I could play football or baseball, swim— but there's always some kind of a situation that would break my thoughts, break my concentration." Wrestling demanded all he had, gave him "a high I couldn't get from any other workout."

"That's the one thing I probably miss more than anything else, that I can't do anymore. I can't get those feelings any other way. Doing anything. Riding a bike. Sitting in a sauna. It was a super high. I never felt like I felt after a wrestling match or practice."

Wrestling, like boxing and soccer, is constant exertion over an extended period of time. Absent a dramatic throw or pin or flurry, the sport tends to give the impression of two athletes moving in a heavy medium, like molasses, without much resolution. All that straining and pulling, reaching and twisting—how strenuous can it be?

Very.

Wrestlers routinely lose three to six pounds in a match, working against the resistance of someone of equal weight. Action through three periods is continuous, barring injury timeouts, out-of-bounds calls, or those times when the referee sees that neither wrestler can gain advantage in a position and calls a stalemate. (Penalty points for stalling also are issued.) Fatigue, as well as the opponent, becomes the enemy. It is one of the indelicate truths of the sport that the exertion required sometimes produces flatulence of seismic proportions.

In college, matches consist of seven minutes of regulation time: a three-minute first period when the wrestlers begin on their feet (neutral position), and two two-minute periods, when the wrestlers, depending on a coin flip, choose the neutral position or one of two mat positions, offensive or defensive, from which to start. The defensive wrestler (DW) is on all fours and stationary at the center of the mat, while the offensive wrestler (OW) sets up on the right or left side of him, with at least one knee on the mat to the outside of the opponent's near rear leg and his head on or above the midline of the DW's back. The OW places his right or left arm— and "his" is the operative word, although females have started attending camps nationwide, and 629 participated on boys' high school teams in 1996–97—around his opponent's stomach. The palm of the OW's other hand is placed on the DW's near elbow. At the referee's whistle, they begin wrestling.

The object of wrestling is to outpoint or pin an opponent. Here are the main ways to score points:

• A *takedown*, worth two points, occurs from a standing, or "neutral," position, when one wrestler takes another to the mat.

• An *escape*, worth one point, is a staple of mat wrestling, and often occurs when the wrestler in the defensive position breaks from the clutches of the wrestler in the offensive position. The bottom wrestler doesn't have to completely free himself to score.

• A *reversal*, worth two points, occurs when the wrestler in the defensive position—either on the mat or in a near-standing position—rises from underneath to gain control.

• A *near-fall*, or a *controlled pinning situation*, is worth two or three points. Two points are awarded if one wrestler holds the other in a high bridge or on both elbows on the mat; if one shoulder or the head touches the mat and the other shoulder hovers at an angle of forty-five degrees or less from the mat; or if part of both shoulders or shoulder blades are held within four inches of the mat. Three points are given if any of the three criteria are met for an uninterrupted five seconds.

• *Riding time* produces a point for the wrestler who "rides" his opponent from the offensive position and has a minute or more advantage of riding time over his opponent.

A *pin*, which ends a match, occurs when a wrestler holds part of an opponent's shoulders or shoulder blades to the mat for one second, as counted by the referee. The referee, who blows a whistle to start the match, also signals points. He or she wears a differently colored band on each wrist, matching the red and blue ankle bands worn by opposing wrestlers, and by holding up fingers of the red or blue hand indicates points for the appropriate wrestler.

Wrestling is as old as humankind. Hieroglyphics thousands of years old have been found that depict wrestling scenes. The Bible refers to wrestling several times, either literally or metaphorically, depending on the interpretation. In Genesis, Jacob sustained a hip injury in wrestling with God's messenger —but he apparently picked up riding time, for though the messenger said, "Let me go, for it is break of day," Jacob wouldn't break the hold until he was blessed. In 1849, in "The Building of the Ship," Longfellow wrote:

> Build me straight, O worthy master!
> Staunch and strong, a goodly vessel,
> That shall laugh at all disaster,
> And with wave and whirlwind wrestle.

Sigmund Freud, rest his id, wrote in 1905, "No one who, like me, conjures up the most evil of those half-tamed demons that inhabit the human breast, and seeks to wrestle with them, can expect to come through the struggle unscathed."

Through the centuries, wrestling has been refined but never completely tamed. It remains basic, one wrestler against another, no equipment required except singlets and headgear. Athletes who despair of depending on teammates often find themselves on wrestling teams. Coaches insist it's a team sport, and partly that's true, because it's conducted in team competitions, but wrestlers know that at its heart wrestling is an individual sport. A wrestler wins alone, a wrestler loses alone. If Jessie Whitmer loses in a tournament, not one teammate consoles him—nor does Whitmer act as if he expects or wants attention. He sags to his chair and buries his head in a towel and eventually relatives circle and draw him aside. Asked about such seeming insensitivity, Mike Mena explains, "I don't go over for a couple of reasons. The primary reason is that he's coming to terms with his humiliation, and he probably wants to be left alone. If I lose, I don't want anybody telling me 'Nice job.' I lost. It wasn't a nice job."

Wrestling's fundamental holds and moves are myriad, and though simple to explain, difficult to execute. There are *head snaps*, when a wrestler cups his hand behind his opponent's neck and pumps it toward the mat like a basketball, hoping to rock him off balance. There are *single-* and *double-leg* attacks and takedowns, including times when a wrestler shoots for a single-leg with the goal of ending up with both legs. With an *underhook*, a wrestler slides an arm under an opponent's arm and lifts the shoulder to open more avenues of attack. A *high-crotch* is a takedown move, created when a wrestler drives an arm between his opponent's legs, and lifts and throws him to the mat. In a *duck-under*, a wrestler gains hand control and then "changes levels" in the sport's vernacular: Dropping into a crouch, he ducks under his opponent's arm and locks it behind his own neck, setting up a takedown. The *arm drag* also hinges on the success of hand-fighting: A wrestler reaches across with his left hand, for example, and secures his opponent's right wrist, then drags the right arm past his own body and seizes the right elbow with his other hand, with the goal of slipping behind the other wrestler. The *front headlock* also is popular: A wrestler snares his opponent's head in the crook of one arm and with the other hooks one of his opponent's arms. The attacking wrestler then locks his hands to close the trap on his opponent's head and arm. One of the more colorfully named holds, the *fireman's carry*, demands that a wrestler drive into his opponent and turn and carry him briefly across his back to the mat for a possible pin.

When both wrestlers start on the mat, the bottom man on all fours (the defensive wrestler) may attempt a *sitout* by swinging his hips and legs free and spinning to square himself to his opponent. In a *switch*, the bottom wrestler thrusts his hips forward, reaches back and grabs the other wrestler's knee and executes a reversal. The top man may choose to "break down" the bottom man with a *chop and bust*—by pulling back, or chopping, the arm he holds by the elbow and jamming his knee into the other wrestler's rear, and driving him forward to his stomach. From this position, the top man may attempt a pinning hold like a *double arm-bar*, Gable's favorite match-ending hold when he was wrestling, in which he underhooks both of his opponent's arms from behind and drives him forward and turns him toward the mat—"running" the arm-bar, it's called. The bottom wrestler's shoulder blades feel as if they are being winched into his spine; his face flames with mat burns. In another pinning hold, the aptly named *cradle*, a wrestler has his opponent bundled for a pin: One arm stretches across his opponent's face, the hand securing the far elbow; the other arm hooks a leg at the knee. With his knee behind his opponent's head, the wrestler in control forces the head toward the captured knee as the outstretched arm brings his opponent's elbow toward his face. Finally, the hands lock to secure a pin.

Like few other athletes, wrestlers are sensitive to touch and pressure, how someone moves in their grip. The books make it all seem so simple: Set up a move. Make the move. Finish it. An underhook tie-up leads to a high-crotch setup leads to a double-leg takedown and pin. A head snap setup leads to a fireman's carry leads to a takedown and near-fall. In reality, however, each movement provokes a countermovement, and a wrestler has to counter the countermove with something the books haven't considered. Experience and instinct become a wrestler's best friends, which is why it is no accident that someone as fundamentally sound as Lincoln McIlravy got that way only through 225 matches in high school alone.

In the hands of expert technicians, wrestling takes flight. In rare cases, it is almost transcendent. Wrestlers talk about finding a "groove," the sort of groove baseball players talk about when they take a perfect swing, or basketball players talk about when they play a perfect half. "You've got to feel the moves. You've got to *be* the moves," former Iowa State wrestler and Olympic gold medalist Kevin Jackson says.

"The thing about wrestling," Bobby Douglas says, "is it's movement and feeling, and I don't think unless you've been a wrestler you can begin to understand that. . . . The only way I can relate that is to say that my wife and I were watching a movie, and this guy was riding a horse, and he was standing up in the saddle. And she says to me, 'Is that how you ride a horse?' And I said, 'Hell, no! You don't ride a horse like that. Sometimes you ride a horse like that if the horse is going up and down and your butt's sore. But what you've got to do is to get in rhythm with the horse, and when the horse goes down, your butt goes down. And when it stops, you don't slam down on it . . .'

"And when you're a good wrestler, you get that kind of feel for [your opponent]. It'll be almost like you're thinking the same thing that he's thinking. And you have to keep up with his thoughts. You have to think and know what he's thinking about doing to you."

Every year, coaches at all levels try to spruce up the rules to make matches more entertaining and increase attendance. Years ago, they eliminated points for riding-time advantages beyond a minute, in an attempt to inject more action into matches. But regardless of the minor manipulations, on most campuses college wrestling creates all the excitement of a fraternity tug-of-war. The sport's one big event, its coming-out party, the popular NCAA Division I championships, comes in March.

Intercollegiate wrestling programs have been declining in number. In three years from 1994 to '96, wrestling was dropped at twenty-four schools, half of them at the Division I level. That was third-highest among eighteen sports, behind golf (dropped by thirty-one schools) and indoor track (twenty-nine). Coaches and other wrestling supporters rant that Title IX, the federal law that guarantees women equal opportunity to compete in sports, has a choke hold on amateur wrestling and other "minor" men's sports. Title IX requires that schools make available to women the variety of sports and levels of competition equal to men's programs. Critics complain that in their rush to avoid lawsuits alleging discrimination, many schools have not just added women's athletic programs but have also eliminated nonrevenue men's sports programs like wrestling to bring the numbers in line. Wrestling is vulnerable because it awards multiple scholarships, and there are no women's teams or equivalents.

Invariably, wrestling coaches cite the fact that since Title IX was passed twenty-five years ago, their sport has been axed at 462 schools. What could this be, wrestling defenders ask, but a law gone awry, a quota system that destroys men's programs? The National Wrestling Coaches Association and USA Wrestling, respectively the national and international arms of amateur wrestling in the United States, have formed a joint task force to lobby legislators for change. Nevertheless, the question remains: What is wrong with wrestling that it immediately becomes such an expendable sport?

At the pre–high school and high-school levels, the sport is faring better, although even in Iowa—an anchor state for wrestling—coaches complain that some schools have to consolidate teams to field adequate numbers (Traer-North Tama–Gladbrook-Reinbeck, for example), and that kids aren't as willing to make the necessary sacrifices for wrestling as they were in the past. The Iowa state high-school meet in Des Moines still sells out every year. And the wrestling? "The quality is there, but the quantity isn't," says Dale Wambold, a former high-school coach in the state, and his sentiments are echoed by many.

America's two prime wrestling hotbeds have consistently been Iowa and Oklahoma. Going into last season's sixty-seventh NCAA Division I Wrestling Championships, Oklahoma State had won the most team championships with 30, followed by Iowa (16), Iowa State (8), and Oklahoma (7). Oklahoma State also led in individual champions with 117, trailed by Iowa (61), Oklahoma (60), and Iowa State (55). They all have done it with primarily home-grown talent. Gable and Oklahoma State coach John Smith competed for their state universities, and the athletes they recruit tend to reside in-state. Six of Oklahoma State's ten starters during the 1996–'97 season came from Oklahoma, and the same number of Iowans started for the Hawkeyes.

Two of the greatest wrestlers that Oklahoma and Iowa have produced—John Smith and Gable—grew up in towns as the sons of white-collar fathers. Nevertheless, it was the agrarian roots of both states that helped establish wrestling's foothold. Wrestling requires nothing more elaborate than two willing participants, and farm boys with free time fit the criteria. Frank Gotch, who popularized professional wrestling in the early 1900s, was born on a farm near Humboldt, Iowa. He wrote in his autobiography, *Gotch: World's Champion Wrestler,* that he learned the sport from another Iowa farmer-turned-wrestler, Martin (Farmer) Burns: "I was only 20 years old and didn't know any more about professional wrestling than a dog about singing or a pig about Latin. I had wrestled side holds with the big lads of the neighborhood and played rough and tumble at the auction sales, but what I didn't know about wrestling of the Farmer Burns kind would fill a mighty large volume."

Farm boys make good wrestlers, because they are strong and accept hard work. Jessie Whitmer is just the latest in a series. "When you get off a farm, you know how to hay-bale —and you're throwing boys in wrestling with calluses on your hands," Whitmer says. "I baled hay, and that and detasseling corn brought out guts in me."

For Whitmer's coach, just getting up in the morning was increasingly an act of courage. One December morning in 1996, Gable heard his left hip crack and felt a rush of pain, a weakening in the joint. He took Motrin, and went to University Hospitals to see an orthopedic surgeon named Larry Marsh. Marsh felt and flexed the joint, ordered X rays, and put Gable on crutches. Nothing was broken, but Marsh suggested that Gable, even at his relatively young age of forty-eight, was a prime candidate for hip-replacement surgery.

Over the next seven weeks, Gable's salmon-colored medical folder would fatten with test results. Marsh, a tall, balding forty-three-year-old orthopedist from upstate New York, made the diagnosis: degenerative arthritis, or osteoarthritis. The hip had simply worn out—or, more accurately, *been* worn out. The severity of the injury filled even Marsh, a ten-year veteran of replacing nature's work at University Hospitals, with wonder.

"The initial orthopedic surgeon's response to this would be, 'Wow! He's only forty-eight. Look at those bad hips!' " Marsh said. "It's extreme to say it's the worst case I've ever seen, but there's no question they're bad."

Even in a patient seventy-five years old, Marsh said, a hip like Gable's would be regarded as severely arthritic. "But it still might not be as bad as what Dan Gable has at forty-eight."

With classical-music tapes playing in the background, Marsh dug out two sets of X rays, showing Gable's hips eleven years ago and today, secured them against a milky-white screen, and switched on a light. Like images from Halloween, the lower part of Gable's skeletal structure glowed bluish green.

"It would be nice if he had a normal side to show, but he doesn't have a normal side," Marsh began. "Neither of these hips are normal even at this stage [eleven years ago], but they're much closer to normal years ago than they are now."

Even in 1985, cartilage—the tough, white, elastic material that cushions the ends of bones—was disappearing in the left hip. Extra bone was forming, as the hip attempted to repair its injuries. Shadows on the X rays, showing a narrowing of space in the joint, documented the changes. "And he also maybe has some small cysts," Marsh said, tapping the earlier left-hip X ray. "Those are also part of the arthritic process." The right hip didn't look good even by comparison. "Anybody would look at that and say that's a significantly degenerative hip and this is bad."

More recent X rays showed that Gable's right hip had formed much new bone and cysts and looked significantly worse than it did eleven years ago. And the left was hopeless. "New bone has formed on the inside. It's pushing the joint out of the socket, so the joint is going lateral compared to where it was here, before, and that's just from all the bone that's forming in there. Of course, the [cartilage] space is completely gone.

"And there are big, big cysts around everywhere. This is a pretty severely arthritic hip."

Marsh cautioned that a hip replacement—because it eventually would loosen and give out and require another, inevitably less-successful replacement—was "ideal for sedentary patients in their sixties and seventies, but they're not ideal for thirty year olds or forty-year-old wrestling coaches."

Nevertheless, the pain that Gable was experiencing drove him to accept the possibility. He wanted to wait until after the season, but whenever he tried to stand after sitting for a while, he nearly yelped in pain. He couldn't find a comfortable position in which to sleep, and he tossed and turned and waited for the light of morning.

During the first week of December, the pain was so great that Gable stayed home for a few days. Kathy went to his office to pick up mail and run errands, and Mackie, age eight—the youngest, named Mackenzie after Gable's father—played nurse, fetching what Gable wanted so he wouldn't have to walk. His stomach wasn't any better. He decided to skip practice: "It's not good for the team to see me this way." He talked on the phone to his assistant coaches, Jim Zalesky and Tom Brands, and found out what happened in practice, and a day or so later he had them out to the house to lay plans in case he didn't feel up to the weekend trip to Penn State and Lock Haven.

The team took off on Thursday morning without Gable. Zalesky, a three-time national champion under Gable at Iowa, was put in charge. Round-shouldered and understated, Zalesky loomed as the leading choice to succeed Gable. He had gone undefeated at Iowa during his last two seasons, 1983 and 1984, and then served as an assistant for two years under Gable before joining the University of Minnesota staff for three seasons. He returned to Iowa in 1990, and was a hot enough property to be hard in the running for the University of Oklahoma head job before pulling his name out.

Zalesky and the Hawkeyes were pinned in Chicago's O'Hare airport for six hours by bad weather. Zalesky called Penn State coach John Fritz, saying that the Hawkeyes would be late for weigh-ins. Fritz proposed that PSU's wrestlers weigh in on Thursday night, and that Iowa's wrestlers wait until Friday and be given a one-pound weight allowance. That spelled problems for Iowa, however, because then its opponent would have ten extra hours to eat and gain back strength. "He must really think I'm stupid," Zalesky confided to Morrie Adams, a radio announcer who accompanied the team. Both teams weighed in on Friday.

Adams had been broadcasting Iowa wrestling's home and away meets for several years, but his association with Gable went beyond the microphone. Adams, fifty-six, his head a thatched thicket of gray and white, described himself as a "licensed independent social worker in Iowa, and I do individual therapy." In his private practice in Iowa City, he did marriage counseling and family therapy, worked with clients suffering from anxiety and depression, and saw individual athletes, including Gable's wrestlers. When one of Gable's stars, as a freshman, lost the first home match of his career, Adams told the high-school champion that he had the physical and technical skills to succeed, but that he also needed to "re-focus, develop the mental skills to stay tough and win." Adams hypnotized one of the other wrestlers to relax him. "He's a very bright young man, and I've been trying all year to get him to be stupid when he steps on the mat . . . Because what happens is he gets paralysis with analysis. You can just see that in his eyes when he starts."

Adams didn't bill the Iowa wrestlers or the wrestling office. Gable remained apart. "Closest thing Gable said to me was, 'I don't know what you do, but I'll let you keep doing it,'" Adams said.

Listening both nights at home, Gable took notes from Adams's broadcasts on KXIC-AM in Iowa City. "Listen," Adams told his radio partner, Mark Allen, off-air, "we better know what we're doing if *he's* listening."

On Friday night in University Park, Pennsylvania, against fourth-ranked Penn State, a record PSU crowd of 11,245 watched the unbeaten Hawkeyes roll to their third straight victory, 22–15. Gable stressed to his assistants before they left that if the victory were assured, the best thing would be to forfeit at heavyweight and keep Wes Hand from facing the Nittany Lions' 1994 heavyweight champion Kerry McCoy so early in the season. "Hand's not ready yet," Gable reasoned. "And he hasn't earned the right to wrestle somebody that good." Tom Brands broke the news to Hand, taking Royce Alger along for support. Hand was furious but powerless. Mark Ironside got a scare when, rolling through a move on the mat, he gave up a hip tilt to Dana Weber and was nearly pinned. But Ironside stormed back for a technical-fall victory, 30–14, worth five points of Iowa's ultimate seven-point margin.

On Saturday night, the Hawkeyes met eighth-ranked Lock Haven in a match moved eighty miles from campus, to Hershey, Pennsylvania, to accommodate the large crowd anticipated. A turnout of 3,113—more than respectable by Division I college standards and in the range of what Iowa drew at home—showed up. Adams dragooned Ironside and McIlravy, both easy winners, to tell a certain coach listening in Iowa City how the team looked. They ratted on no one. Then Adams summoned Mike Uker to the microphone. The night before, Uker had dropped a 6–3 decision to Penn State's Glenn Pritzlaff, who was rebounding from off-season shoulder surgery. But against Lock Haven, Uker pinned Neil Barnes with just over two minutes gone in their 167-pound match.

So, Adams asked Uker on the air, when did he sense that Barnes was succumbing?

"Well," Uker said, "he started out OK, but then he got tired and started sucking swamp water."

It was time to go home.

• • •

The team flew back on Sunday, the same day that Gable kept a 9 A.M. appointment in the gastrointestinal department at University Hospitals. He felt bloated and still had diarrhea, but at least there was no pain or blood. More tests. As for his left hip, Gable over the weekend began thinking about getting a new hip before the end of the season. He checked the calendar. "I plan to knock this down in two or three weeks—get it over with and back," he said. Within a month, Dr. Marsh had scheduled surgery for Thursday, January 23, four days after an important midseason tournament, the National Team Dual Championships, in Lincoln, Nebraska. Gable would be on crutches for three months, but he hoped to rejoin the team well before the Big Ten championships—the conference's NCAA qualifier—on March 8 and 9 in Minneapolis.

With Marsh, Gable rarely asked questions about anything outside the immediate problem. He had a hip that hurt and needed fixing; how soon could it be done, what was the timetable for recovery, when would he be back? "I get the impression he's a no-nonsense guy," Marsh said. "He needs to know what needs to be done, and let's get on and do it."

Marsh didn't dwell on the surgeries that Gable might need after the hip replacement. The right hip, by all odds, would be the next to go. The knees were in terrible shape—what remained of them, that is. It almost was as if Gable had worked all his life toward this confluence of pain and replacement. It was almost as if he felt he deserved it. After the 1972 Olympics, when he finally had surgery on his left knee, doctors spent hours cleaning debris from the joint. Days later, he was wrestling again, beginning his job as assistant Iowa wrestling coach under Gary Kurdelmeier. The knee was heavily taped, but the stitches ripped anyway. The wound was resutured, and Gable kept wrestling. As his coaching career progressed, and new injuries sprang up and old ones worsened, Gable had what amounted to a standing appointment with doctors at the close of each season. Almost inevitably, he would have offseason surgery—knees, neck or back, shoulder, even lip surgery to remove nonmalignant growths stemming from when he bit through his lip while wrestling.

Deep into the 1980s, Gable wrestled hard on the mat to show his athletes of all weight classes what pressure they should feel, and where they should feel it, in the application of a hold. Or just to make them realize how hard they had to wrestle if they intended to dominate a match.

"When I was a freshman [in 1980] he just never stopped wrestling, and a long time after that," said Ed Banach, who under Gable won national championships at 177 and 190 pounds. "One year when I was a junior or senior I hurt his knee—I heard it pop—wrestling in the middle of the summer, and I felt bad, and I said, 'I don't want to wrestle you anymore.'

"And he goes, 'No! No! Just wrestle.' I was going over to a meet in France, and I had to get ready, but I couldn't find anybody else in the room to wrestle. So then he fell on top of me and tried to turn me . . . and he beat me up. He turned me every which way. We wrestled twenty-five minutes, until I was so tired I didn't even move. That was the last time I wrestled him. But I didn't miss it."

Now that he was a coach himself, at the University of Wisconsin, Barry Davis got on the mat the way Gable used to. The difference was that Davis, an NCAA champion at Iowa once at 118 pounds and twice at 126 pounds, weighing a little less than Gable, wouldn't take on any man who weighed more than 150 pounds. "When you get to 158, they start being too explosive, they can hurt you," Davis said. "When I was wrestling at Iowa, Gable was doing that all the time."

It was a carryover from his college days, when Gable scoured the wrestling room for workout partners of any size and weight. He wanted to improve his conditioning and technique, and he needed opposition and resistance. He wrestled men many times his size (5-9, 140), including his Iowa State and Olympic teammate Chris Taylor, who weighed more than 400 pounds. ("I can do pretty good with him for about the first thirty minutes. After that, he tires me out and I can't do anything," said Taylor, who died in 1979.)

Gable, as athlete and coach, had been on crutches countless times, but he was having trouble adjusting to the aluminum crutches that Marsh gave him. They hurt his armpits as he stabbed and swung his way along. Marsh readjusted them so Gable wasn't pitched forward at such an angle, and that seemed to help.

Gable never asked why all this was happening to him, and he never blamed the sport that had bequeathed him a crumbling old man's body at age forty-eight.

"Don't ... don't ... we don't need to ..." he sputtered early on a Sunday morning in December, when the subject raised was the wreck wrestling had made of him. "I'm not any more beat up than a guy who works a construction job for thirty or forty years of his life. A lot of working-class people have the same problems."

He was determined not to be a "Molly Putz"—a phrase his late mother used to indicate a weak-minded person. "Most people, back fifty years, they didn't even live to forty-eight. I'm fine. I'm the picture of health. I've been in a contact sport for over thirty years. I haven't done stuff all that hard—real hard—for ten years. Most people are old and gray when they're forty-eight years old. Hell, I'm starting life. I'm just making changes in my, uh, lifestyle ..."

Later, in a more transcendent moment, he thundered, "Pain? What's pain? I've had pain all my life. I've been hurt all my life. I'm never going to have the pain gone. The pain's not going to be gone until I die. I've got too many joints that are beat up. It's just the way it is."

In some ways wrestling had been good to Gable. He received $84,414 a year to coach. He had three years left on a five-year deal. He was given membership in the University Athletic Club, he had two dealer cars at his disposal, and his family's expenses to out-of-town competitions were paid. His wrestling camps, run through the university, fetched him another $80,000 to $100,000 annually. His wrestling-shoe contract with Asics brought $35,000 and he received undisclosed amounts from a weight company and from speaking fees. He and his family lived in a two-story, cedar-sided home two miles north of Iowa City. Fox and deer and raccoon left tracks in the snow. A hot tub sat outside the back deck, near a miniature grotto-like enclave with a statue of the Virgin Mary—Kathy's work, Gable said.

A few meters away was what the family called the "clubhouse," cedar-sided to match the house. The Gables zealously guarded the phone number to the clubhouse, for it was the lair of the patriarch. Gable worked at a desk in the main room. He and Brian Mitchell, Jennifer's boyfriend, would converse here; Bob Bowlsby, the athletic director, sometimes shared a beer in the clubhouse with Gable and talked business. A T-shirt from Mickey Mantle's restaurant was framed and hung on a wall, and a Mantle-model bat that Gable swung as a kid stood in a corner; Gable grew up loving Mickey Mantle, and he cried when Mantle died in 1995. There was a wood-burning stove and two saunas, steam and dry, a shower, and a workout room with weights and mats and an exercise bike. Winding iron steps led to a loft with two single beds.

Gable had been married to Kathy for twenty-two years. She wanted him to step down, rid himself of the physical and emotional stress of coaching, but remain in the Iowa athletic department. She told Marsh that her husband was in more pain than he admitted to. She had heard Gable, groaning, get up one night and thump downstairs on his crutches and return.

"What were you getting up for, so early?" Kathy asked at breakfast. Her hair, thick and dark blond, was cut short. Her voice simmered with both question and accusation.

"Well, I was so thirsty I needed to get a drink of water," Gable replied.

"Well," she said, "why didn't you wake me up and I would have gone downstairs and gotten it *for* you."

"Oh, you were were sleeping so sound . . ."

"No!" she countered. "Because if I would have been sleeping sound, I wouldn't have heard you, and I did. Just wake me up."

Gable promised he would. But about avoiding the exertions and conditions that led to so much pain, there were no promises. Kathy knew better than to assume anything; she had undoubtedly made her wishes clear, and like everyone in Iowa she could only wait until Gable made up his own mind about his future.

chapter 3

I N THE WEEK preceding the Iowa State meet,
Gable resumed command. The more he saw and thought, and
the more he heard from his assistants, the more he deplored
how some on the team had competed, even though they had
won. Joe Williams, for example: With the leverage of his long,
heavily muscled limbs, he should have been pinning opponents,
dominating them. But the passion was missing. A two-point
decision over Penn State's Brian Romesburg, a three-point victory over Lock Haven's Brian Leitzel; it was as if he were
punching a tme clock. Williams didn't like road trips—maybe
that was it. Maybe something else. "He needed me to get him
ready," Gable said. Knowing how low-key Williams was, Gable
drew him into conversations between drills in the wrestling
room and supplied firm but light-handed criticism. "Keep the
pressure on him, Joe—that's it."

Mike Mena, holding on to win close matches at 126, was
making noises that he'd like to drop back to 118. Meanwhile,
Kasey Gilliss was drowning in his first year as a starter. He had
a 1–3 record, and Gable toyed with the possibility that Eric
Koble—a dark-featured kid with a smile so wide it seemed to
jump the margins of his face—might slip in at 142. Ersland,
after two major decisions at 177, had lost twice and "wasn't

wrestling well," in Gable's estimation. Fullhart, at 190 the winner of four in a row, was just "OK." Jessie Whitmer, Mark
Ironside, and Lincoln McIlravy all were unbeaten, at 118, 134,
and 150 respectively, and Ironside and McIlravy were emerging
as the team's role models for domination, with five pins, two
technical falls, and one major decision between them. Mike
Uker had his moments at 167, with a couple of pins. Wes
Hand, the heavyweight, took the forfeit against Penn State in
the right way, as a challenge, and impressed Gable when he
rallied from a 4–0 deficit to beat Lock Haven's Ricky Krieger,
8–7. Gable knew what he was doing: It was not the first time
that he had benched a starter early in the season to protect his
confidence leading up to nationals.

But something else pained Gable as much as his hip or
stomach: the team attitude. He sensed that his wrestlers were
almost too loose. Arch rival Iowa State was coming to town
on Saturday, ranked third in the country behind Iowa and
Oklahoma State. It was no time to be loose, not against a
Bobby Douglas–coached team that last year parlayed five qualifiers into a second-place finish in the NCAA championships.
Gable assembled his team at practice early in the week. He told
them that they could drink and have girlfriends—fine—only
they couldn't expect to win by the top-heavy scores that Iowa
teams should win by. "This is your wake-up call," Gable said.

Despite all that, Gable was fond of this group. He believed
it was important to spur the horse once early in the season to
see how it would react. In fact, his athletes usually accepted
hard work and followed orders and, in Gable's mind, were
"good guys, every one of them."

Gable felt connected with this group—as he had not been
with certain members of teams in the 1980s. He knew all about
the time that Gilliss yelled a pickup line out a car window and
realized too late that the target was the wife of a postgraduate
wrestler at Iowa named Eric Akin. He knew that Fullhart felt
trapped by his time commitments and intended to switch ma-
jors from engineering to finance, and Gable wanted to sit down
with Fullhart and his advisors. Only word from high in the
athletic department that this might be viewed as meddling

made him back off. Up and down the lineup, Gable enjoyed a great rapport with these athletes young enough to be his sons. On one road trip, driving a van from the competition site to the hotel, Gable quizzed Koble about his life as a junior at the University of Iowa. Suddenly, Gable swung his head toward the back seat and Koble.

"You and your girlfriend split again?" Gable asked. Koble nodded. He couldn't guess where this was leading. How did Gable find out? "Well," Gable went on, "what I'd say is either patch it up or drop it. This going back and forth can be tough."

When Gable pulled over and got out to pump gas, Koble tracked him with his eyes. He wasn't worried that Gable—hardly a Lothario in his single days—was playing Dr. Ruth. "I trust him. He's done a lot of things and knows a lot of things," Koble said. "A lot of us go to him with personal problems." It was just another way that Gable tried to understand his athletes, to help make them better.

With Iowa State approaching, Gable began spending more and more time in the wrestling room working with his athletes, and less and less time in his cubicle office answering correspondence and returning calls and shoveling through the avalanche of administrative work. "Paperwork is my bad point," Gable admitted. "It will probably drive me out of coaching more than anything else. I just can't keep up."

Down the hall and around the corner from the office was the wrestling room, Gable's laboratory and refuge, his second home. Country music thrummed and twanged over the sound system by the hour. Plastic barrels of Gatorade and water waited to be tapped. Gable kept the thermostat set at approximately eighty degrees—twenty degrees cooler than in the Iowa State wrestling room where he spent his collegiate days. It was a matter of balance in Gable's mind: The room had to be hot enough to get the sweat going and the body prepped for a strenuous workout, but cool enough so that wrestlers could labor for hours and not quit. But it still was stifling, and the yellow brick walls seemed to throw the heat back onto the black mats like hot gravy.

Practice began at 3:30 P.M., sharp, and ended between 5:30 and 6. Gable, glancing at a clipboard he held in one hand, briefed the team each day on what the newspapers were printing about them or how insiders were viewing the chase toward the national title. Leaning forward on his crutches, his rapt audience seated before him on wooden bleachers, Gable ran down what had happened to each starter in his last meet or what future opponents offered. It was never personal; he rarely mentioned names. Just, "OK, 118 [Whitmer], you need to be more explosive when you. . . . Now, 126 [Mena] . . ."

Much of the practice was spent doing "live drills," one-on-one wrestling with no referee, the wrestlers running through myriad moves and countermoves. Thanks to the unfathomable exertion wrestling demands, by the end of practice puddles of perspiration dotted the mats, and when wrestlers walked in the sweat from their own bodies, the sound was that of footfalls on a sidewalk in a spring rain.

Tempers ran hot, offense was taken easily, fisticuffs began infrequently and ended quickly. Two reserves, Bill Kucinski and his workout partner, Nick Dohrmann, stopped wrestling and began throwing punches. Dohrmann landed the best punch, a long left, and Kucinski went to the locker room to cool off and returned in fifteen minutes; the two shook hands and resumed wrestling. Kucinski, 134 pounds, whose blond hair skimmed the tops of his shoulders, had fought like this only once before in his life. "It's just the intensity level sometimes gets up there," he said. "And when you've got two athletes competing that tough and giving it their all . . . I mean, Gable says it best when he says it's like a battle. One guy is basically trying to beat the crap out of the other guy."

Kucinski—who wrestled at the same Chicago-area high school, Mt. Carmel, as Williams—witnessed a recent fight in the wrestling room between freshmen Lee Weber and Justin Decker. "Weber bit the top of Decker's head," Kucinski said, half-smiling. There was blood. Gable, Kucinski said, was not pleased. "Sometimes after an incident like that, guys won't be able to wrestle because they'll have stitches, or cuts that can get infected. Stuff like that he [Gable] doesn't like. I mean, he likes the heat and intensity of it, and at the same time he doesn't like to see something like that where it might take us out of practice."

Emotions were pitched highest in "the room" at weight-cutting time, when Iowa wrestlers typically lost ten pounds or more in two days to reach their mandated weights. As the season progressed, NCAA weight allowances tightened, until by the time of the NCAA championships, wrestlers had to make "scratch" weight—not an ounce over the limit. Gable often used the word "ornery" to describe his wrestlers' attitude as they worked to drop pounds as quickly as possible, to prolong their recovery time.

In the process, more than a few Hawkeye wrestlers—to use another Gableism—"broke." One such incident occurred in March 1983. Iowa wrestlers were training for the Big Ten championships—not just to win them, that was expected, but to place all 10 wrestlers in the NCAA championships. But the boat had sprung a leak. Iowa's 118-pounder had quit. Gable shuffled his lineup and ordered Mark Trizzino to drop from 134, where he had wrestled all season, to 126. It was hard enough for Trizzino, a short, squat, wide-shouldered, and thickly muscled athlete, to make the 134-pound limit, let alone a weight-class lower. He pushed himself to the brink in practice, and his T-shirt became so matted with sweat that his chest hairs showed through it like dark seaweed.

He left the mat to get a drink of water. Gable pursued him. He wanted him to slide into his plastic tops and bottoms and keep the sweat going. The confrontation began at the drinking fountain. "Put 'em on!" Gable demanded, referring to the plastics. Trizzino shouted no. They began pushing each other. Trizzino tried to shove Gable backward over an exercise bike, but failed. "I tried to grab his hair," Trizzino remembered, "but he didn't have any."

The two careened through the locker-room door, and the sounds of thrashing and raised voices reached the wrestling room, where everyone stopped to listen. "Don't anybody go in there," said J Robinson, one of Gable's assistants at the time. No one was remotely tempted. Eventually, Trizzino appeared—wearing plastics.

Wrestling's image has been hurt—and its popularity among young wrestlers and their parents doubtless compromised—by the physical and emotional stress of weight cutting. In forty-eight hours or so, wrestlers use measures bordering on the extreme to shed ten or more pounds—which are usually dismissed as "water weight." John Elton, wrestling coach at St. John's University, a Division III school in Collegeville, Minnesota, calls it "the black plague of our sport." John Smith, the Oklahoma State coach, began cutting weight as a fourth grader in Oklahoma.

"I definitely wouldn't recommend it to families who have kids in wrestling today," he says. "I think I was a little bit unique in that wrestling got ahold of me early and nothing really bothered me. I didn't like it, but I didn't feel burned out from it.

"But I don't think it's a healthy situation, to cut weight too early. I'd never have my kid cutting weight that early, just put it that way."

Why do many collegiate wrestlers cut so much weight instead of wrestling in a heavier weight class? The rationale is that they would probably lose if they did, because wrestlers normally heavier and stronger than those wrestlers are cutting—"sucking down," in the sport's jargon—to get to that weight themselves. The ideal is for a wrestler to drop to the lightest weight possible without robbing himself of strength.

This sets the stage for the sort of weight-cutting methods never dreamed of at Weight Watchers. At Division I schools, it is not uncommon for wrestlers cutting weight to layer heavy cotton or wool sweats over vinyl or plastic sweats, put on a stocking cap, and pedal an exercise bike in a boiling-hot wrestling room. It doesn't take long before sweat flows; when the wrestler sits down and pulls the plastic from his wrists, he releases a torrent of trapped perspiration. It's as if a garden hose has been turned on.

Gable and other coaches insist that they're following the latest scientific advice in the matter of weight cutting and that athletes are closely monitored for signs of trouble. Kristen Payne, the Iowa wrestling trainer, who watched weight cutting at two other schools before she came to Iowa, says that Gable has asked her opinion on weight-cutting issues, and that the two have reviewed the pertinent literature. But, she adds, because of her gender she doesn't roam the locker room freely, "so I don't know how much of the real aggressive stuff is going on."

In speaking to youths at Gable's summer wrestling camps, Payne doesn't hedge. "I tell them, 'I'm not going to stand here as a medical professional and tell you that it's healthy to cut weight like this. But there is a safe way to do it.'

"It's not healthy to get on a bike and shed [weight] and sweat. But this is the reality of the sport. It's happened for years, and there have been relatively few serious medical problems."

Long-term, the danger of developing eating disorders exists. While much attention has been paid—and rightly so—to females who are bulimic or anorexic, the fact is that wrestlers or former wrestlers are being seen at eating-disorder clinics. And short-term, the rapid heating of the body in a hothouse environment could signal disaster.

"The fact that nobody has died within anybody's memory —I think part of that is because the athletes are in such phenomenal shape to begin with," St. John's University's Elton said just four months before two college wrestlers, in the throes of weight cutting, died within four weeks of each other. "In the middle of weight cutting, if a wrestler had his temperature and pulse and blood pressure taken, and an electrolyte reading, he might be put in intensive care with an IV."

That is, if he'd already cut enough weight.

As many as thirty or more wrestlers filled the wrestling room during the 1996–97 season. Most were varsity athletes on partial scholarship, many of whom had won multiple highschool titles. A significant minority, like Terry Brands, were

postcollegians who were training for important matches leading to the U.S. team selection for the 2000 Olympic Games in
Sydney, Australia. Under NCAA rules, postcollegians at Iowa
and elsewhere technically could not work out against varsity
wrestlers because, under such circumstances, the former would
be considered coaches. (However, several exceptions took the
teeth out of the measure.) The Olympic hopefuls chose Iowa
because of the competition and the atmosphere in the room,
and because of Gable's presence. These wrestlers were usually
in their late twenties and early thirties, and had put their professional careers on hold to train in the room. For many, like
Eric Akin, this was not their only sacrifice.

Akin, a former Iowa State wrestler with a washboard of
muscle from his shoulders to his groin, rented a farm with his
wife, Stephanie, and their two children. Stephanie worked two
jobs to support the family until five-month-old Chase was
born. Stephanie's job in a women's clothing store in Iowa City
meant that Akin sometimes had to take both children to the
wrestling room while he worked out or cut weight. When he
took a sauna a few feet from the locker-room door, he would
put Chase into a stroller and watch her through the square
window in the sauna. Jake, age five, would run back and forth
to his father with news flashes. Eric worked in wrestling camps,
Gable's and others, filing down the technique of high school–
age youths. One day Gable, who lived nearby, dropped in to
see Eric and Stephanie and the kids. Stephanie was working.
Chase reposed in a blue baby seat on the sofa; Eric rubbed her
chest and cooed to her. Gable smiled.

"I like seeing a wrestler play with kids," he said. "I like
to see them playing daddy." Then he abruptly changed the
subject.

"You're flurrying better than I've seen you," said Gable,
who kept close watch on Eric and the other members of the
Hawkeyes Wrestling Club. "But when you're stalking, you're
still too high. Bend those knees."

Gable leaned forward and made faces at Chase. Akin still
was thinking about bending those knees.

"People ask me the difference between Iowa State and the

club program at Iowa," Akin said. "I tell them I was a boy wrestling at Iowa State. But when I came here with Gable, I became a man."

The Hawkeyes mowed down Iowa State, 26–13. A crowd of 7,241 in Carver-Hawkeye Arena–named in honor of a deceased multimillionaire who threw no small amount of change at the wrestling program—watched Iowa win its nineteenth straight dual match against the Cyclones and thirty-eighth in a row overall. Lincoln McIlravy climbed back into serious competition by defeating State's Chris Bono 8–2. Bono, a Floridian, stood five-feet-four, a wide, moving-truck of a man who couldn't blink an eye without a muscle jumping. When McIlravy took off last year for Olympic training, Bono claimed the 150-pound NCAA title as a junior. This was the meeting everyone expected would be repeated in this year's NCAA finals up the road in Cedar Falls. McIlravy managed a takedown in the final minute of the first period and added two more later in the match, boosting his collegiate record against Bono to 3–0.

The most competitive match was at 126, where Mike Mena went two overtimes to defeat 1996 NCAA runner-up Dwight Hinson, 2–1. Each had a one-point escape through regulation and a two-minute, sudden-death overtime. In the second sudden-death overtime, a thirty-second tiebreaker, Mena won the referee's coin toss and chose to station himself on all fours in the center circle, the down position. Hinson assumed the offensive starting position: He knelt on his left knee on Mena's left side, and slipped his long right arm loosely around Mena's waist, and stretched his right leg on the outside of Mena's left leg. At the whistle, Mena exploded from Hinson's clutches in the first eight seconds, and the escape gave Mena the match.

Gable expressed pleasure—or at least satisfaction—with the performances of six Hawkeyes, including McIlravy and Mena. Whitmer ingratiated himself with a 17–8 major decision over Cody Sanderson, a redshirt freshman who had finished third in the Las Vegas Invitational and was 12–4 heading into

the match. Whitmer not only dominated but did it in Ga-
blesque manner, overwhelming Sanderson with a ten-point
third period. At 158, Williams pinned Matt Patitz, who wrestled at 177 and 190 during the previous season and wouldn't
find a starting home at any weight this season. Regardless of
the competition, Gable liked Williams's tough-guy attitude,
the way he "beat up on the guy." Fullhart, at 190, won by the
kind of margin (18–7) that satisfied Gable, and Ironside, at
134, posted his fourth pin in five matches.

Four performances disappointed Gable. Kasey Gilliss lost
his fourth match, 3–2, but worse, he had lost his touch with
big scoring moves. Mike Uker dropped a 14–9 decision to
another newcomer at 167, Bart Horton. Gable figured Tony
Ersland would have problems at 177, and he was right—Ersland lost by 15–4 to Barry Weldon, who placed fifth in the
national championships a year ago at 167. And Wes Hand
stumbled again at heavyweight to drop to 2–2.

Now it was back to the wrestling room. There, the pace
of work quickened as the Christmas holidays approached.
There was reference material now, videotapes of this season's
matches, and Hawkeye wrestlers drifted into the wrestling office throughout the day to fire up the VCR and watch and
critique their performances.

In the wrestling room, Gable sat in the second row of the
bleachers and watched practice, letting Zalesky and Brands do
his legwork. He ordered Gilliss to lower his stance, hoping it
would unleash the freshman's offense and ground his defense.
In two weeks, the week after Christmas, the thirty-fourth Midlands Championships would be upon them.

Personally, Gable seemed to be settling into his decision
to have his left hip replaced. "I don't see myself not getting
around. I might as well do the damn thing," he said. "I won't
let it limit me too much."

He was, however, torn by a decision he had to make about
the hip replacement. Would he be better off if surgeons cemented the artificial hip—made of cobalt chrome—in place,
or if they allowed the replacement to be absorbed into the
remaining bone structure? Older patients often opted for ce-

ment because they were not extremely active and wouldn't unduly stress the artificial hip. The "absorption" option appealed to younger patients like Gable who wanted to remain somewhat active. Gable faced a limited lifestyle anyway; Marsh, his orthopedist, didn't want him running or engaging in weight-bearing sports, leaving Gable with swimming and bicycling. An avid angler and outdoorsman, he could fish, of course, but portaging was out.

Wincing after practices, Gable climbed aboard the exercise bike set back from the mats against a wall and rode for a half hour. There he was, swaying and rocking with the exertion of pushing his arms and legs against resistance, the top of his bald head gleaming with sweat, pushing, pushing, the large flywheel on the bike crying in higher and higher pitches of pain.

Whitmer didn't have to turn around to know.

"That's got to be Gable," he said. "Nobody else cranks on it like that."

chapter 4

IT WAS the Midlands Wrestling Championships
—which annually draws together the top teams in the country
for early-season tournament competition—that first established Danny Mack Gable as a presence, a future force, in
college wrestling.

The year was 1966, and he was an eighteen-year-old freshman at Iowa State. Under NCAA rules at the time, he couldn't
compete as a varsity athlete—except in tournaments open to
all amateurs, not just collegians, like the Midlands—until his
sophomore year. An unbeaten three-time high-school champion at Waterloo West, he was heavily recruited, but chose to
stay close to home. His parents—Mack, a rough-and-tumble
investor and real-estate salesman, and Katie, who kept an im-
maculate house and balanced the books—sent him off to Ames
in a new Mustang. Gable slipped back home on weekends,
especially when it was the off-season and he wasn't immersed
in training. Early in his tenure at Iowa State, Gable seemed to
regard his parents' ranch house at 2241 Easley Street, a half
block from the high school, as more a base of operations than
the family home.

Or so Katie felt when she wrote him on November 12,
1967.

To this day, the four-page, handwritten letter holds a treasured place in the Gable household. Before each daughter graduates from high school, she receives a copy of what Katie wrote to her only son decades before—a reminder of parents' expectations. One can almost see Katie, poised over paper, a cigarette burning between her fingers, upbraiding Gable for his callousness: "I can see no reason for your mouthing or lying when your [sic] asked a question that could be answered with a civil answer, such as 'where have you been?' or 'what time did you come home. . . .' "

When he returned home on weekends from college, Katie sensed in Dan a self-importance she sought to banish. His behavior, she wrote, had "been to the point of you really must thing [sic] you're something else. . . . Everyone has a lot of respect for you. Don't let these kind of week-ends spoil or change people's minds about you."

"It straightened me right around," Gable said. "She always knew how to do that."

In the crowded wrestling room run by Iowa State coach Harold Nichols, Gable initially was just one of many stars in the Cyclones' constellation. Nichols—a rooster of a man, short and chesty—had assembled talent two and three deep at each weight. Rare was the wrestler who had not won two or more high-school titles and, in some cases, earned NCAA All-American honors by finishing among the top eight in his weight class. In fact, the 1966 Cyclones team Gable joined had three runners-up returning from the previous season's squad that had placed second in the NCAA championships at Ames.

One of them was Dale Bahr, who at 145 pounds found himself wrestling the lighter Gable in practice. "Quite frankly, when he came into our room as a freshman, he wasn't that good," said Bahr, who assisted under Nichols before becoming the University of Michigan coach. "I used to beat on him in practice. He couldn't get away from me. I could reverse him, but he kept working and working and working, and when one guy would get tired and stop and get a drink and come back, [Gable] would be working with another guy.

"And if that guy got tired, or maybe hurt or something, Dan wouldn't stop and wait for him to go get taped, he'd just go get somebody else. In the course of practice, he'd wear out two, three, four of his teammates."

Les Anderson, a two-time NCAA champion at Iowa State, became Nichols's assistant and toured the wrestling room, demonstrating holds and techniques. He was tough and smelled of cigarettes. Gable impressed him immediately. "He was the easiest person I ever coached. The reason for that is, number one, his intelligence, and number two, his intense desire not to lose—which was far more important than a desire just to win.

"He had superb balance. He'd go through something once, twice, and lo and behold, he'd have it after a short moment. It was like he'd practiced it 10,000 times like most wrestlers. That kind of body awareness. . . . He didn't have quickness. He didn't have speed—average at best. He had no muscle definition coming out of [high] school. He wasn't particularly strong. But if there was only one gift that God would give you, let that be it: balance."

Going into the 1967 Midlands, Gable knew his shortcomings, or at least had begun questioning areas of his wrestling. He won his first eight collegiate matches, competing in invitationals at 130 pounds, to stretch his winning streak, counting high school, to seventy-two. And yet . . .

"Right out of high school, I never had the fear of getting beat, which is how most people lose—they're scared of somebody," Gable remarked. "But I really didn't have a clue how I'd do in college. I mean, I knew I could beat guys in practice, and I did well, but there were guys I had trouble with."

It was Iowa State's second appearance in the Midlands, which then was held over the winter holidays in the new field house at La Grange (Illinois) High School in suburban Chicago. Gable, his reddish hair neatly combed and swept over the right side of his forehead, his sideburns extending past his earlobes, his ears beginning to cauliflower, easily pinned his first two opponents, setting up a quarterfinal match against Larry Baron of Southern Illinois University at Carbondale.

Gable won the 130-pound quarterfinal match 8–3, and that's when tournament founder and director Ken Kraft took notice. "I knew Baron because I'd seen him wrestle in high school," said Kraft, wrestling coach at Northwestern University. "He was a tough kid. And so I watched his match with Gable, and it was a competitive match, and Gable was just a little bit better. And I knew that by winning in the quarters, Gable was going to meet somebody very solid in the semifinals. I think it was Behm."

Don Behm was a returning All-American at Michigan State who would finish second in the country in the 1967 NCAA championships and win a silver medal in the 1968 Olympics. He manhandled Gable early on, taking a 5–1 lead before Gable countered a move that Behm had previously scored on—a fireman's carry—and nearly pinned Behm. Tie match, 5–5, going into the third and final period. Gable, seizing the offensive, scored an escape and takedown and upset Behm, 10–5.

"Behm was a real good technician—slick, solid, all that stuff," Kraft said. "And Gable just shut him down."

In the final, Gable met the redoubtable Masaaki Hatta, the two-time NCAA runner-up for Oklahoma State at 123 pounds who won the national title in 1962. Hatta had age and experience on his side. Before the match, Les Anderson took Gable aside.

"I knew Hatta like a book—I'd tried to beat him for two or three years at Iowa State," Anderson said. "I took Dan into the locker room. I said, 'Lookit, this is his stance. He'll wait for you to shoot, he'll wait to take you down.' And I said, 'This is what will work, an ankle-high single [takedown]—attack at his ankle.' And he said, 'What is that?'

"So we stand up on the concrete floor in the locker room. I go through it, real slow. He hits it five, six times, right on that concrete floor, right before the finals. And he hits with it in the match. He scores four takedowns with it. 'Holy crap!' I go. 'I not only got a wrestler, I got somebody coachable.'"

Gable, immediately toppling Hatta and surging to a 2–0 lead, went on to an 8–3 victory against the defending two-time Midlands champion.

Gable remembered that before the match "some radio guy said, 'Hey, come on! We'll get you on the radio here!' So I went over real quick, because my match was coming up. He said, 'I just want to ask you one question. Is it true that you've never been beat before?' And I just said, 'Yeah. It's true that I've never been beat until now.'

" 'Until now,' I said. And I didn't say that I was going to get beat for sure, but maybe, you know. It's like, you go into something, you're a little bit unsure of really where you're going to end up."

Back in Ames, a day or so after his triumph, Gable and a few of his teammates, including Bahr, were walking around campus. Because of his shyness and tendency to hang back and "get my kicks watching other people," Gable offered an inviting target, as Bahr recounted: "Everybody would be touting him, after the Midlands, as the coming of the best wrestler ever, and they'd see somebody and they'd say, 'Do you know this is Dan Gable right here?' And somebody would pretend to be holding up a microphone, and they'd say, 'Hey, this is the great Dan Gable. Dan, say a few words for us.'

"Dan never spoke up. He was embarrassed about it. He liked the kidding, though."

Mack Gable attended most of his son's matches in college, and so did Katie when she could. They did not push him into wrestling or athletics of any kind, Gable said, but supported him once he chose wrestling. Mack secured a chinup bar above Dan's bedroom door so that his son could work on his arm and shoulder development. There were wrestling mats in the basement, where Gable and his friends and sometimes Mack himself could roll around, and there was a sauna and weights.

Mack was short, heavy-set, and had thinning black hair. Katie was a thin, high-spirited woman who passed on her narrow hips and prodigious work habits to her son. When she died of cancer in 1994, she was reported to be doing one of two things—either working in the yard or typing business papers for Mack's real-estate company.

The Gables were generous with their son, allowing his

wrestling buddies to stay at the house at no charge to train with him for days, weeks, sometimes months. Katie would arise first and prepare breakfast, sometimes cracking a beer and placing it on the windowsill and coaxing it through the morning. So remembered Chuck Jean, a raw, brawling talent who holds the distinction of winning four national wrestling titles in two different organizations—two NCAA titles at Iowa State and two National Association of Intercollegiate Athletics titles at Colorado State.

"'Bout 11 A.M. or so, Katie would finish that beer. A six-pack a day for her, that'd be it," Jean said. "[Dan] Gable, he'd tell me to keep an eye on Mack's drinking. I had a hard time with that. Ol' Mack and I saw eye-to-eye on things like that."

The Peterson brothers, Ben and John, stayed with the Gables for a month, training with Dan for the 1972 Olympics. "For a week or so, we'd sleep in until breakfast," said Ben, a former Iowa State wrestler who, like Gable, won a gold medal in '72. "Mack started getting us up when he went to work. 'You're supposed to be in training. You aren't even running,' he told us. We started running at seven in the morning, on a cinder track. It was a major turning point. This young man's dad was making a major investment in what we were doing, and he didn't want to let us sit around. Otherwise, we had nobody we were accountable to. Not a coach or anybody. Like he said, 'I'm doing this because I want a gold medal, too.'"

Katie prepared four meals a day, but she was too busy to eat the breakfasts she made—eggs, bacon, toast, and cereal. The other meals consisted of meats and salads and potatoes and desserts. If she wanted to smoke, she did it outside, or in a remote part of the house where she wouldn't harm or offend her muscular boarders.

After Katie died, Dan asked Peterson, a Baptist minister in Wisconsin, to give the eulogy. Peterson was honored. "I said that I lived in their home for a month. I said that of all the ladies I had known in my life, I couldn't remember any lady who was more committed and faithful to her husband and son than Katie Gable."

• • •

But both Mack and Katie drank, Mack sometimes to excess and in the presence of Dan's friends.

"One night we were over there and we were shooting pool," said Marty Dickey, a Waterloo businessman and long-time friend of Gable's. "And Mack came down, and he's had a few beers. Dan introduced him to a kid named Mike Graham. And Graham put his hand out, and Mack started to arm-drag him and took him to the floor. And he didn't even know the kid.

"And Dan just went, 'Oh, my God!' And Mike, he just went, 'What the hell did you do that for?'

"Our parents drank all the time. We didn't give it much thought. We thought it was funny, but it embarrassed Dan."

When he coached wrestling at Oklahoma State, Myron Roderick got a call just before bedtime the week that his Cowboys were to face Gable and Iowa State. It was Mack Gable. Roderick knew him from when he, Roderick, was trying to recruit Dan Gable. Roderick suspected Mack had been drinking.

"He said, 'Hey, coach, I know we're coming down there, and you're going to hire crooked officials, but we'll still whip your asses,'" Roderick recalled. "I wasn't mad or anything. That was just Mack. I told him, 'You got one part right, the crooked officials part. I don't know about whippin' our asses.'"

Gable and his older sister, Diane, watched their parents fight with words and with fists. Katie and Mack raged at each other when he arrived home in the wee hours from his nocturnal ramblings.

"I remember the police coming many times," said Dan, who never developed much of a taste for alcohol. "I can remember having to go to the hospital several times, for stitches, for whatever." The stitches, he explained, were for his mother or father, whoever had been hurt. "I don't know if my mom got hit too much. But my mom used to throw a lot of stuff at my dad."

With their children, Mack and Katie didn't spare the rod. Or the ring. Or the soap. Or the yardstick.

Mack wore a ring. If his son misbehaved, Mack made a fist and down came the ring on the boy's head, leaving its mark then, and to this day, perhaps.

"He'd get mad. . . . Obviously, I deserved a good crack, but not on the top of the head," Dan Gable said. "I mean, nowadays, it would be bad. But . . ."

One rainy day, young Danny Mack Gable glimpsed heaven in the form of a road being torn up.

As he tells the story, "We had tremendous rains, and these big gaps in the ground were filled completely full of water, and I was dinking around the construction site and fell in the hole. I was real young. I could swim pretty good, but I had all my clothes on. I was real muddy, and I couldn't get out of that damn thing.

"So, a construction guy came over and grabbed me and pulled me out and wanted to know where I lived. I only lived up the street, and he took me home. And, boy, did I get hell for that. I got a lot of hell for that. The ring down on my head."

Katie punished swearing the old-fashioned way, by forcing soap into her children's mouths. "I ate a lot of soap," Dan said.

"My mom also broke rulers, twelve-inch rulers, and yardsticks over my head. She broke more than one of those damn things. . . . So I wasn't as scared of my mom as I was my dad. Because rulers didn't hurt as much as rings."

Danny Mack Gable wanted to believe nothing as much as this: that his parents were good parents, and if he peered through the looking glass long enough, he could see reason and virtue in his and Diane's upbringing.

"Times change, you know," he said. "People come to your house and say, 'Oh, my God!,' but in those days it wasn't unusual. . . . They treated me great. They gave me every opportunity to be successful, [though] not from their actions at the beginning. More by what they put me in and said to me when I got home.

"But when it came down to always doing the best things

—no. They didn't do all the best things. But, you know, who does?"

The Midlands Wrestling Championships had not kept team points for the last three years, but this time around, a team champion would be named. It would create more interest in the event, officials thought, add a splash of gin to the tonic. But the suspense wasn't killing anyone. Top-ranked Iowa (5–0) was bringing in one defending NCAA champion (Williams), one two-time past winner (McIlravy), a three-time All-American (Mena), and a two-time All-American (Ironside). The No. 2 team in the country, Oklahoma State, had passed up the post-Christmas Midlands to stay warm and compete in the Reno (Nevada) Duals. But four other top ten teams in the *Amateur Wrestling News* coaches' poll were entered in the Midlands: Iowa State, Illinois, Michigan State, and California State—Bakersfield.

The Iowa team took vans from Iowa City to the Sheraton North Shore in suburban Chicago, where they would stay for two nights, riding in shifts to compete Saturday and Sunday at the Welsh-Ryan Arena on the Northwestern University campus. It was a full boat; Gable brought seventeen wrestlers—ten starters, six reserves, plus Eric Akin, the Hawkeye Wrestling Club member, who, under NCAA rules, had to drive separately. But the traveling party lost one of its regulars, Brian Mitchell, who forsook Jennifer Gable and Iowa wrestling to ride with his parents, Bob and Diane, to watch Iowa play Texas Tech in the Alamo Bowl football game in San Antonio, Texas. Mark Mitchell, Brian's older brother, was a reserve linebacker for Iowa.

Several Midlands coaches and officials met Friday night in a chandeliered conference room in the North Shore Hilton, a fifteen-minute drive from the Sheraton. Gable and several confreres sat at a long, wide table, amid the rubble of paper and pens and coffee cups and pop cans. Civilians sat at three computers, tapping out reams of information that would be sifted through and amended until the seedings were finally settled upon at each weight class. Ideally, the wealth in each of the ten classes would be spread, and the No. 1 and 2 seeds would weave their way through the top and bottom of the brackets and meet in the final.

Dan Gable, looking worn and restless with pain, sat with his back to the doors, his crutches propped against a pillar. Occasionally, he arose, hobbled a few steps, and returned to his chair. Across the table sat Tim Cysewski, the Northwestern coach who wrestled at Iowa from 1973 to 1976, Gable's years as an assistant under Gary Kurdelmeier. With his full head of black hair and spryness, Cysweski looked much younger than Gable, his near-contemporary.

Cysewski (pronounced "CEE-ses-ski") good-naturedly needled Gable, saying the rumor was that the Iowa coach had already had hip surgery. Well, the rumor was false, Gable said over the tops of his glasses.

"My grandmother was a hundred years old and had one— a hip replacement, and she's still living," the Northwestern coach said. " 'Course, she didn't have such a great hundredth birthday."

When Cysewski pushed to know how fast Gable planned to be back on the mat after surgery, Gable retorted, "as fast as I can," failing to mention that Marsh had warned him never to get on the mat again.

"No, but how long exactly do you plan to be off, before you're back on the mat?" Denny Moore asked. Moore, the University of North Carolina–Greensboro coach, a large man with a mellifluous voice, pulled his chair closer to Cysewski and peered across at Gable.

"Two weeks," Gable stated flatly.

"Two weeks!" Moore repeated, shocked. "The man is unbelievable!"

Someone in the room was smoking. Gable rubbed his eyes. "When I was wrestling," he said, "and I had my knee operations, I had a choice—three months, or a shorter recovery time and they'd take the cartilage. I said give me less recovery time."

"I got virgin knees," Cysewski said. "I know just what'll

happen. I'll get on the mat with some kid and I'll blow them both out on the mat."

Around 9 P.M., Ken Kraft, the tournament director, announced that the work was going slowly, and that "we might be here a while is what I'm saying."

At 9:30 P.M., Kathy Gable swung by the hotel, with Annie, seventeen, in tow. Jennifer had been dropped at the Sheraton North Shore with the two youngest Gables, Mackenzie and thirteen-year-old Molly. Kathy parked and picked her way carefully across the icy lot and went inside. She dropped Annie off at the coaches' meeting and soon was on a pay phone just off the lobby. What she heard drained the blood from her cheeks. She issued a mournful, "Oh, no . . . Oh, no . . ." as her face turned as red as the plaid jacket she was wearing. She began crying. "Does she know? Does she know?" she asked.

She hung up and walked across the lobby, around a corner and down a hallway to the meeting room. Gable glanced up from his chair. He knew something was wrong. He never got the chance to ask what.

"There's been a death," his wife said, choked with tears. "Not in our family. In Jenni's boyfriend's. Diane was killed. Car accident. Near Sheridan, Iowa."

Gable removed his glasses and put them on the table. He rose and looked with anxious eyes at his wife, but made no move to embrace her, not yet. He asked about Brian, his fishing partner, and if he was all right, or if anyone else had been killed. Kathy shook her head no. Gable led her to the end of the table and sat down again, trying to digest what he had heard.

The room had fallen silent. Computers had stopped clacking. Kraft approached, and his movement seemed to break a spell.

"Kathy, I'm so sorry," he said. "You never know, one day to the next."

Suddenly, as if unfrozen by Kraft's sympathetic overtures, Annie fell to the carpet in a fetal position at Kathy's feet and emitted a long, low, seamless moan of unbearable pain, of suffering unrelieved. Kathy bent and soothed her and brought her to her feet. Kathy turned to her husband and, anticipating his question, said that Jennifer hadn't been told—and that they would have to be the ones to do it.

In the van on the way back to the Sheraton, Kathy drove while Gable used a car phone to call a Des Moines hospital and find out the conditions of Brian and his father. From a shift supervisor, Gable wheedled the news that Bob Mitchell, an Iowa City builder, was stable but had a concussion and deep cuts, and that Brian had suffered neck injuries but that he was wiggling his toes—a good sign.

"What if Jenni had been along," Kathy wondered, staring straight ahead into the oncoming headlights.

"Don't say that," Gable said. He had a catch in his voice.

Kathy left her husband off at the hotel entrance and parked. He adjusted the Cossack-like hat he wore and leaned into the work of moving forward on his crutches.

"I'm glad nothing happened to Brian," he said, the cold wind eating his words. "Boy, she really loves that guy."

Moving through the lobby and up to his suite, Gable ran into clumps of his wrestlers wanting to know details. Three times he told the story, and how he found out about it, before he reached his door. Jennifer was on the other side. He walked in and shut the door and, a few minutes later, reappeared in the hallway.

"Jenni heard it and passed out," he said. "Just boom, like that. Right to the floor. Said she thought something like that had happened."

He thought for a moment.

"News like that, I would have expected [it to be] my dad," he said. "He's a walking time bomb. He doesn't take care of himself as well as he should."

The next morning, Saturday, Kathy left with Jennifer and Mackenzie and drove to Des Moines to visit Brian and see how she could help the Mitchells. Before she left, she told her husband, "I don't know what happened to Annie. Usually, she doesn't lose it like that. She's tougher than that."

Gable now had Annie and Molly in his charge, as well as

seventeen wrestlers who would compete in as many as eight matches apiece over two days. Because everyone had been up late on Friday night, waiting for the pairings and news about the accident, Gable handled the pre-tournament team meeting in the hallway, the night before. Then he let the team sleep in until they met in the lobby at 8:30 A.M. for the trip to the arena. The trainers, Kristen Payne and her assistant, Jerod Gayer, set up a buffet in the Gables' suite, and wrestlers wandered in for fresh fruit and cereal. Hand was the last to appear, a heavy-lidded bear on the prowl for food. He poured a bowl of Sugar Smacks, bade hello to those about, and returned to his room, all in the space of five minutes.

Welsh-Ryan Arena was clamorous. Annoucements streamed over the public-address system. This coach was supposed to report here, that coach there. Eight gray mats filled the floor where Northwestern played its home basketball games. In all, 360 wrestlers from 60 schools and wrestling clubs competed as individuals for team points. An estimated crowd of 3,500 filled the 6,000-capacity gym. The Iowa delegation staked out the north end of the balcony, and the trainers marked the spot with plastic sacks of bagels and energy bars, and energy drinks in plastic barrels. It would be home for the next forty-eight hours.

Gable lurched about on his crutches, visting with men he had wrestled and coached with and against for most of his life. Several were bandylegged, with orthopedic problems of their own, and they asked Gable how he was doing with his bad hip and what was in store. Gable spent no small amount of time during the first session in the radio roost of KXIC announcer Morrie Adams. Not until the big matches of the quarterfinals and beyond did Gable begin sitting on the "bench"—a folding chair set at the corner of the mat—when an Iowa wrestler competed. "Too many things going on," Gable said. "Too many guys wrestling all the time, and it's too hard to get around."

Later, he brightened and added, "Friend of mine back home I talked to, he said he wouldn't have known exactly what was going on unless I was talking on the radio."

Bill Kucinski led off Iowa's bid, losing his 134-pound match to eighth-seeded Ryan Shapert of Edinboro. After his 10–2 defeat, Kucinski dropped to one knee, panting, then faded into the traffic of wrestlers, coaches, and trainers in the back corridors. He was paying the price, he said, for cutting more than ten pounds to make weight. "My chest is burning. My throat's dry. I'm starting to feel bad. Is it chilly in here?" He looked up. A pulled hamstring soon would take him out of the tournament, and he would fade back to reserve status.

Meanwhile, the Hawkeyes' front-liners began establishing a beachhead. Whitmer, second-seeded at 118, peeled off a 16–6 victory. Murderers' Row—Ironside, McIlravy, and Williams, all top-seeded—won their opening matches with ease, Ironside by pin, McIlravy by technical fall, and Williams by an eight-point decision. Mena, seeded second at 126 pounds, impatiently waited for his first match, pointing out to his teammates in the north balcony that while other Hawkeyes had wrestled three times already, there he sat.

"All these wrestle-backs and a double-elimination tournament," he said, referring to the system in which a first-time loser would be placed in the consolation bracket and have a chance to wrestle back for as high as a third-place finish from there. "Why? Who wants to see losers? Who wants to wrestle if they can't win?"

Gable skipped and hobbled on his crutches to see Mena win his opening match over Dale Eggert, 15–2. Mena axed Eggert with a leg sweep, eliciting a loud, "Mena! Nice move!" from his coach. Eggert, a forty-year-old wrestling coach at Libertyville (Illinois) High School who represented Northwestern's Wildcat Wrestling Club, was making his twelfth Midlands appearance. He was the tournament's oldest wrestler, a man who refereed several of Mena's matches when Mena was on summer break from high school.

"You can't beat us young guys," Mena said, passing Eggert at the edge of the mat after the match and patting him on the rear.

For the next hour or so, Gable dropped in on several matches involving Hawkeyes, tucking important moments away for future use and shouting so loudly from the bleachers and sidelines that the boom of his voice could be distinguished from distant ramparts in the gym.

He arrived late to Koble's match against thirteenth-seeded Vince Taylor of Pensacola Christian College. Koble's development was particularly vital, considering that Gilliss hadn't buttoned down the 142-pound berth.

It was the third period. Koble led, 5–3. Both were off their feet and on the mat. Koble was like an angler who had hooked a large fish and didn't know what to do with it. He held Taylor by a half-headlock with one arm, while a leg had hooked Taylor's left leg. Koble was unsure which end to work. Gable knew.

"Keep your weight on his head! Keep your weight on his head! Keep your weight on his head!" Gable yelled through cupped hands, and half to himself said, "Koble looks dead. Look at that. Dead. Get off your ass."

Now to Koble: "Suck it up, Koble! Get a score *right now!*"

Koble scored a little later and won, 7–5.

From the scorers' table, Gable, craning over his crutches, watched Hand get bounced into the heavyweight consolation bracket after losing 4–2 to second-seeded Steve Neal of Cal State–Bakersfield. In short order, Gable joined Jim Zalesky in the hallway to comfort and confront Hand.

"The guy could be a national champion, and you almost beat him," Gable said, his voice rasping, verging on hoarseness. "And you could have if you would have shot more—just one decent shot . . . You've got to be *confident.*"

Gable began hobbling away, then paused and wheeled and said, "A long, tall guy like that, you've got to get under him."

"I spend all my energy trying to hold him off," Hand said, his first words since losing, and they wedged like a sliver in Gable's brain.

"Yeah, and it's called hand-fighting," the coach said. "It's a basic skill!"

After Saturday's two sessions, the Hawkeyes had nine of ten wrestlers in contention to place—everyone except Gilliss. Six Hawkeyes had reached the semifinals: Whitmer, Mena,

Ironside, McIlravy, Williams, and Fullhart. Three others—
Uker, Ersland, and Hand—had a chance for third. Hand gal-
loped back into the coach's favor by beating tenth-seeded
Trent Hynek of Iowa State, 10–3.

Early Sunday morning, Gable lifted weights and baked in
a sauna at a nearby health club, then opened his suite for a
team meeting before the group headed to the arena for the
afternoon semifinals. The wrestlers sat or sprawled on the carpet, in chairs, and on a rollaway in the main room. Gable put
down a bagel he had been nibbling on and pinpointed what
each of his starters should expect in upcoming matches. He
warned Williams about Eastern Illinois's Matt Hughes, seeded
fifth. "He's going to want to slow it down and make it a
one-point match and try to beat you. He's got some big moves,
you know, upper-body, but he doesn't defend the shot that
well, except that he slows people down." Gable described the
mistakes he had seen the previous day. "Some of you guys,
the thing I've been noticing, the biggest mistake, even with
Williams, is you work real hard to get a shot, and you get it
almost ninety percent of the way to taking this guy out, and
then as soon as you get almost to to the point of taking him
down you stop and hesitate. And then all of a sudden, the last
five percent, ten percent is real hard to get. . . . We're putting
ourselves in a position to score, and that's better, but we've
got to capitalize and really act like when time's running we've
got to score."

The meeting broke up, and the wrestlers went back to
their rooms to pick up their gym bags. Gable started working
on his bagel again, but then a call came and he stopped to talk
to Brian Mitchell. Brian wanted to hear how the team was
doing, and Gable sketched it out. Gable asked about Mitchell's
injuries; Brian told him he had suffered torn neck ligaments,
nothing worse.

Gable asked about Bob Mitchell, who was driving the van
that skidded on ice and crashed, killing Diane. "Did he break
up when he found out?" Gable asked into the receiver. "Really? Well, you've got to do that once in awhile. You've got to

get it out of you, guy. . . . Well, you guys have some women in your life now. You've got my wife, and Jenni, and some others."

Molly walked in from the bedroom she was sharing with Annie as Gable was hanging up. He enlisted her to help him put on his shoes again. "I can't bend over yet," he said. "It's my back, today." She bent down.

"Hurry up," he told Molly, wiry and blond, who was chomping Gummi Bears candy. "Hurry up. I've got to go. Take care of me. God gave me these women for a reason."

Molly: "No."

Gable: "I'd bat you if you were a boy saying that. But instead I'll give you a quarter for this."

Molly (picking up the half-eaten bagel): "Is this your bagel? How long ago did you eat it?"

Gable: "I've been eating it for an hour. How do you eat those Gummi Bears in the morning? I can't believe you eat Gummi Bears in the morning."

Molly: "It's not morning. It's, like, 12 P.M."

Gable: "I know, but Gummi Bears? Why even eat them? Hey, are they good?"

Molly: (Nods.)

Gable: "Come on! Hurry up! I can get these socks on if I wanted."

By the time Gable and his daughters ride the elevator to the lobby, the team is waiting, and the exodus for the last day of Midlands competition begins.

The date of the Midlands semifinals and finals was December 29, but Gable and the team had March 20 to 22 in the crosshairs—the dates of their NCAA championship title defense. Even now, on a crisp, sunny Sunday in Chicago, all thoughts were on Cedar Falls. That meant thinking about Oklahoma State, out of sight at the Midlands, but not out of mind. The second-ranked Cowboys were clipping along with strong showings in a couple of tournaments and easy dual victories over the University of Tennessee–Chattanooga and

Georgia State before chopping down bigger timber, No. 10 Oklahoma and No. 7 Michigan State, by big scores: 32–11 and 39–0 respectively.

"Oklahoma State is knocking at our door," the Iowa coach said privately, and with worry. To his team, he said, "There's a big article in the paper today about how Oklahoma State's been kicking everybody's ass and how good they are and so on. That team's not here, and Iowa State didn't bring all their people, Illinois didn't bring all their people, so just because the score is the way it is now, doesn't mean it's [the NCAA championships] a shoo-in. . . . We're trying to win here, do the best we can. But it's all for the end of the season.

"Every match is important, but we're still learning. Gathering information all the time."

The Hawkeyes polished off the Midlands with three champions, all from Murderers' Row. McIlravy tore into Arizona State's unseeded Michael Douglas for fourteen takedowns en route to a 28–13 semifinal victory. In the 150-pound final, McIlravy beat Iowa State's NCAA champion Chris Bono again, this time 7–1.

McIlravy was back, all right. His father, Ken, bearded, in a western shirt and jeans and boots, watched approvingly but not excitedly. His son grew up strong, doing chores on 16,000 acres of South Dakota ranchland, home to beef cattle as well as the McIlravys.

"As a pee-wee wrestler, Lincoln wasn't very good," his father said. "He was 22–20 as a seventh grader, a 98-pounder. Then he was 37–2 in the eighth grade. Won the state title. Won five before he was done.

"Five schools recruited him: Iowa, North Carolina, Wisconsin, Oregon State, Nebraska. Gable came to our house, and we played it straight with him. He fired us up. We had a party when Lincoln signed. Eight or nine people were there. Gable, I remember, wanted a picture taken."

The father stopped and thought a moment.

"Gable is the most fascinating person I've ever met," he said. "He's not always right, but he is always Gable. He pushes guys to their physical and emotional limits. And he always gets his way."

Gable gave Lincoln a loose handshake as he came off the mat after beating Bono. McIlravy had taken down the defending national champion once in each period. The Iowa wrestler credited Gable with steadying the team through the trauma of the Mitchell family's accident.

"He was our security blanket. He gave us a level of comfort," McIlravy said. "He's done everything. He's lost a sister. After his mother's death—it was expected and all—he didn't skip practice."

Ironside pushed his record to 10–0 with five victories in the Midlands, capping his weekend with a 12–4 major decision over Iowa State's Dwight Hinson in the 134-pound final. In a rematch of last season's NCAA 158-pound championship, Williams converted three double-leg takedowns into a 7–4 victory over Ernest Benion of Illinois. The previous March, on the floor of Target Center in downtown Minneapolis, Williams edged Benion for the NCAA title.

That he was black and from Chicago made Williams's third Midlands championship even sweeter. "A lot of kids from my neighborhood who look up to me come to the Midlands to see me compete," Williams said. "There's not that many black athletes out there in wrestling, so that makes me want to train harder and make more people say, 'Well, man, look at him. Maybe I could do it.'"

Whitmer, Mena, and Fullhart each finished second in their classes. Whitmer's domination in an 8–2 semifinal victory over Illinois's Lindsey Durlacher sent Gable into the loudest and happiest of orbits.

"Keep him on the mat! Keep him on the mat!" Gable bellowed as Durlacher, overpowered by Whitmer's strength, scambled toward the edge of the mat. "Pin his butt! Strongest man in the world!" Then, in an aside: "Whitmer looks like a guy in puberty yet. What is he, four–eleven?" Back to coaching: "Jessie! Jessie! Get his legs outta there! Get his legs out! Strongest man in the world!!!!!!"

Gable's enthusiasm was tempered in the final, however,

where Whitmer had a glaring weakness exposed in a 1–0 defeat to Michigan State's David Morgan. Morgan escaped from Whitmer in the second period and made it hold up. The trouble was that Whitmer couldn't escape from Morgan in the third period, when the MSU wrestler had the up position, kneeling beside Whitmer, who was on all fours and waiting for the referee's whistle to try to break away. After the referee had raised Morgan's left hand in victory, Whitmer stalked off the mat, snatching the warm-up jacket thrown his way but not looking at who threw it.

Mena, a two-time Midlands champion at 118 and top-seeded at 126 this year, was upset by Arizona State's Shawn Ford in the semifinals, 5–3. Mena defeated Akin, 5–0, for third place, ending a stressful tournament during which he had again began to float the notion that he might be better off wrestling at 118. (Gable shook his head. "All I know is that I've been three years with him trying to cut to 118, and it's been hell. If he showed me he could do it without a coach hitting him over the head, OK.")

Fullhart kicked and threw his headgear after his 3–2 defeat at the hands of top-seeded Jason Robinson of Edinboro in the 190-pound final. The referee shook a cautionary finger at the retreating Fullhart, who had won two of his four Midlands matches by disqualification and injury default.

Wes Hand finished a respectable fourth, winning a big match in the consolation semifinals against Syracuse heavyweight Jason Gleasman, who, like McIlravy, had put his collegiate career on hold the year before to train for the Olympics. Gleasman wound up making the U.S. Greco-Roman team, but did not place in Atlanta. In Greco-Roman competition, wrestlers concentrated on upper-body attacks, and moves had names like the "trapped-arm gut wrench." The other form of international wrestling—freestyle—more closely approximated college, or "folkstyle," wrestling. Hand took Gleasman into overtime, when the Iowa wrestler presumed to attempt a most astonishing feat: to throw a man whose own throws had made him an Olympian. Maybe Gleasman was caught by surprise; for sure, everyone else was. Hand, unseeded, executed a two-point takedown with a throw, and stashed away a 3–1 victory over the third-seeded Gleasman. "I'm on a high," Gable enthused breathlessly. Tom Brands, his assistant, echoed one of Gable's lines that ricocheted around the Iowa camp for days. "Hey!" Brands yelled, pointing gleefully at Hand. "He Grecoed a Greco!"

It seemed anticlimatic, but important nonetheless, that Uker pinned two of his seven opponents and finished seventh at 167, while Ersland, losing three matches by a total of six points, placed eighth at 177.

The Hawkeyes boarded vans for home in the cold Chicago night with an easy team victory—they racked up 176 points, well ahead of runner-up Edinboro's 95.5 and third-place Cal–Bakersfield's 91. Iowa State finished fourth with 89 points, Illinois sixth with 79, and Michigan State eighth with 73.5. Overall, the Hawkeyes had won 52 of 70 matches; their starters were 45–11, with 6 pins. In ten matches, varsity wrestlers had won by ten or more points. If this wasn't domination, it would do until a better imitation came along.

"I'm gaining confidence in this team. They're gaining confidence. There are some positives," Gable said. "Five or six guys are getting tougher, and nine guys placed. I'm on a definite high."

Gable gave the team a break at New Year's, but reeled them back on Monday for two-a-days, leading to weight cutting on Thursday, weigh-in on Friday, and then a bus trip to East Lansing, Michigan, for Saturday night's dual against Michigan State. A week after that, the pace would quicken: the National Duals January 18 and 19 at Lincoln, Nebraska, where Gable would see Oklahoma State for the only time before the NCAA championships, then hip surgery on January 23. He planned to return for the February 8 home duals against Illinois and Arizona State. He would miss the Minnesota, Wisconsin, and Northwestern duals. His stomach still hurt, seven weeks now. It would be better after surgery, doctors told him.

"I don't want to procrastinate," Gable said. "I want to get on with it."

But he still dithered about if and when he would leave coaching. The question made the rounds of fans and coaches at the Midlands, and Gable's longtime friends and enemies kept watch and waited. This much seemed certain: Gable realized his body was telling him something, shouting at him to give it up, and it probably would be sooner rather than later that he did so.

The previous spring, hitting the road for athletic department fund-raisers, Gable deflected questions about retirement by saying that he and Iowa athletic director Bob Bowlsby were going to go fishing, drink a couple of beers, and discuss matters. Then Gable would say, "You know, it wouldn't hurt my consideration of this matter if there was a new boat waiting there for us to fish in." They never went fishing, but Bowlsby drove out to Gable's, and the two took a sauna in the clubhouse and cracked a couple of beers, and Bowlsby presented the Iowa coach with a new boat—a toy boat with a toy trailer to go with it. Then Bowlsby said, "There! Now I expect you to negotiate in good faith."

Next to Gable's retirement, the hottest question was: Who would follow him? Or, more precisely, would it be Jim Zalesky or Tom Brands? It had to be one of them, doubtless the one recommended by Gable, but he wasn't saying.

It was a daunting proposition, following someone of Gable's stature. "Look at any sport on the college level, and there's never been a dynasty that's continued after there's been a change of head people," said J Robinson, Gable's longtime assistant and friend until the two had a falling out, who eventually became the University of Minnesota wrestling coach. "It's just going to be that way. I don't think that whoever gets the job knows that's going to happen.

"The best time to get the job is not this time, it's the next time."

The coaching scenario could be played out in a telephone booth. Gable hired Robinson, who left and hired Zalesky, who had wrestled and coached under Gable, for the Minnesota staff. Zalesky tried unsuccessfully to recruit the Brands brothers for Minnesota, then bounced back to the Iowa staff and coached

Tom and Terry. Now Zalesky and Tom Brands sat across a tight aisle in the Iowa wrestling office and waited for the end of the season to see how the cards fell.

Brands and Zalesky represented different tributaries of the same river. Brands had emerged as the Iowa wrestling icon of the '90s; born in Nebraska and raised in Iowa, the product of a broken home, he was tough and driven to succeed. Even as his brother narrowly missed making the 1996 U.S. Olympic team, Tom ran the string all the way to a gold medal in Atlanta. Gable, on hand to give advice but not as an official coach, nearly hyperventilated at one point watching Brands.

Zalesky could serve as a poster boy for Iowa wrestling in the '80s, as inward in his approach to the sport as Tom Brands was emotive. Zalesky learned his wrestling at Prairie High School, up I-380 from Iowa City, a school known for its hard-nosed Czech athletes. Had it not been for neck and shoulder injuries, Zalesky might have pocketed an Olympic medal himself.

While each assistant coach lived and worked outside the mainstream in his hidden and primitive sport, each now was experiencing a common American nightmare: hanging around until the boss croaked or quit; pledging undying fealty to the boss and the business, passing off personal goals as secondary, and denying obvious tensions in the office.

Brands did admit that after the Olympics he went to Gable for answers.

"I was real anxious about him retiring, and I went in and I said, 'This is driving me crazy. People are asking me about this.' I just came off the Olympics, and I was kind of a hot name, and everybody was asking me what was going to happen. He calmed me down good. He looks at things so rational.

"Basically, what he said was that he's probably not going to be coach next year."

Gable made no promises, Brands said, except to say that either he had a hand in picking his successor or "he wouldn't step down." And there the conversation ended.

"I've always been a good sport when things are out of my control," Brands said. "Well, it's out of my control. I've got to do the best I can, and if Jimmy gets the job and hires me, fine. I'll be an assistant for another couple years or so or whenever an opportunity arises.

"I'll put this in the hands of the higher power. But I love it here. I love these guys. That's no secret. They work hard. That's what I like about it."

Zalesky had seniority, with seven years as Gable's assistant and head recruiter, compared with Brands' five years. Over the last three years, Zalesky said, Gable had talked about getting out, but the conversations were more frequent and serious this season as Gable's health declined. Zalesky would not discuss his chances or his future, saying only he would wait to see what happened.

Zalesky and Brands acknowledged each other's presence and exchanged information about schedules and wrestlers, but otherwise spun off into their own realms and responsibilities. Gable was coming into the office less and less, and eventually Bowlsby—out of both necessity and what Gable viewed as an attempt to entice him to stay—gave Gable office help in the lean form of Bill Wilkinson, a skilled sports-management graduate, who straightened Gable's office and prioritized his appointments and speaking engagements. Wilkinson sat in Gable's chair, worked at Gable's desk. Gable didn't reclaim his office; if he wanted to confer, he sat in the visitor's chair. "That's how it'll be until everything's straightened out," the coach said.

In early January against a Michigan State team that had been in free fall and was shut out at Oklahoma State on December 14, Iowa scored a 26–10 victory—the top-ranked Hawkeyes' thirty-ninth straight dual victory and sixth of the season. But top to bottom, Gable saw ghosts and goblins in his lineup. Whitmer, who a week earlier had suffered that 1–0 loss to State's David Morgan at the Midlands, was swamped in their second meeting, 18–7. Morgan improved to 19–1, cementing his place among the top three in the country in the 118-pound class, behind Clarion's top-ranked Sheldon

Thomas and Oklahoma State's Teague Moore. Whitmer slipped to 9–2.

Mena and Ironside scored easy victories at 126 and 134, with Ironside improving to 11–0 and ranked No. 1 in the country. Gilliss was struggling in his 142-pound match against Sam Hakim, a fellow redshirt freshman whom Gilliss had beaten 5–4 in his opening Midlands match. McIlravy was in the locker room with a headache, a chronic condition he had aggravated in the Midlands final. McIlravy, who worked out sparingly during the week, had weighed in and was ready, but Gable told him he wouldn't use him unless the world was collapsing. Whitmer had lost a major decision, and now Gilliss trailed Hakim 3–0 late in the third period. The world as Gable knew it was collapsing. Gable dispatched trainer Kristen Payne to tell McIlravy he would be wrestling.

"I said to Lincoln, 'Coach wants to wrestle you,' " Payne said. " 'You are cleared medically, but I need to know if you're OK with this.' And Lincoln said, 'Yeah. I'm fine.'

"If he was mad, or if he had said, 'I just don't want to wrestle,' or if he was angry [and said], 'Why does he want to wrestle me?,' I would have gone back to the coach and said he's not ready."

As McIlravy was warming up, Gilliss rallied for a 5–3 victory to even his season record at 6–6. McIlravy, now committed emotionally to wrestling, responded with a 17–2 decision over Adam Elderkin at 150. Williams followed with another of his it's-too-close-but-we'll-take-it victories, 7–3, to remain, with Ironside and McIlravy, unbeaten for the season. Uker won easily, 12–4, at 167, but Ersland stumbled, 6–1, at 177, and Fullhart lost his second straight 3–2 decision, this time to Brian Picklo, in a match that left Gable fuming about the officiating. Hand—still feeling the sharp pain of a neck and shoulder injury suffered in the Midlands—managed a 12–6 victory to cap off Iowa's victory. The Hawkeyes, at least until the National Duals, would hold on to the top spot in the rankings.

On Sunday's bus ride home, Gable had the driver turn up

the radio. The Green Bay Packers were playing, and Gable, who worshiped at the shrine of Mantle, also reveled in the announcer's roll call of past Packer greats: Hornung and Taylor. Starr and McGee. And Lombardi, always Lombardi.

"I just tingled when I heard their names," Gable said. "I said to myself, 'Hey, Gable, they didn't get to be good by easing off.' Before that I was thinking I'd take it easy on my athletes. I had a two P.M. practice scheduled Monday. Now I made it for nine A.M.—the earlier the better. And we'd get something done."

chapter **5**

T HREE DAYS AFTER Michigan State, Gable convened practice on the concourse ninety-three steps above the
basketball floor at Carver-Hawkeye. The wrestlers would begin
their first of two workouts today with sprints. Then back to
the wrestling room to drill and run, building to the National
Duals over the weekend. The Duals featured sixteen of the
top Division I, II, and III teams in the country jousting in
single-elimination team competition, the two unbeaten teams
meeting for the title on Sunday afternoon. It figured to be a
showdown between Iowa and Oklahoma State, Dan Gable versus John Smith.

"You're going to have four matches in twenty-eight
hours," Gable told his team. "We'll see now how tough you
are, see if you can shut anybody out this year. You've got to
wrestle hard all the time. Even if you get tired, you shouldn't
show it.

"It's a matter of pushing through the match and doing
what you've got to do to win instead of letting up. You may
get tired. So what? We expect to be tired, but we expect to be
able to continue until a match is over as well. Got to get in the
right frame of mind here. Get tough on you. One lap. OK. Hit
it!"

The pack of twenty varsity wrestlers, most in sweatshirts and sweat pants, took off in a drum roll of feet. A cold winter sunlight lay in rectangular sheets on the floor. Mark Ironside led them around the quarter-mile concourse, as he led most such drills. Last was Jeff McGinness, the former 126-pound national champion who did not look as if he would ever see 126 again. Gable noted without rancor above McGinness's panting, "Jeff's real out of shape. You can tell he's redshirting, kind of taking advantage of it. Imagine the shape he'll be in in the fall."

For a half hour, Gable had them run around the concourse, then up and down the ninety-three steps, then around the concourse and back to the steps. Always the mantra: "OK, hit it! . . . OK, hit it!"

It was part of Iowa wrestling lore that Gable had his wrestlers do "buddy-carries" up the arena stairs. Indeed, Gable used to participate himself, jumping on the back of a wrestler and riding him like a runaway stallion to the top of the stairs, the coach dragging his feet up each of the ninety-three steps to toughen the workout. But there were no buddy-carries this time. "They have to wrestle afterward," Gable said. "That's too hard after buddy-carries."

After a half hour, Gable ended the sprints and stair-climbs and told the wrestlers to change into their wrestling shoes and meet in the wrestling room. Gable looked down at the sweat speckling the floor. "You can tell they're into it. You can tell they're working when you see that." He shook his head. "Should've made them do one more. Would've if I'd wanted to torture them. I just didn't want to torture them today."

In the wrestling room, Jim Zalesky and Tom Brands had swabbed the mats to reduce the possibility of staph infections, which produce angry-looking sores and swelling. The wrestlers already had paired off by the time Gable rolled in on his crutches. Hand, the heavyweight, wore a foam-rubber collar to protect him from chronic "stingers"—the feeling of an electric shock traveling down the arm, causing loss of strength, brought about by nerve-damaging blows to the shoulders and neck.

Gable, in a dark sweatsuit and desert-brown boots, sat in

the second row of the bleachers and watched Jessie Whitmer squirm and twist from a sitting position on the mat but not escape from a reserve who, reaching around Whitmer from behind, trapped one of the starter's hands against his stomach. Hard on Gable's mind was Whitmer's Midlands match against David Morgan, when Whitmer couldn't free himself in the third period. "If he's got your hand, don't come up to your feet," Gable said, Whitmer looking up at him. "Break the grip, and then come to your feet."

Gable called the group to order. "Each guy do his favorite move twenty times," he began, and when that was over, he ordered escape moves—"standups or sitouts, make sure you keep your hips under you, walk your feet out." There was low-ankle shooting from standing positions, and hand-fighting, the basic skill that Gable wanted Wes Hand to further develop after his Midlands loss. The session finished with more sprints, one end of the room to the other, eleven times, Mike Uker crying out over his black mouthguard. And then curls in the weight room behind a low brick wall on the other side of the mats, and rope climbs and chin-ups.

They broke for lunch. Gable went to a downtown pizza joint, took the salad bar, a small cheese-and-sausage, and a glass of Mountain Dew. He sounded worried on a number of fronts. Mike Mena's weight, for one. The senior had just one more chance to win an NCAA title, after getting as close as third as a sophomore. Mena hadn't stopped agonizing about whether 118 might not be his best choice after all, especially in light of his Midlands defeat at 126.

Gable met with Mena and explained that because of a recent rules change, it might be even harder for him to drop and hold weight this year at 118 than it was last. Under the new NCAA weight policy, during the second half of the season, a wrestler had to weigh in 75 percent of the time at the weight at which he intended to compete in qualifying tournaments and at the NCAA championships. Gable saw no advantage for Mena to drop to 118, risking loss of muscle, then climb back for another weigh-in at 126.

Gable forked his salad to his mouth. "You shrink a guy

down six, ten times, every week jumping them up and down, it will take a real toll on them."

Of course, Gable had self-serving reasons as well to keep Mena at 126. Whitmer, despite recent setbacks, had shown he could win at 118. And he had paid his dues.

"Whitmer, he's kind of got my heart," Gable said. "You know, he's a good kid. Done whatever I've asked him ever since he's been here. More experience, he could have been better. Probably should have been in the lineup more often.

"But Mena was always in there. I probably should have made sure I wrestled him [Whitmer] in more tournaments and stuff. Because once he's in the lineup, like right now, we're getting all the bugs out of him."

In the end, Gable said, it would be Mena's choice if he wanted to drop to 118 and challenge Whitmer, although Gable had made his position clear. "I'm really against it. I'll explain it over and over again until he figures it out. And then, if he still wants to go that way, that's fine."

Mena already knew the pitfalls of marching out of step.

"You don't want to get him [Gable] mad at you, because if you do, it's just like the whole world is mad at you for some reason," Mena said. "It's like, if Gable's happy with your performances, then everybody is. Other coaches, teammates, administrative people. Everybody.

"But if he's not happy, it seems like everybody knows about it. There's people in the administrative office that he's good friends with, and when you're doing well, they're saying Hi to you. But when you're not doing so well, nobody's talking to you. If you can keep him happy, everybody else seems happy, too."

Other parts of the lineup needed to come together as well. At 142, Kasey Gilliss was unsteady. Eric Koble, his backup, had shown flashes until he was hurt, and another reserve, Jamie Heidt, had edged into the picture. Another candidate, Ben Uker, Mike's younger brother, would suffer a broken jaw in practice a few weeks later and miss the rest of the season.

"Gilliss has won five of his last seven matches, which isn't earth-shattering," Gable said. "But it's better than losing the first three of four [as Gilliss did]."

At 177, Tony Ersland, a dues-paying senior like Whitmer, had the only losing record among the starters, 6–7. Gable toyed with opening the weight to challenges from contenders such as Matt Hoover, a sophomore who had just returned from academic ineligibility. "Even if Hoover does win the trial and gets in the competition and doesn't do very well, I might as well go back to Ersland and go with the heart, because Hoover's got two more years of eligibility. Hoover's a good kid, too, but I can't just go with who's good kids."

Mark Ironside had emerged as the favorite among the coaches, a wrestler wringing the most from his ability, an example of what hard work brings. Whitmer had, proportionately, more power; Lincoln McIlravy had more instinctive elan. But Ironside had a pilot light for wrestling that never went out.

After lunch, Ironside threw his jacket into a chair across from the secretary's desk in the wrestling office and disappeared into a small room to feed the VCR the tape of his victory in the Michigan State dual. Slouched deep into the cushions of a couch five feet from the screen, Ironside watched without emotion as he worked the opponent and the referee for points. Tom Brands walked in and sat wordlessly beside Ironside. In a moment, they were on the carpet, Brands showing him how to keep an opponent on the mat in a situation similar to the Michigan State match.

They untangled. Ironside crawled back into his couch-slouch. He had another two hours until practice.

More and more, the Iowa coaching staff was becoming concerned about McIlravy's headaches—both as a personal health problem and as a condition that could dynamite the team's national-title hopes. Brands, in sketching the status of the team, said, "We've got one guy really ready to go now, and that's Ironside. That's my viewpoint. I don't know what Gable would say. Whitmer can't get up from the bottom. Mena doesn't know if he's going to eighteen or twenty-six. Forty-

two [Gilliss], well, that's obvious. Fifty [McIlravy], he's dominating, but that [headache problem] concerns me. I say a
prayer about it every night."

In the wrestling room, McIlravy was pulling back from
hard wrestling and instead was taking long turns on the exercise bike. Just the exertion that wrestling required—never
mind the head blows themselves—gave him severe headaches.
He approached Kristen Payne, the trainer, and asked her to
make an MRI appointment for him, "for my peace of mind."
He wanted a neurologist to look at images from inside his skull
and determine if he had any organic problem like a tumor.
When he did step onto the mat, McIlravy wore headgear he
had fashioned from a life vest that gave him more cushioning
than the standard-issue model.

It was no secret that Gable was counting on McIlravy for
the National Duals. At a team meeting before practice, with
McIlravy in attendance, Gable began with a not-so-subtle reminder to his 150-pound star and others of what was expected
of them at the Duals and throughout the season.

"This team is unusual from the standpoint that we are
making history in terms of positive things right now. I mean
... we're going to have to have seven guys in the national
finals this year—even though we're going for ten—to beat the
record of six. We're going to have to win six titles to beat the
record that we've had before.

"All you have to do right now, though, is to go undefeated
and win the Big Ten and Nationals [NCAA] and you've set
some positive records. You've got to stay strong mentally.
You've got to learn to suck it up to a certain extent."

After practice, Gable, hobbling badly on his crutches,
went to his office and called a friend and booster and revealed,
"I'm worried about Lincoln. He told Kristen something today
that kind of bothered me. He said he wanted to be wrestling
in four, six, eight years from now, in 2004 and 2008.

"He doesn't want to do something now that ruins that.
Well, you start thinking like that, and you get your ass beat.
You've got to plan for today, take it as it comes.

"I might talk to him. Somebody's got to be the asshole, and the asshole this time is me."

The injuries to McIlravy and Wes Hand were creating what Payne called the most confrontational environment she had had in two years of working with Iowa's wrestlers. There were no shouting matches between Gable and Payne, but their relationship was uneasy and sometimes strained.

Like many trainers, Payne walked in quicksand. On one hand, the lean, wise-cracking trainer sat on the bench and clenched her fists and cheered for the athletes she bandaged and iced. On the other, she was a medical professional forced to deal with injuries and make decisions that could harm her team's chances to win. In addition, besides her university salary, she received $4,000 from Gable to work at his summer wrestling camps.

Around the time of the National Duals, Payne and Gable were at odds over how to handle Hand's injury. Payne prescribed rest and anti-inflammatories for the searing pain that ran up and down his arms. Gable thought he should wrestle his way through it and learn to cope, as he would have to in a match. The coach's general view on injuries was that "there was a fine line where you don't want to be easy on them and where you want to use what's available scientifically."

The situation peaked when Gable and Payne met before practice and Payne presented her argument that Hand—who on Sunday had stopped at Gable's house for a massage and a dip in the hot tub—should sit out practice. Gable seemed to agree. "The plan was for him not to wrestle that day," Payne said.

There were forty wrestlers in the room, a busy place. Payne didn't see Hand until a few minutes into the session. He was wrestling. (Hand's choice, Gable said.) "I was angry," Payne said. "Then Hand fell on the mat with another stinger, and he said it was the worst one he ever had.

"I know tons of trainers who deal with that sort of thing with the coach on a daily basis, but I never had with Gable. I talked to him the next day. I didn't confront him, but I told my assistant I might leave if he didn't need me.

"We met in the training room. I told him I was upset. I told him I walked out of the office thinking one thing, then another happened. He told me about his frustrations with injuries. He related all the things going on, and about Oklahoma State coming up, and he talked like we could lose.

"He didn't apologize, but I wasn't looking for an apology. He listened to me, and he respected what I had to say."

Payne liked Gable and thought he "never would endanger any athlete," and that his temptation to send Hand onto the mat could be understood given that the symptoms of a stinger were not obvious—no bruises, no swelling. "I'd say on ninety percent of the things I say, he agrees with me," she said. "If we disagree, usually he starts at one end and I start at another, and we meet in the middle. We just didn't this one time."

Gable had thrown his support behind Payne when she interviewed for the trainer's job, and once before practice he told Hand to apologize to her for missing an appointment for his injury and not telling her. During practices, Gable, no stranger to stingers himself, watched Hand carefully, and asked both Payne and the wrestler for reports.

"How's the neck?" Gable asked at the beginning of practice. "Time we went to the Gable method. Hot-cold-hot-cold for two hours. Mountain Dew and whiskey, Mountain Dew and whiskey. Dew and whiskey. Back and forth.

"Do that for twenty-four hours, and I guarantee you won't feel pain anywhere."

The Hand incident notwithstanding, as National Duals week progressed, Gable seemed to radiate enthusiasm for the sport that had claimed roughly thirty-five years of his life and a good share of his skeletal structure. He continued to make the wrestling room his command base. He watched and directed practice, and when the room cleared, he lifted weights and rode a bike. If Gable went to his regular office at all, it was to return calls and phone Kathy to tell her he was coming home, normally around seven or eight P.M. Then he put on his stocking cap and coat and met the biting Iowa night. With surgery just over a week away, he was gorging himself on wrestling until the last minute.

He sat one late morning in the room and watched Mike Mena and Eric Akin dive and scramble after each other on the mat, a sweaty storm of lightning reversals and thunderclap grunts. For Gable it was magic.

With Mike Uker sitting beside him, grinning silently at the intensity and ferocity of the exchanges, Gable said, "I love that. I *love* that! Move and countermove. Gets my blood pumping!"

The coach talked later with several wrestlers who had inquired about the whereabouts of a freshman.

"He told me he was quitting two weeks ago," Gable said. "I told him he was taking a leave of absence. He said he wanted to live more of a normal student's life. What the hell is a normal student's life? You can't quit something like wrestling. Not something you've been doing all your life. We argued about it. Normal student's life . . ."

Gable once left his crutches behind and padded on stocking feet onto the mat and helped Zalesky and Brands make a point to Fullhart about scoring at the edge of the mat. Quickly, a semicircle of a dozen wrestlers formed to watch the coach demonstrate, using Lee Fullhart, Zalesky, and Brands, yanking them by the arms to place them properly. Then Gable turned it into a five-minute lecture on the dangers posed by Oklahoma State.

"Oklahoma State are masters of putting people on their ass, with a high-crotch [takedown] or something else," he said. "You've got to remember, wrestle them smart."

Midway through the week, Mike Uker received permission from Gable to talk to the team. He hooked his black mouthguard over the waistband of his gray gym shorts and snaked down the bleacher steps, past his brother Ben, his broken jaw wired shut, and other teammates who squeezed together to make a path. Mike Uker, shrugging and uncomfortable, began by addressing a point that Gable apparently had harangued on after Michigan State: If Oklahoma State beat

Michigan State by 39–0, and Iowa beat the Spartans by 26–10, then, in a numerical hocus-pocus, OSU was 23 points better than the Hawkeyes.

"I was just thinking about this weekend and the past week and how he was pretty pissed off after the meet, that he thinks that Oklahoma State is twenty-three points higher, something like that. . . ." Uker began.

"No, I didn't," Gable said from stage left, bent forward on his crutches.

Undeterred, Uker continued, "It fired me up and made me mad because, like Gable says, we are the sport. And I think it's time for some guys, including myself, to start going out and wrestling to our ability. Basically, I just want to kick some guys' butts, kick some ass this weekend. . . . It's hard coming to practice and all that and getting pumped up, the same way you're going to be before a match.

"But if one guy can turn it around here and there, then I think we can come together as a team."

"That's about it?" Gable asked, apparently hoping that a pep talk from a senior would inspire the team as much as a lecture from the coach might.

Mike Uker took his seat. Gable stated that he was looking forward to meeting Oklahoma State in the final, that they were much the same team as a year ago, and that "if they've improved that much since then, I'll have to give them credit."

"I just hate Oklahoma State," came a voice from the bleachers.

The same day, Wednesday, Gable led the team through a serious round of weight cutting in preparation for Friday afternoon's weigh-in at Lincoln, Nebraska. The NCAA gave wrestlers a one-pound weight allowance in January, but beginning next month, "scratch" weight would have to be made all the way to the national championships in March. None of the Iowa wrestlers seemed in danger of not making weight and missing competition. Lincoln McIlravy, who planned to compete, had been 16.5 pounds over his 150-pound limit the week before—doubtless because of his limited mat activity—but now he was 14 over and could shed that easily, he thought, over the next fifty hours.

Gable stripped down to neon blue briefs and disappeared into the sauna to keep his wrestlers company and to make sure none "broke," in the vernacular of Iowa wrestling. Occasionally, an athlete, weakened in mind and body and riding the emotional edge, bolted from the room, nearly incoherent. Later in the season, when he was still recovering from surgery, Gable peered through the pane of glass into the sauna. Most of the wrestlers sat inside, drenched in sweat and sitting on slatted wooden benches. No one spoke. "How's everybody in there?" Gable shouted, without opening the door and losing precious heat. "Who's hurting most? Gilliss? Why is Gilliss hurting? Uker—keep your head up! How's Joe [Williams] doing? You've got to work through the pain. OK. Each one say your name and weight. . . ."

And the first one began: "Tony Ersland, 177 . . ."

Uker had seen teammates break. "They yell, go crazy," he said. "You have to relax. Otherwise your heart pumps too hard and you panic."

After a few minutes, the wrestlers, lobster-red, left the sauna and wrapped themselves in diaphanous sheets and lay on the mats. It was a toga party without the booze and music. Gilliss lay for eight minutes, eyes shut, exhausted.

"Another eight minutes, Gilliss. Let's go!" Gable yelled, and back Gilliss went to the sauna. Most went in for fifteen minutes, out for five. They ate from platters of fresh fruit and drank hot tea.

"We do this to feel good," Gable said. "We get the muscle soreness out of our bodies. We do it for a change of pace. We do it for mental toughness. We do it for camaraderie."

Most of the Iowa wrestlers professed that Gable's infirmity and impending surgery hadn't distracted them or hurt the team. They revered him, and one went so far as to call him "the Messiah of wrestling." It was left for Royce Alger, the strength and conditioning coach and a holdover from the raucous teams of the mid-1980s, to bring the coach to earth.

Alger asked Gable why he started wearing boots.

"Hasn't it occurred to you why?" Gable answered. "I wear them so there's no need to bend down to tie my shoes."

"Who puts on your pants?" prodded Alger. "Your old lady?" No one else on the staff or team would dare to make such an assault on the Messiah of wrestling. Gable expected it from Alger, a chunky blond with a crooked smile.

"Nnnnn . . ."

"Unbelievable," Alger cut in. "Does your old lady put on your underwear?"

"I do that. It's hard. Very hard."

Gable turned and lunged into his crutches for the getaway. He didn't hear Alger say, "He just doesn't know how to take me sometimes."

Thursday, January 16, the day of Gable's final hospital visit before surgery, dawned bitterly cold and sunny, the kind of frozen wintry scene that looked better in a picture than it felt in person. Kathy Gable left her husband at the door of Pappajohn Pavilion at University Hospitals and parked in the ramp and joined him to register at 7:30 A.M. The hospital was just coming to life. There was the low murmur of voices in the registration line, and the thick smell of hospital air.

"Hard getting up today?" the receptionist asked the man standing before her, up to his armpits in crutches.

"It's been hard getting up for thirty years," Gable replied. "It takes a while."

A nurse, Katy Carlson, with short, cropped blond hair and a stethescope around her neck, led the Gables to examination room C4, crowded with an examination table, a desk, and two chairs. Carlson helped Gable off with his heavy, puffy coat, observing that he looked like Nanook of the North. She filled out forms on a clipboard and asked for next of kin. Gable's brow furrowed.

"That's me, unless you've got another wife," Kathy said.

The nurse asked, "Do you or have you ever drunk alcoholic beverages?"

"Yes. A case a day," Gable answered with a straight face.

Carlson played a ten-minute tape on a VCR. It explained the details of the surgery and defined Gable's condition, osteoarthritis, as "a joint disease associated with aging." The words hung in the air. The forty-eight-year-old wrestling coach said nothing.

The narration continued: "To correct the hip joint, the ends of the bone forming the joint are removed and replaced with metal and plastic pieces similar in size and shape to your original bone. We call each replacement a prosthesis. Your orthopedic doctor will explain the best type of prosthesis for your hip."

"Yeah, I'm going to do it, boy," Gable told the screen.

Gable learned about the implements he would be getting to make his dressing chores easier and, it was assumed, keep Royce Alger at bay. Included was a "long-handled reacher" for pulling up his socks, a long-handled shoehorn, and an elevated toilet seat. ("Holy shit!" exclaimed the future user, no pun intended.) "While you sleep," the narrator continued, "place a pillow between your legs to keep your hips aligned. You may resume sexual activity as long as you follow your hip precautions." ("You gotta be shitting me!" To Kathy: "Can you believe they put that in there?")

After watching the tape, Gable was handed a sheet of paper and told to complete his medical history. He sat at the table, pencil in hand; Kathy, in slacks, perched cross-legged on the exam table. It took a while. He had to remember all the surgeries. There was elbow surgery in 1968 or '69, he couldn't remember which. Both knees in '73. Left knee and mouth in '79 and '80. Right knee in '93 or '94. Shoulder in '93.

Mike Pyevich, a fifth-year resident in a yellow gown, came in and read the report and repeated it to Gable. Gable touched the parts of the body involved and gave more details. Pyevich asked if Gable had problems with anesthesia, and the Iowa coach said that morphine and Demerol made him sick and hallucinate. "Just as well you're taking some sort of an overall anesthetic," Pyevich said. "That way at least you won't hear the pounding of the hammer, or the saw."

Pyevich, who would assist Marsh with the surgery, told Gable the risks and answered questions. Gable worried about the chance of infection. Minimal, Pyevich said, but it still existed. "We give you antibiotics before, during, and after the operation," the doctor informed him. "We operate as quickly as we can. We operate with sterile techniques, of course. We have these big, high, laminar-flow rooms, to try to sweep bacteria away. Between us and Mayo, we have the lowest infection rates in the country, but it's not zero. It does happen."

Physical therapy would begin twenty-eight hours after surgery, on Friday afternoon.

"Big wrestling meet that night," Gable said.

"I doubt you'll be making it."

"OK, listen," Gable said. "The only thing that I need is the radio to listen to it."

"No problem."

"Gotta have a radio."

Pyevich told Gable that he would be staying in the hospital for five to seven days. No physical therapy on the weekend, because the staff was off Saturday and Sunday. Gable wondered if Payne, the Iowa trainer, couldn't come in to help.

"Yeah, but she's mad at you right now," Kathy said, referring to the Hand tiff.

"No," Gable said. "We . . . she made up. She couldn't stay mad. She called me out of the locker room last night."

Another resident, Dr. Bob Hart, slipped into the room. Gable mentioned that his knees hurt so much they woke him at night, but that the pain wasn't as great as that in the left hip. Hart observed that it wasn't unusual for a hip in need of replacement to hurt worse than a bad knee. Just prior to that, Pyevich had told Gable that after surgery, "whatever the deep groin pain that you feel now will be gone. It will be replaced with the new surgical pain. You'll be sore on the outside of your hip because that's where we have to cut through muscle and have to cut the bone. . . . You're swapping pain, but usually people say, 'My hip feels better.' "

One of Gable's 117 collegiate victories at Iowa State. Here, he dominates his opponent with an arm bar, his most punishing move.

An anguished Gable finishes second for the only time in his career, as Larry Owings accepts congratulations at the 1970 NCAA championships.

1.

2.

3.

Gold-medalist Gable (*right*) poses with Iowa State teammates and fellow Olympic medalists Ben Peterson (*left*) and Chris Taylor at the 1972 Olympics in Munich.

4.
Where boys become men: the Iowa Hawkeyes wrestling room, lorded over by Gable, crutches and all.

5.
Fatherly love: Gable preps senior Jessie Whitmer for his match against Iowa State.

6.

7.

Iowa's Murderers' Row: *Above left*, Mark Ironside (134 pounds) celebrates his first NCAA championship; *above right*, Lincoln McIlravy (150 pounds) in training for his third national title; *below*, Joe Williams (158 pounds) pounces on an Oklahoma State rival.

8.

9.

Iowa's Lee Fullhart, the 190-pound sophomore, throws Oklahoma's John Kading to the mat during their NCAA championship match.

Mike Mena—who contemplated dropping down to 118 pounds, but barely made 126 for the Big Ten championships—scores a few points on Iowa State's Dwight Hinson.

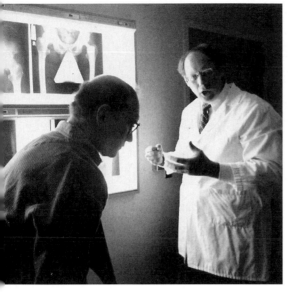

11.

With his hip X rays showing deterioration, Gable listens to orthopedic surgeon Larry Marsh explain the procedures of hip-replacement surgery. Gable had the operation midseason so he could be back and ready for the NCAA finals.

With Gable in the hospital, three members of his staff carry on without him during a dual meet: (*from left to right*) Tom Brands, Royce Alger, and interim coach Jim Zalesky.

Iowa heavyweight Wes Hand begins a takedown that helps carry him—and his team—to a two-point victory against Iowa State in the last meet of the season.

13.

14.

By twists and turns . . . Iowa's
Kasey Gilliss (*bottom*) brings
Iowa State's David Maldonado
over the top and onto his back
en route to a thirty-seven-
second pin in the first round of
the NCAA championships.

15.

Mike Uker takes an injury
timeout to massage his left
shoulder during a tense match
in the NCAA tournament.

16.

Tom Brands embraces Gable as they rejoice in Iowa's fifteenth national championship in Gable's twenty-one years. Trainer Kristen Payne exults at right.

The Gable women—back in 1993—gang up on the man of the house: Gable's wife Kathy watches with daughters Jenni and Annie, as Molly and Mackie pile on their father.

July 15, 1997: Dan Gable announces at a press conference that he will take a leave of absence from coaching, perhaps making the 1996–97 season his last.

Hart asked if Gable had back pain. "I've always had back pain. Just from wrestling, I'm sure." Hart made a note to schedule Gable for lower-back X rays that very day, at the same time he had other X rays of his hip taken. "One of the things that we sometimes do to improve range of motion is to use a little dose of radiation afterwards, to stop bone formation," Hart said. "We do that particularly in guys who seem to make a lot of bone, have arthritis in a number of places."

Hart's beeper went off, and the session broke up. The nurse warned that Gable shouldn't be seeing a lot of visitors after surgery.

"My wrestlers will see me," Gable said sternly.

An occupational therapist showed Gable how to use some of the long-handled implements he saw in the tape, and he was shipped off for a final round of X rays. He ate lightly in the hospital cafeteria and had more tests after lunch in addition to giving blood that he would get back during surgery. Then he and Kathy tried to find their way out of the sprawling complex, where information kiosks stocked detailed maps of the institution.

Along the way, paintings and sculpture sprang up like summer gardens. Long ago, before the hospital went through yet another of its building phases, a glass display booth in the lobby contained the bronzed hands of several noteworthy artists and physicians connected with the University of Iowa. One pair of hands reached up and out, as though toward one's throat. They were Gable's hands.

"Probably in some attic around here now," he said, and headed into the low-setting afternoon sun.

It was just the start of his day. Presiding over the last practice before the team left for Nebraska, Gable wore sweatpants and a white T-shirt as well as a turquoise bandage on his left arm where he had had blood drawn. "Mena!" he shouted, after practice began, "that's your shot, don't let him use it on you!" "Nice move, McGinness!" "Hip tilt him, Joe!"

Gable flopped on a table and got a rubdown from the team masseur. He turned his head toward the mats. "Stalemate!" he yelled toward two wrestlers locked together on the mat. "Get up. Start over."

Gable in his time had learned a lot about starting over. He also knew about a kind of pain that went far beyond what surgery, or wrestling, could possibly offer.

chapter **6**

$\mathbf{M}$AY 30, 1964, was a hot Saturday night in Waterloo, Iowa, in the middle of the long Memorial Day weekend. Diane Kay Gable, a nineteen-year-old with a wide, welcoming smile who wore her dark brown hair cut short, stayed behind when her parents and her fifteen-year-old brother left for the family's rented fishing cabin 100 miles northeast of Waterloo on the Mississippi River, near Harpers Ferry, Iowa. Diane would join them later.

Danny was gone. What a relief. She didn't need a kid brother around on a night when she planned to have fun. She had baby-sat for Danny when he was younger—and what a disaster that was. She would invite one of her boyfriends over to the house, where she and the young man would take a seat on the couch in the living room and turn off the table lamp, confident that Danny was tucked in. Which was what he wanted them to think, as he sneaked out of his bedroom . . . and into the living room . . . and reached for the lamp switch and . . . *surprise!*

But she loved her brother and went to his wrestling meets, because wasn't she partly and indirectly responsible for his success? When he was in the fourth grade, ten years of age, and Diane was an eighth grader, she asked in several boys she knew from school who were wrestlers. The guys soon began rug-wrestling with one another, as wrestlers will, until the cry went up, to the effect, "Hey, there's Diane's little brother! Somebody go take him on!" So Danny, who loved all sports and even made believe he was a swimmer in the basement where there wasn't any water, now was trying wrestling. There, in the Gables' living room just a few steps inside the front door, he dropped to the carpet and assumed the position of the offensive wrestler, one arm locked around an older, bigger boy who was on his hands and knees. Crouched like lions, they were. The larger one sprang into action, or tried to. Danny held on. All around the room the bodies thrashed. And still Danny held on.

After she graduated from Waterloo West in 1962, Diane attended the Humboldt Air Line School for flight attendants in Minneapolis. She soon soured on the experience and returned to live at home and work for her father's real-estate business. "She hated that damned place, Minneapolis," Mack, seventy-one, a stroke victim, recalled in 1997 in his halting speech. "She just didn't want no part of that deal."

Like her brother and parents, Diane was caught in the cycle of family violence. On December 23, 1962, Waterloo police were called to 2241 Easley in response to a call from Diane. According to sketchy police records, she reported that her father had struck her. No charges were filed.

Diane wasn't seriously involved with anyone on that Memorial Day weekend, although she had been seeing a twenty-year-old man who lived in nearby Cedar Falls. They had their third date on Saturday night, driving around in his car and returning to the Gable house near midnight. They sat in the living room looking at new-car advertisements, because Diane was in the market for one. A car pulled up, and a tall, husky youth in black-framed glasses like Buddy Holly's got out, knocked on the door, and went inside. Tom Kyle lived in the neighborhood, the son of a bank president and his wife. Earlier that evening, Kyle, sixteen, and several of his friends had stopped over at the Gable home and gone out with Diane and brought back some beer.

Diane called a girlfriend, trying to line her up that night
—early morning, actually—with Kyle. Diane also planned to
drive later that morning to Harpers Ferry to meet her family.

It was now 2 A.M. Diane's date for the evening had left,
and she was alone with Kyle. The Sunday *Waterloo Courier* was
delivered at 6 A.M., but no one opened the screen door to
get it.

Later that Sunday, in Harpers Ferry, Mack began to
worry. Diane hadn't shown up. There was no phone in the
cabin, so Mack drove his wife and his son to a pay phone a half
mile away, and he called a neighbor and asked him to check the
house. Diane's car was in the driveway, and the neighbor said
he could hear the radio, but no one answered his knock.

Mack asked him to get inside. How? The neighbor didn't
have a key. Break the window by the back door, reach in, and
let yourself in, Mack said. Within minutes, the neighbor circled
through the kitchen and into the living room and discovered
Diane's body on the bloody carpet. There were two stab
wounds in her chest; she was partially clothed; her face had
been bitten.

Katie and Danny remained in the car, watching Mack hang
by the phone with another man whose name has been forgotten. Mother and son wondered what was taking so long. The
pay phone rang, and the other man answered, and he hung up
and conferred with Mack, and the two walked toward the car.
The man's expression had dissolved into something frightening
to behold. It spoke of news so terrible that words bent and
withered with the weight of it.

How bad? Katie and the boy wanted to know.

Well, the man said, she's been hurt.

Well, obviously, but how bad?

Put it this way, came the reply, she's not alive.

The boy long since forgot the man's name, and what, if
any, attachment he had to the family, but the boy would never
forget those words. Not simply, I'm sorry, Diane's dead. No
—*she's not alive.*

As the boy became a man, other memories clung.

"All of a sudden, mom went hysterical," Dan Gable remembered. "She ran out of the car, ran down the road where the cabin was. We drove the car down there, and she ran into the cabin, and when we went in, she was beating her head on the wood floor.

"We had to take the hundred-mile ride back, and about thirty miles back, I was in the backseat, and we were having a conversation, and all of a sudden it hit me, out of nowhere, that maybe I know who did it.

"I said, 'Dad, I think I know who might have done it.' And he goes, 'What?' He stopped the car beside the road. He said, what did I mean? Who did it? I said, 'Well, Dad, a couple times I been walking with a neighbor to school, and the neighbor has been sayin' things about what he'd like to do to Diane.' They were sexual things. Like he wanted to get into her knickers. But I just looked at 'em like boy talk. Maybe flattering, in a way.

"And he, my Dad, kind of cracked me one. 'Why didn't you tell us?' Kind of pinning the blame [on me] at the time. But I took it with a grain of salt. I didn't think there was any meaning in it."

Within three hours, police picked up Kyle at the grocery where he worked and questioned him. He confessed and was charged with murder. In his statement, Kyle said he had been drinking, and that he choked and then stabbed Diane after she began screaming about the damage some of his friends had done to a screen window in the house earlier that night when they had returned from buying beer. Rape, though not proven, was widely assumed. The murder weapon was never found.

Kyle waived his right to a jury trial and went before Black Hawk County District Court Judge Blair C. Wood, who would determine if Kyle was guilty of first- or second-degree murder and sentence him. The three days of hearings began on October 4, 1964—the same month in which Kyle turned seventeen. The murder and trial rocked the blue-collar community of 75,000, located on the winding, cement-gray Cedar River, the home of Rath Packing and John Deere tractor. Two prominent families were involved, linked by a brutal murder. On newsstands, *True Police Cases* magazine carried a major story with pictures and text, and the cover teaser, "IOWA'S WEEK-END PARTY OF PASSION AND MURDER."

On the first day of hearings, Kyle, flanked by his parents and attorneys, stood before Judge Wood, who asked if the defendant understood the charge and the possible consequences, death by hanging or life in prison?

Kyle's voice was flat. "Yes, sir."

The county attorney maintained that Kyle was guilty of first-degree murder and the "perpetration of mayhem," meaning attempted rape. Kyle's attorneys denied that premeditation was involved, portrayed their client as an unstable personality whose dark side was worsened by drinking, and held out for second-degree murder or manslaughter.

Mack Gable was among the 100 or so spectators who attended on opening day. Katie Gable went sparingly. As Mack remembered, "No. No. She couldn't take it. I shouldn't say she couldn't take it, but, you know, we had had enough damn trouble." Dan appeared once in court, a time he wouldn't forget. He recalled the surges of anger—"seeing that guy sitting up there in the front, on the stand. It was a nightmare. It was a nightmare."

Security was tight. Sheriff's deputies and city police took Kyle from the county jail to the courtroom and back. Two other law-enforcement officials stood guard at the courtroom entrance. Another Waterloo cop sat inside the courtroom railing, near Kyle.

A stream of twenty-four witnesses testified about their impressions of Kyle and the events of the evening in question. Two youths said that he had made remarks with strong sexual overtones about Diane. The defense, claiming "diminished responsibility" but not insanity, called a psychiatrist who treated Kyle when he was twelve years old. Dr. Billy Grimmer, a resident at University Hospitals in Iowa City, testified that Kyle had stolen a car, was truant from school, and exhibited "sociopathic tendencies."

On the Monday morning of October 25, 1964, at ten A.M., Kyle, who had not testified, stood again before Judge Wood.

Did Kyle have anything to say? Kyle said he did not. Wood then found Kyle guilty of first-degree murder and sentenced him to life in prison. Wood said in court that the death penalty would accomplish nothing. "The tragic injury to the dead girl and her family would in no part be repaired by hanging the defendant. . . . The fact that our statutes carry provision for death by hanging did not prevent the commission of this crime."

According to the *Waterloo Courier*'s account, "Controlled tears glistened behind the boy's horn-rim glasses, but he and his parents, Mr. and Mrs. John C. Kyle, restrained any show of outward emotion when the verdict was announced."

The courtroom was crowded. Mack Gable heard the verdict announced. His wife remained in the corridor outside the courtroom. Reporters asked him his opinion of the verdict, and he said, "I don't see how they could have given him anything less than life."

Now came one of the hardest parts of all, resuming life. New carpet replaced the one stained with Diane's blood. Mack wanted to sell the house; Dan fought against that, and won.

"I was just going to sell the damn house and get the hell out of there," Mack said. "He wanted to move into her old room, where she . . . God! That was spooky. But he said it felt like he was, like he was closer . . ."

"I just thought, 'Does she want it to change our whole lives, or does she want us to work through this?' " Dan Gable recounted. "I mean, I proved that I could handle it, because I moved into her room. Just to prove to my parents that we needed to stay there and we needed to support her and not run out on her and not close the door on her. My dad made an office out of my bedroom."

Katie was shattered. She would feel the hollow pit of loss no matter where the family lived. "She was heart-sick real bad," Mack said.

Staying at 2241 Easley, she seemed to have a mission. "You don't think that every day my mom lived in that house she wasn't looking for the knife?" Dan said. "And we think it was one of our knives he used, and that it'd been cleaned. You know, we might have spread some butter with the same knife that killed my . . ." More than thirty years later, he still could not finish the sentence.

Mack, meanwhile, experienced guilt that he couldn't shake, guilt that may have had roots reaching back to whatever happened between him and his daughter that sent police to his door. But now the guilt had a name, and the name was Tom Kyle. "I suppose because I'm a father I should have watched out for her better," Mack Gable said. "But she was twenty or so, you know . . ."

Mack and Katie put more restrictions on their son, for he was all that was left. "My life tightened up," Dan Gable said. "It made me even more of a horse with blinders, as far as wrestling went. Not just from a competitive point of view, but also to keep my mom and dad together. It seemed like they were drifting apart, mom and dad constantly drinking more, fighting about the situation, blaming each other. Kind of funny: After I left high school, they started really gettin' along good, and they realized they liked each other a lot."

Mack resumed showing up at Waterloo West practices; both he and Katie went to matches and followed Dan all over the country when he wrestled at Iowa State. They rarely mentioned Diane's death to people outside the family, and if they did, only fleetingly. Yet pictures of her remained on display in the house.

"When Dan started competing in wrestling, especially in his college days, I think everybody kind of mellowed out," said Dan's wife, Kathy. "[As] they got engrossed in Dan's career, it kind of made them forget what happened to Diane."

Several of Gable's Iowa wrestlers, past and present, said that Gable mentioned his sister to them as a point of inquiry: Had they heard what had happened? Then, little else. Mike Narey, a nonwrestling friend of Gable's since their Iowa State days, recalled a time that he and Gable were driving from Waterloo to Iowa City and the subject of Diane came up.

"He says, 'Did you know about my sister?' " Narey said.

"And I said, 'Yeah.' And he never said another word. Didn't say another word all the way back to Iowa City. He didn't want me sticking my nose into his business, so I didn't."

More than a dozen years ago, Gable was sitting in the St. Louis airport with his team. They were waiting to change planes to fly to Stillwater for a dual the next day against Oklahoma State. Gable, flipping through the pages of the *St. Louis Post-Dispatch*, happened upon a story about a rapist eluding police and terrorizing women in the city. Gable shook his head and looked up. He wore an expression of ice and fire.

"I don't understand," he said. "Guy like that. If somebody even tried to touch Kathy . . ." He fell silent for a moment. Then: "Well, nobody better want to do that."

chapter 7

THE 1996–97 IOWA WRESTLING schedule could have been constructed as a Gable farewell tour. The Hawkeyes opened their season in Lake Okoboji, where Gable had trained for the 1972 Olympics and taught at wrestling camps. Northwestern University, where the Midlands was held, was the site of the 1970 NCAA championships; Gable had won 181 straight matches in high school and college, but there lost his last match as a collegian, 13–11, to an unheralded University of Washington sophomore named Larry Owings. Now came Lincoln, Nebraska, where in the National AAU Freestyle Championships in 1970 he won his 149.5-pound weight class by pinning four opponents and winning three matches by a combined score of 25–1. It was Gable's first major competition since his shocking and widely publicized upset by Owings. "Even though I couldn't wipe that loss totally off, [the freestyle title] brought back my ego," Gable said. "It brought back everything I'd been training for—all my life."

As a topping to the 1996–97 season, the NCAA championships would be held in Cedar Falls, Iowa, next door to Waterloo, within 20 minutes of 2241 Easley Street. Mack Gable and his son's old friends and former teammates would be there for support, as would Gable's old high-school coach, Bob Siddens. Gable and Siddens had maintained a close relationship over the years, and Siddens, a large man whose well-muscled chest preceded him, still called the younger man "Daniel." "Daniel," Siddens told Gable as he left the mat after winning his third state title for West, "I probably will never have any-one like you again." For the last year and a half, even before his body began crumbling, Gable eagerly anticipated the NCAAs in Cedar Falls as a good way to go out—preferably raising high the championship trophy.

On the way to Lincoln, Gable busied himself in a front seat with the paperwork he had neglected at the office. "Do you know the three keys to success?" he asked Kathy as she drove him in the morning darkness from home to the bus idling at Carver-Hawkeyes Arena.

"Organize, organize, organize," she said.

"No. Prioritize, prioritize, prioritize," Gable corrected her. "That's why when you walk into my office and don't see everything neat and tidy—why? I'm working with my athletes. *They're* my priority."

Kathy would drive the family van separately to Lincoln, bringing Mackie, Molly, and Jennifer, as well as Brian Mitchell, who wore a neck brace after the accident and appeared solemn and contemplative. Annie would ride in the bus with her father and the wrestlers, who let her sit in on their card games. Before the bus left, Kathy made a run for bagels and muffins and donuts, for Gable and whoever else wanted them—though it wouldn't be the wrestlers, because an early-afternoon weigh-in loomed and many had just worked out and taken a sauna to shave off more weight. As the bus pulled from the lot, a man-ager handed out meal money: twenty-six dollars a day for in-state athletes, forty for out-of-state.

Dawn broke cold and clear. Across Iowa on I-80 heading west, the land flattened and emptied. Gable, groaning as he moved in his seat, began reading correspondence. "I've never gotten so much mail from old people," Gable mused, after reading a handwritten letter from a seventy-three-year-old re-tired farmer from Randalia, Iowa, who had had both hips re-placed last February. The farmer wrote: "I started driving again in April, and went back to bowling and dancing in July. I think you will recuperate faster as you are younger."

Two seats behind Gable, Tom Brands slipped a *Car and Driver* magazine out of his travel bag and began reading about truck conversions. Mike Uker drank a cup of water that he tapped from the plastic keg that the trainers put at the front of the bus. As the bus jostled along, he stood and tipped the paper cup to his lips once, twice, three times, getting every drop. Then he asked permission and dipped into Brands's bag for something to read, selecting *Braveheart,* and he returned with it to his seat.

Food was on his mind.

"After the workout last night I went to Hy-Vee and bought some strawberries, some kiwi, and watermelon," Uker said. "Then I went back for another workout, and I slept pretty good. It wasn't hard to go back. It's hard if I haven't eaten and then try to get through it. I try to keep a regular schedule, and I never work out in the morning. Some of the other guys got there to work out at six. Not me."

Uker turned down, with reluctance, a muffin that Annie offered. Gable, overhearing, swiveled in his seat and said, "They're up here. I leave it up to you." Even though Uker had gone up two weight classes to make room for Lincoln McIlravy at 150, he had to watch his weight. "Cereal would've been good, but it leaves me with cotton-mouth. Then all I can taste is cement."

From the front of the bus to the back looked like a battle-field. Ten wrestlers lay on the floor, with their coats and carry-ons for cushions and pillows. The only way to reach the bathroom in back was to march along the arm rests, assuming a wrestler didn't have his feet over them. Mike Mena, the loner, sat in the very back. He wore a T-shirt, dark sweatpants, and black boots. He had told Gable that he would wrestle at 126. He knew the price of resistance; also, he had had a good week of practice, and his weight was under control. In the middle of the week, he jumped on the digital scale in the locker room and watched the flashing red stilt numbers stop at 139. "Sahhhhhh-*weet!*" he exclaimed, and jumped off. He could make 126 easily enough by Saturday. Before this morning's workout, he weighed 135. Now he was 132. With the one-pound allowance, he was five pounds over the target weight of 127. Again, no problem.

He smiled and leaned back in his seat. "Hmmm, not cutting as much weight, and I'm still winning—sounds good to me," he said.

The bus reached Lincoln at 12:15 P.M. The team checked in quickly at the motel and immediately rode to campus to begin the tail end of weight cutting, the hardest part, where every half-pound was a mountain. Approximately 200 wrestlers milled in and around the wrestling room at the Devaney Recreation Center. McIlravy, still bothered by his headaches, and Joe Williams led the Iowa charge to the saunas. Both wore gray sweats over plastic suits, and soon the sweat was flowing. McIlravy emerged shortly and put a towel over his head and rode an exercise bike. Mena, dripping sweat in his red briefs, was ready to step on the scale. "Golf really is easier," he cracked.

After Williams had made weight and showered, he headed for the bus with the rest of the team. Gable, trying to jar life into his 158-pound national champion, fisted him on the arm as he passed and called after him, "Let's go four-and-oh and [score] twenty-four points," Gable said, meaning he wanted Williams to aim to win all four of his matches by pins worth six points each. "Four-and-oh and twenty-four."

The official name for the tournament was the Cliff Keen NWCA (National Wrestling Coaches Association) National Duals. Keen, now deceased, served for forty-five years as the University of Michigan wrestling coach and was among the first in his sport to explore other entreprenurial avenues, including a line of athletic products that has long thrived. This was the fifth year that the tournament would be held at the University of Nebraska, but it was rumored to be heading next year to Iowa City, in hopes of higher attendance.

Seven of the top-ten teams in college wrestling had en-

tered. Besides No. 1 Iowa and No. 2 Oklahoma State, there
were Iowa State (No. 3), Penn State (No. 4), Minnesota (No.
6), Michigan State (No. 7), and Michigan (No. 8). Because the
tournament was set up in a dual-meet format with the winning
teams advancing through the championship bracket, the result
would not neccessarily fortell the finish in the NCAA championships. There, team depth counted more than team
balance, for if a wrestler lost a match, he still could keep competing and ring up points for his team from the consolation
bracket.

Nevertheless, the National Duals, with half of the Division I field populated by ranked wrestlers, presented a national
showcase. "This has an NCAA feel to it," Michigan coach
Dale Bahr said. "It's got the NCAA announcer [Ed Aliverti,
a bass-voiced former music teacher from Edmonds, Washing-
ton]. It's got the NCAA's top teams. It's just two months
early, is all."

A dinner was held Friday night at a downtown Lincoln
hotel, the Cornhusker, to bring together the coaching staffs
and honor individuals before the meet. Kathy Gable drove the
van from the motel, with Gable in the front, and Jim Zalesky
and Tom Brands in the backseat. Gable, in a white shirt and
dark print tie, indicated that he might hold heavyweight Hand
—still bothered by stingers—out of the early matches and save
him for the tough ones at the end. "Sorry it has to be that way.
But I'd rather have him ready to wrestle. That's life, and you've
got to be realistic."

Kathy maneuvered the van onto a street a block from the
hotel.

"Why don't I just let you off in front, and I'll park and
walk to the hotel?" she asked her husband.

"Bullshit!" Gable said in a surprisingly loud voice. "This
is a dangerous town."

Both Dan and Kathy got out; the assistant coaches parked
and caught up with the Gables at the hotel. After a white-
tablecloth dinner of buffet-line chicken and steak, a few of the
coaches were called to the podium to speak. Gable, sitting with

his wife and assistants in back, designated Zalesky to go forth. "I don't want to hobble up there," the coach said. "And my stomach hurts."

Zalesky, buttoning his sport coat on the way to the podium, mentioned how pleased the Hawkeyes were to be participating in their third straight National Duals, and then put the Iowa–Oklahoma State rivalry on full boil.

"With Oklahoma State not wrestling us this year, guess we'll have to meet them here," he said. An audible "ohhhhhhhhh" swept the room. John Smith, the Oklahoma State coach, did his best to look unruffled, but shot a quick, daggered look across the room at Gable. Gable had said that he thought the Cowboys were dodging Iowa with their schedule; Smith maintained that OSU had too many paybacks and couldn't fit the Hawkeyes in. At a reception preceding dinner, Dan and Kathy chatted with Smith about their families; Dan said his daughters were fine and that Annie was starting college next fall. Kathy asked Smith about his infant son, Joseph, born on December 28, the Smith's first child. It was a stiff conversation between the two highly competitive coaches.

Back at the motel, Gable met with his team. There was nothing formal about the announcement of place and time; usually the wrestlers just hung around the hallway on Gable's floor until somehow, through word-of-mouth or telepathy or both, everyone wound up in the same room at the same time.

Gable stood leaning on his crutches in front of his wrestlers. He had taken off his suit coat and cuffed his sleeves to his elbows. Iowa had drawn seventeenth-ranked Clarion in the opening round. Clarion was a tough Pennsylvania wrestling school that wouldn't pose many problems for Iowa except at 118 pounds, where Sheldon Thomas, the defending NCAA champion, had a 16–0 record this season and was top-ranked in his weight class. Gable drilled Whitmer, seated on the bed in front of him, with a stare. Whitmer, loser of two straight, would have to wrestle Thomas.

"He's not strong physically, but he's a goer," Gable said. "And he shoots low, and he rides, and so when you get to the second period . . ." Thinking of Jessie Whitmer's recent losses, Gable urged him to take the up, or offensive, position when possible. "With [the last] two matches, we've kind of . . . we think we could have won both of those matches maybe if we hadn't taken down. But we learned a lot about you. And, uh, that's the way it is. It's still not the national tournament. And we think that, uh, you can win a national championship.

"So right now, you better be ready. And you gotta be strong up here," Gable said, pointing to his own head.

Without naming him, Gable indicated that Clarion coach Jack Davis counted "four guys on his team"—that is, athletes who could hold their own with Iowa. "You look at their lineup, they're eighteen, twenty-six, thirty-four, and heavyweight— the four guys," Gable indicated "So, forty-two, fifty, fifty- eight, sixty-seven, seventy-seven, and ninety apparently are girls." He felt Payne's gaze upon him. "Did I say that? Girls? Boys, I meant. Right, Kristen?" The room broke up.

Gable brought fifteen wrestlers to the meet, planning to substitute and save injured wrestlers for the toughest matches. Joining Lincoln McIlravy and Wes Hand on the injured list was Lee Fullhart, who had not completed a practice all week because of a sore back and fatigue brought on, he said, by the stress of school.

"Now, Lincoln," Gable said, scanning the room for his two-time national champion. "Don't think that you're not going to wrestle the first match. I mean, who knows? Can't tell if I'm going to have to use you. . . . You'll obviously know after about the third tough weight, or in the beginning. And as long as you guys are wrestling well, you'll be fine, and we'll get Koble in there right away."

First thing Saturday morning, Whitmer got two slaps across the face from Gable and then a 10–0 whipping from Thomas. Thomas powered into Whitmer for a single-leg take- down in the first period and nearly pinned him, and it was 6–0 going into the second period. Whitmer chose the up position, but he couldn't manufacture points, and Thomas got riding time in the third period. Afterward, Whitmer slumped into a folding chair next to Gable, who gave him time to replay the match before discussing it with him.

Iowa powered its way through the next three weights, meaning that McIlravy could rest. Eric Koble stepped in and won at 150, 12–5, part of an eight-weight winning streak for Iowa that ended when heavyweight Mike Christensen, subbing for Hand, lost a decision. An interesting development took place in Uker's 16–1 victory at 167. Fighting off a takedown, he suddenly exploded and "pancaked" his opponent—in one blinding move lifting him and bringing him crashing to the mat —and nearly pinned him.

"Hey, Uke, your guy smiled as you were throwing him," Gilliss said.

"He was?" Uker said. "So was I."

The 30–7 victory boosted the Hawkeyes into an after-noon match against Nebraska, a 19–16 winner over North Carolina. Gable grumbled after Clarion that Whitmer still hadn't learned to escape, and that Kasey Gilliss still hadn't learned basic skills. The only intensity came from Joe Williams, an unusual source given his propensity to lighten up on the road, but a 24–9 winner nonetheless. Gable went over to watch Oklahoma State finish off Fresno State, 35–0, the fifth time this season that the Cowboys had won all their matches.

"They're not doing much, but they're winning the close ones," he said.

The NU Coliseum, site of the National Duals, was aptly named. Four mats lay under a high roof supported by ten concrete pillars. The only seating was in the balcony, and there was an ambience of ancient Rome about the scene, as the homestanding Cornhuskers were fed to the Hawkeyes, who took an easy 40–3 victory on Saturday afternoon.

Iowa's entire first string wrestled. Hand lost to the fourth-ranked heavyweight in the country, Tolly Thompson, 11–5, while McIlravy showed little rust in a 24–8 runaway. Ken McIl-ravy stood a few feet away from the mat, frowning behind his bristling gray-and-white beard. Gable was willing to let Lincoln name his practice schedule to accommodate his headaches, but he thought it was important for his 150-pound star to keep competition-tough, even though the team was in mid-romp. The situation apparently reminded Ken McIlravy of last week's match at Michigan State, when in a much closer contest at the time, Gable summoned Lincoln to wrestle.

"Gable doesn't want to win by this much," the senior McIlravy groused, holding his hands six inches apart. "He wants to win by *this*." His hands spread wider. "I'm concerned with my boy's health. I'm just baffled why he wrestled last week. I wasn't there, but I told Lincoln that for you to wrestle in a dual that was essentially meaningless against an opponent that wasn't in your class was a no-win situation for you."

The elder McIlravy had disagreed with Gable before. In Lincoln's freshman season, 1992–93, Gable had pulled him out of a redshirt year to wrestle in the NCAA championships at 142 pounds. Gable figured the team was stronger with McIlravy in the lineup, but it meant that Troy Steiner, a senior and defending national champion at the weight, had to cut to 134. Ken McIlravy thought his son was too young to be thrown into such competition, and that Steiner deserved better. As it turned out, Lincoln won a national championship, Steiner finished third, and the Hawkeyes won the title.

"Don't get me wrong," Ken McIlravy said. "I like Gable. Of all the coaches I know, he's more concerned with people than ninety-five percent of the others. But . . ." He trailed off.

Ken McIlravy went back to watching wrestling.

The victory over Nebraska propelled Iowa into the Saturday-night semifinals against Minnesota, coached by Gable's estranged friend and former assistant, J Robinson. Robinson, a Californian who wrestled at Oklahoma State, had been one of Gable's roommates at the 1972 Olympics. He served as Gable's top assistant for eight years (1977–84), teaching the Iowa way of wrestling. Bowlegged and mop-topped, Robinson—the "J" without a period continued a parade of family names beginning with the letter—was a tough Vietnam veteran who tended to bark commands. Many of the wrestlers he oversaw, including Zalesky, loved him.

During his years with Gable, Iowa ran off seven straight NCAA championships, a string that ended two years after he left. Robinson called those years "like Camelot." The wrestling office resembled a day-care center, with Gable's and Robinson's youngsters playing on the floor and forcing visitors to take a serpentine course to their destinations. Robinson's 170-acre ranch, home to buffalo and thirty-eight wild mustangs, was headquarters when wrestlers and coaches wanted to roast a pig and drink some beer. Robinson and his wife were close friends of the Gables, ever since Robinson and Gable served as assistants under Gary Kurdelmeier. In 1976, when Tom Kyle, Diane Gable's killer, briefly escaped from prison, Dan worried about Kathy's safety; Kyle, it was rumored, had vowed revenge for his life sentence. The Robinsons invited the Gables to stay with them until Kyle was caught, and the Gables accepted.

However, their relationship fractured in 1984, the year that Gable, busy with his work as U.S. Olympic freestyle coach, turned the Iowa team over to Robinson—and promptly took it back after a loss at Oklahoma State. But the crushing blow to their relationship occurred after the season, when Robinson resigned in a dispute with the university, which wanted to take financial control of his intensive wrestling camp. With his entrepreneurial vigor, Robinson had developed a summer program of rigorous training and competition for youths, and he enlisted Iowa wrestlers and coaches to help.

Robinson was furious that Gable did not support him, while Gable was incredulous that Robinson would not budge. Each believed the other to blame for the imbroglio. Even as Robinson prepared to hold a press conference to state his reasons for leaving, Gable shook his head in his office. "I tried to get him to compromise," Gable said. "He wouldn't. He's got to give a little. He's so damn *stubborn*."

Gable abhorred losing to any team. Oklahoma State topped his list, but next probably was Robinson-coached Minnesota—Gable still ranted about the officiating of a match the Hawkeyes lost in 1994 in Minneapolis. But Minnesota was a young team this season, and one of their leaders, 118-pound Brandon Paulson, an Olympic silver medalist in Greco-Roman, was slowed by a bad ankle that would require surgery ten days after the National Duals meet.

Gable appeared on the sidelines without his crutches, and he was the Gable of old—involved in every match, shouting himself hoarse. Whitmer led off with two takedowns in the first period and coasted to a 9–4 victory over Paulson. Even after Whitmer had lost badly at Michigan State, Gable told him that he had a national championship in him, and it was beginning to look as if Gable was right. Mike Mena did twenty-five pushups after his 11–2 victory, and Ironside notched his seventh pin of the season, most on the team. Gillis lost, 10–6, to Jason Davids, second-ranked nationally at 142.

McIlravy (14–0) then squared off against Chad Kraft (14–2). McIlravy was top-ranked in the country, Kraft was fourth. McIlravy, looking tired and ashen and complaining of headaches, held slim leads, but in the third period, he wobbled at the edge of the mat after taking an accidental blow to the head. He looked dazed, disoriented. Ken McIlravy instinctively tensed forward. "Something's the matter," he said. "I'll straighten this thing out with Gable."

Lincoln held on for a 4–3 victory, and left the mat immediately. He unsnapped his customized, heavily cushioned headgear and slung it toward the bench. He tromped downstairs, not to a locker room, but to the first room he found. It was an aerobics studio, with mirrors on three walls. Now McIlravy could be viewed in triptych: He was stretched out on his back with his head resting on his workout clothes and his gym bag, sweat running from his forehead into his eyes and making him blink. His dark blond hair looked as if it had been mussed by an unseen hand. His expression lingered between anger and confusion. His head hurt, he said, a dull, right-sided pain, every twenty seconds. He complained of recent depression and sleeping as many as twelve hours a day. He usually kept a daily record of who he wrestled and how he did, but he hadn't made any entries in the four weeks he had been easing off.

Ken followed Lincoln and then turned to leave him alone with his thoughts.

"I feel like I'm at fifty percent," the wrestler said, shaking his head. He admitted that he had drifted through the third period, losing track of time and score, and that he had just wanted the match to end—and how unusual that was, because he usually just thought about scoring and scoring again. "I hate wrestling when I'm not up to par. In my mind, I lost. Four weeks off makes a difference, especially the way I wrestle. It worries me to have [headaches] when I wrestle a guy like that, who butts heads all the time . . ."

But what consumed McIlravy, as the matches continued a floor above, was Gable. McIlravy said he had trouble communicating with Gable about the issue of his health and readiness for Minnesota. Gable, McIlravy said, would ask, "How's your head? Can you wrestle today?," but what McIlravy said he wanted to hear was, "Is your head hurting? Would you like to take some time off?"

"Gable doesn't look at me as an individual," McIlravy said. "That's the way he's gone along for twenty years in coaching. There are a lot of candyasses on the team. Hand is a baby right now. If everybody was OK [on the team], and I was the only one who wasn't, it wouldn't be a problem. But this way, he's hard to convince. There's no bruise, no swelling."

Although angry, his voice was steady and subdued. The large, empty studio seemed to swallow his words.

"The real truth is, it doesn't matter how the team does. They're good guys. I like them. But I care about how I do, and if I win the nationals. Everybody does, I bet. I hope so. I hope they feel the same way."

McIlravy's more immediate problem was the impending finals on Sunday, where Iowa was expected to meet Oklahoma State. McIlravy clearly didn't want to wrestle, didn't feel like it. Could he convince Gable? Should he even try? Would Gable listen?

"He wouldn't ask me to do what he wouldn't [do]. I know that. He'd wrestle through this. I know he would. But look what it's gotten him. Look at him. He's a wreck. I don't want to end up like that in twenty years. I want to be a person."

By the time Gable left in the van with Kathy for the motel, he knew two things: First, the Hawkeyes—23–12 winners over Minnesota—would meet the Cowboys—28–9 winners over Iowa State—in the final. Second, injuries were becoming the storyline for the season. Gable clearly felt the tightrope under his feet: McIlravy had shown that he wasn't ready for prime time, and yet, as Gable pointed out in a team meeting the week before, McIlravy always kept himself in a state of high readiness even without practice. Headaches obviously were to blame, but there the certainty ended. A month of holding him out of practice apparently hadn't helped. Neurological tests turned up nothing. Iowa's three-year dual-meet streak and No. 1 ranking would be on the line in less than twenty-four hours.

What was a coach to do?

"How long has it been since December 29?" Gable wondered aloud in the van, as Kathy drove. That was the date of the Midlands finals, when McIlravy reaggravated his head injury and virtually dropped out of live wrestling in the room. His troubles had begun in December, when he suffered a concussion in practice. He had a family history of migraines, and sometimes his head hurt with exertion. It was now January 18. "It's been that long since he's practiced," Gable said, and stared out the passenger window.

There was little indication, as the van poked through the night, that Gable sensed the rebellion brewing in McIlravy, although he soon would.

The subject turned to Oklahoma State. The Cowboys had beaten Iowa State by nineteen points, while in December, the Hawkeyes had whipped ISU by thirteen.

"That's OK. Comparative scores don't mean anything," Kathy Gable said, trying to cheer her husband.

Gable came to life. "That's right. We should win at one-fifty, one-fifty-eight, one-ninety," he said, including McIlravy in the mix. "Damn it! We're going to *kick ass!* I needed that."

Gable noted that John Smith had kept his younger brother, Mark, seventh-ranked at 177 pounds, out of the Iowa State match, where he would have faced third-ranked Barry Weldon, 18–1 this season. Smith apparently wanted to save Mark, an up-and-down competitor, from the likes of Weldon, and send him in fresh against Ersland.

"That was a smart coaching move," Gable said. "Not that I like giving too much credit there. But he was looking out for his brother."

Gable had been mentioning Oklahoma State for more than a week, anticipating the championship. His passion and angst surprised at least one veteran Iowa wrestler, who wondered if Gable wasn't taking the midseason match too seriously. Perhaps he was, but throughout his career, Gable and Oklahoma State had been inextricably entwined.

As if the wrestling rivalry between the states wasn't enough, there was the baggage left over from 1984. That year, Oklahoma State began looking for a new coach, and Gable was widely mentioned as a candidate. It was even reported as undisputed fact that he had been offered $3 million over several years to coach the Cowboys, but that he had turned it down to remain in his native state. However, Myron Roderick, OSU athletic director at the time who later became director of the National Wrestling Hall of Fame in Stillwater, Oklahoma, denied that he had even talked to Gable about the job. "I wanted to ask him about his interest, but he never returned my call," Roderick said. "I never offered him a dime. I darn sure couldn't give him 3 million dollars or whatever. As A.D., if I did something like that, I'd have been run out of town."

Roderick ended up hiring Joey Seay (pronounced "See"), who left the program in probationary shambles in 1991, when Smith took over.

Later in 1984, the tenuous relationship between Gable and Oklahoma State exploded into a feud that thirteen years later had not subsided. At issue was the 136.5-pound berth on Gable's Olympic freestyle team. In the trials, Randy Lewis, a two-time national champion under Gable with a flair for pinning, defeated Lee Roy Smith, former Oklahoma State national champion and John's older brother, by taking two of three matches. Lewis didn't advance to the next round, however, because Smith officially protested the scoring on one of Lewis's moves. Officials, reviewing tapes, agreed and ordered the match to start over, and Smith won, forcing a third and deciding match. Lewis suffered a knee injury and defaulted.

And that would have been the end of it—Lewis defaulting and Smith advancing—except that Lewis, at the urging of his father, also appealed, and the case went to binding arbitration, where a rematch was ordered. Publicly and at the hearing, Gable supported Lewis, avowing that he wanted to see justice done. Lewis won the rematch and went on to win a gold medal, but Gable had stirred a witch's brew by siding with his former wrestler over a wrestler from archrival Oklahoma State. OSU fans charged favoritism, and the incident, many in wrestling think, cost Gable a chance to coach other Olympic teams.

"I didn't have any choice but to say what I thought—I would have been subpoenaed if I hadn't gone," Gable contended.

John Smith, lean and dark, with an aquiline nose broken three times in wrestling, suggested that Gable could have inveighed against legal action with Lewis and his family. Smith admitted that while Lee Roy—now the Arizona State coach—has forgotten the incident, he, John Smith, can't. "Do I look at Gable differently? Not neccessarily. I don't think he's evil. I still look at Dan Gable as a great man, as a great coach. I respect Dan Gable. I don't think he was out to destroy anybody. I just think there were definitely mistakes made in that situation, and I'm bitter about it."

At eight o'clock Sunday morning, Williams and Ironside ran sprints and laps around a grassy field across the street from the motel. The day was warming fast, headed to 50 degrees, melting what snow there was. Around noon, Gable left his room, where he was watching a telecast of the Iowa-Michigan basketball game with Molly and Brian Mitchell, and held a team meeting in another room. McIlravy sat propped against a headboard, staring beyond Gable.

Late the previous night, there was a father-and-son talk. "If you wrestle, I'm gone," Ken McIlravy said, and added that he would never watch Lincoln wrestle again. ("Which was bullshit," Ken McIlravy would later admit. "I was desperate.") The father turned to leave. Lincoln caught him by the coat.

"Dad," he said, "if you don't come to watch, that's fine. You need to make a choice. You need to either support me in whatever decision I make or not come watch anymore. I'm a twenty-two-year-old man. I'm capable of making my own decisions."

"Yeah," the father responded. "But you're not making them."

Now Gable—in a white, button-down shirt and dark slacks—spoke to the group, painting Oklahoma State as a predictable team that largely emulated Smith's style.

"I can't get over, the same old high-crotch," Gable said. "The same dropping down. The same motions. It's just a replica. He—John Smith's—got about eight guys on his team that wrestle just like he did. The short drives and so on. Not physical.

"To me, it's like either we're going to wrestle their style, or we're going to take our style to them. And that's real crucial, and that's why we practice those drills at home. We've done it a long time, and our situation is hands-on. We like to be physical.

"And if we wait for them, it's going to be a mistake. That means we have to go over, tie them up, and make sure that we force action that they don't like. And we want them backing out of bounds . . . We've got to repeatedly do it. We just can't do it once, twice, and three times.

"This is the same team that we pretty much destroyed last year [26–9]. However, it's going to be tough matches today. Not in all cases. I think we can beat the crap out of some of the weight classes. But you're going to have to hole up and you're going to have to be tough."

Gable pressed forward on his crutches in the small path-
way between the beds and the chest of drawers. There was
power in his voice, but not volume. His hands squeezed the
grips on the crutches. He was entering deep water.

"Now here comes the problem, a little bit. Well, maybe
some of you guys, because of injury and things like that . . . we
haven't been able to get you to the point where you can do that
every second. Well, that's where your desire and determination
comes in—right now . . ." The coach put his fist to his chest.
"Heart is what it's all about," he said.

Gable wove threads of what each wrestler should expect
from his opponent into the rambling, eighteen-minute talk. He
critiqued, talking about his wrestlers in third person and then
addressing them personally. "Tony," he said of Tony Ersland,
who lost in overtime at 177 pounds to Minnesoa's Brandon
Eggum, "he's making progress. He's improving all the time.
But you still gotta be able to suck it up. Get down to the
nitty-gritty. When you got that down [defensive] position,
when you flipped, you should have been out. You've got to
suck it up. I shouldn't have been over yelling at you. You've
got to be able to do it yourself."

Gable obviously was worried about injuries and conditioning and sustaining effort. He mentioned 190-pound
Fullhart, who had been limited in practice by a sore back
muscle and lost in overtime to Minnesota's unbeaten Tim
Hartung. ("Hell, I don't have any faults with Fullhart. He just
couldn't stand up—that's the bottom line. You know? He
couldn't get his breath. We've got to get him in better shape
here.")

Gable turned to McIlravy, and the gap between them
seemed greater than the ten feet from the front of the room,
where Gable stood, to the bed, where McIlravy reposed.

"Whatever we need to get you guys going after this, to
get you in the right frame of mind, we've got to [do it] . . .
We're going to have to talk about communication. You know,
Lincoln, that's what I'm most concerned about right now just
from the standpoint of health. It's because we're dealing with
an area that's a little bit more touchy compared to a muscle or

something like that. We don't know exactly what it is. We did some tests, but we don't know."

At 12:40 P.M., the team boarded the bus for the short ride through light Sunday traffic to the Coliseum. The coaching staff and team had packed and would leave for Iowa City immediately after the match. McIlravy wore a green-tweed Sherlock Holmes coat and a tan hat, and he said he felt fine, then reconsidered—"well, about the same."

Gable, at the front of the bus, stood and delivered one final brief talk, urging that the team take comfort and confidence from the year-round wrestling they did, and that any self-doubt they had would be mirrored on the other side of the mat.

Bright sun flooded through the bus windows, but Gable's and everyone else's mood seemed to be darkening.

The bus parked across the street and a half-block away from the Coliseum. The Iowa wrestlers filed out the door and headed across the brown grass of a center divide toward the venue. Gable stood and turned and braced himself against the back of his seat and watched everyone pass.

"Talk to you now?" McIlravy said in a low voice.

"Let's wait until everybody leaves," Gable said.

They conferred for fifteen minutes over the back of Gable's seat. The bus motor idled. Outside, wrestling fans in light coats climbed the Coliseum steps or stood outside and basked in the warmth. Finally, the meeting broke up, and McIlravy left the bus first, weighed down by the large gym bag slung over his right shoulder.

"I'm not going to wrestle," he said. "I think we have an understanding."

Gable, apparently, thought otherwise. "He'll warm up and see how he feels," the coach said. "It's important to [prepare to] *win*, too."

The conversation didn't take Gable completely by surprise. The night before, McIlravy warned Gable that he might not feel like wrestling because of his headaches. But the coach clearly wasn't happy. He took out an apple and began eating.

Stumping along on his crutches, he stopped every few feet to take a bite.

"You've got to stay healthy, that's the point of it," he said. "I didn't miss a meet in college or high school. One hundred and eighty-two meets in a row, and I didn't sit out. I only sat out one match after that, and I stayed up all night icing down, but it didn't help. I was crying when I called and said I couldn't wrestle.

"My feeling," Gable stated, "is he's not taking advice that turns out to be the best, and sometimes he just thinks too much. Kristen is getting between us, telling him things."

But wasn't the point that McIlravy was in pain? Gable was asked.

"I've been in pain my whole damn life," he countered, with agitation.

Inside, as McIlravy stretched, word spread among his teammates that he wouldn't wrestle. Ken McIlravy said his son, in the aftermath of their dispute the previous night, hadn't told him of his decision. The father was told that Lincoln had decided not to wrestle, that he had held his own against Gable. The father said that Payne had been supportive of his son but hadn't meddled, and he took issue with what he regarded as Gable's short-term view of the situation.

"Gable wants to win right now, right this moment. Winning is the only thing that matters. He's putting on a lot more pressure this year, I guess because it's probably his swan song."

A crowd of 1,910 crowded together in the balcony, and for once the Iowa fans in their black and gold had a vociferous rival in the orange-clad Cowboy backers. The latter had the better of it at the beginning. Oklahoma State's Teague Moore, behind early by 4–1, rallied to beat Whitmer, 8–5. Moore rode Whitmer for more than two minutes, after Gable apparently changed his mind from the team meeting and ordered his wrestler to take the down position in the third period. "I made a bad call," Gable said afterward. Mena fell apart in the third period of his match, giving up a stalling point and then a takedown in the last ten seconds, losing to third-ranked Eric Guerrero, 3–2.

Two matches into the biggest collegiate dual meet of the season, Oklahoma State held a 6–0 lead. Clearly, McIlravy's anticipated absence weighed on the Hawkeyes. Ironside, next up, stripping out of his warmups, tried to light a fire. "We'll turn it around, and right now," he told the bench.

In the meeting of first- and second-ranked 134-pound Division I wrestlers, top-rated Ironside and Steven Schmidt were tied at the end of regulation, 6–6. But in the two-minute sudden-death overtime, Ironside summoned strength and quickness and took Schmidt to the mat for an 8–6 victory. Koble, McIlravy's replacement, began loosening up, jumping in place and swinging his arms in circles and across his chest. Meanwhile, Gilliss stepped onto the mat against third-ranked Scott Reyna, a two-time All-American. Alger, in a black leather vest and western shirt, jeans, and cowboy boots, shook his head on the Iowa bench and murmured to no one in particular, "Gilliss, if you ever have a match, let it be now."

It wasn't. Reyna hammered Gilliss, 5–1. Reyna scored three points in the third period, on a takedown and a stalling call, and what Gable feared was coming true: The Hawkeyes, renowned for their conditioning and third-period flurries, were themselves last-period patsies. Even Ironside, the only Iowa winner through the first four matches, was held even in the third period.

On the Iowa bench, morale was plummeting. Unless a way could be found to clone the old Ironside, the Hawkeyes could be headed to their first loss in three years. The last time they were beaten was on February 11, 1994, when Oklahoma State seized a 23–16 victory. Gable showed visible annoyance at a Cowboy fan in the balcony behind the Iowa bench who was shouting loudly and wearing an orange Oklahoma State hat roughly the size of a TV satellite dish. Alger, assessing Gilliss's loss, said in a voice that Gilliss couldn't help but hear, "It's because he fuckin' drinks beer all summer and doesn't get in the weight room."

McIlravy watched without emotion as Koble was jacked three feet in the air by Jimmy Arias and slammed to the mat, bruising his body and most certainly his ego. Arias walked away with a 13–3 decision, and now Oklahoma State led by an identical score. Williams, top-ranked at 158, his face as serene as if he were studying at the library, battled fifth-rated Hardell Moore on even terms through three periods and an overtime. Now it came down to a thirty-second, sudden-death tiebreaker. Williams, winning the referee's coin toss, chose offense, wrapping a long arm around Moore on the mat. Moore had to score to win, but didn't—or did he? He nearly escaped before time ran out, but the referee made no call. Moore thought he had won, and raised his index finger, but at the same time, the referee was reaching for Williams's right arm to raise in victory. Williams, like Ironside, went to 15–0 for the season. Smith glanced down the sideline at Gable and smiled wrly as he pushed his hands together, almost prayerfully. Gable caught the glance but betrayed no emotion toward Smith.

Uker slipped in his black mouthpiece and squared off against Mark Branch, No. 1 at 167, an unorthodox wrestler whom Gable privately thought was the best that OSU had. The last time Gable had seen him was the previous March, in the NCAA finals, meeting Iowa senior Daryl Weber for the 167-pound title. In the first period of the match, there was a popping sound, and Branch writhed on the mat with a blown-out right knee. He had to default and settle for second place against a wrestler he had beaten 9–1 during the regular season. Now Branch was back, against improbable odds, and the venom he might have had for Weber was channeled against Uker. Branch drove Uker to the mat thirty seconds into the match and twice nearly pinned him in building a 7–0 lead going into the second period. OSU fans, led by the man in the satellite-dish hat, chanted "stalling . . . stalling," because Uker seemed frozen by Branch's varied angles of attack and leg tieups.

Uker was sitting on the bench, thawing after a 13–0 defeat, when Ersland dropped a 12–3 decision to Mark Smith. The back-to-back major decisions hoisted Oklahoma State into a 21–6 lead—and Iowa's first defeat in forty-two dual meets was imminent. Fullhart and Hand finished with victories over unranked opponents, and Gable hobbled upstairs to the KXIC radio nest, a 21–13 defeat in the books.

"I guess I don't congratulate you for second, huh?" Morrie Adams said on the air.

"No," Gable said, "you don't."

John Smith lingered on the sidelines, as if his leaving would cause the scoreboard to change. No American wrestler in history, not even Dan Gable, could match his accomplishment of winning six straight world titles, including two Olympic golds. The question often is posed: If they wrestled each other in their primes—at, say, 134 or 142 pounds—who would win, Smith or Gable? Gable probably trained harder than any wrestler in history, and he had an iron will that allowed him to roll on the mat seven days after knee surgery. He was a power wrestler, a pinner.

Smith, who won ninety straight matches at Oklahoma State, would have contrasted nicely with Gable, a jaguar pitted against a bull elephant. Smith was quick and unorthodox, driving in low for a single-leg takedown in the time it took to tie a shoelace. He was most dangerous when he appeared to be in trouble, for with his great flexibility he could turn and twist and contort and spring free, like Houdini from a locked safe. He never had major surgery during his career, and for that he thanked an elastic body that healed quickly.

Based on longevity and international competition—Gable won two world titles, counting the 1972 Olympics, to Smith's six—the Oklahoma State coach loomed as the favorite in a mythical match. But among wrestling coaches, and with few exceptions among coaches in general, Gable reigned supreme. There were his fourteen national titles in twenty years, including nine in a row. Going into this season, Gable was tied for third on the all-time all-sport coaches' championship list with Stanford men's tennis coach Dick Gould. (University of Houston men's golf coach Dave Williams won sixteen national titles from 1956–85, while UCLA men's volleyball coach Al Scates also won sixteen, from 1970–96.) Gable's string of nine straight national titles was second best in NCAA history, tying him with three other coaches—Southern Cal men's track coach Dean Cromwell, North Carolina women's soccer coach Anson Dorrance, and Louisiana State women's track coach Pat Henry. (Arkansas men's track coach John McDonnell won twelve straight NCAA titles from 1984–95.)

Smith took over a struggling Oklahoma State program that had been penalized for NCAA violations not of his doing. In his first season, 1992–93, the Cowboys were banned from postseason competition, but the year after, Smith led them to the NCAA title—an achievement that the team never accomplished when he wrestled. But Smith, at thirty-one nearly young enough to be Gable's son, was still a coaching neophyte, in just his fifth season at Oklahoma State. Standing there on the coliseum floor, he seemed to sense the weight of Gable's coaching record. Smith also knew he would be seeing the Hawkeyes and their balding, limping coach in March, in Iowa, when it mattered.

"Iowa is still a better tournament team right now," Smith said. "They have more people who can make the finals, but we have guys who can do it . . . I think we're at the point where we can count on four or five of our guys. They've established themselves, and they're showing no signs of weakening.

"But we've got to have three—at least two or three—of them come through. We've got to, to be real good. I'm including my brother as one of those three."

Iowa, losing six of ten matches to OSU, had a 28–12 record in individual matches in the National Dual Championships; the Cowboys were 32–8. It was moot what McIlravy's presence in the lineup would have meant, but Gable said he thought the Hawkeyes might have tied or even won with McIlravy wrestling and charging his teammates' batteries.

In his comments to reporters, Gable was even-handed in discussing the McIlravy situation. "He's gotta get right in his mind, and by making a guy wrestle, or telling him he should wrestle if he feels like he don't want to, it just would hurt our relationship and probably give him less of a chance to be the best he can be. So I let the decision to wrestle be McIlravy's.

"Because it involves your head, it scares you more than it does like a wrist or an elbow. You can work through those things. But when you start having things [go wrong] that affect your life functions—you know, for the rest of your life—well . . . Even with my hips and knees, after thirty years they're affected, but not right away like the brain or the heart would be."

It was a quiet bus ride home. Gable drove back in the van with his family, except for Annie, who rode in the bus and played the card game Uno with Williams and Hand and others, turning over an orange plastic Gatorade barrel for a table in the middle of the aisle. McIlravy and his wife, Lisa, in a maternity smock, sat in back and talked quietly. McIlravy might have been the only Iowa wrestler to feel buoyed by the weekend. He thought he had had a good talk with Gable on the bus before the meet, that they were finally connecting. The denouement occurred, McIlravy said, when he told Gable that "my health is not dependent on the team's fortune—it can't be that way."

"And he said, 'Yeah, you're right,' " McIlravy said. "And then he related it to himself. He said, 'You know, right now it's killing me with my hip, because I'm not healing up. I'm on an uneven plane, and I'm not healing.' And he said, 'I can't wait until Thursday when I'll be making progress'—you know, when he's had his surgery. He said, 'So I can really understand where you're coming from right now. You know, I think that's probably the best decision.' "

The Gables, in their van, followed the bus, picked up Annie in the Carver-Hawkeye parking lot around midnight, and drove straight home. The snow cover had increased since Nebraska, and the country back roads were icy but clear. Gable, his voice hoarse from the meet, shifted in the passenger's seat. He was still chewing on the McIlravy situation. McIlravy was right that Gable himself undoubtedly would have wrestled with a similar injury. But McIlravy was also wrong: Gable had treated him like an individual, allowing him to miss a big meet simply because he had expressed such reservations.

After the van was unpacked, Gable stood on the front

porch. A light shone from the hallway. He had taken off his coat and stood bent over his crutches, staring past fences and trees into blackness.

"It'll be a cold day in hell when we lose to Oklahoma State in the nationals," he said in a voice ragged with emotion. "They aren't eight points better than us, even though they surprised me at '18 and '26."

Gable soon would be searching his knowledge and experience for answers. He had spent a lifetime learning that wrestling wasn't all cheering crowds and glory; he knew that it sometimes took a setback to pave the way to success.

chapter 8

T HROUGHOUT HIS wrestling and coaching career, Gable watched and listened and learned what could help him and what could not. Driving across the Iowa countryside one day, leaning over the steering wheel and swinging his head from side to side, he said, "I'm like a wolf." He pointed into heavy brush, as if one was lurking there. "I'm always spying. I'm always watching how people will react to things.

"I watched how wrestlers reacted in the 1970 World Championships. It was in Edmonton, Canada. I was an alternate. I trained with the guys, but I didn't wrestle. After our practices, I went to all the other teams' practices. I'd sneak in and watch them for a while. I was just like a wolf.

"I would stand in the corner. Watching. Watching. Watching. And nobody knew that I was just, like, taking notes. Mental notes. Mental notes. Mental notes. Little did they know that I was going to be kicking their butt the next time in the World finals. I'd watch all these guys make weight. All these different wrestlers from different countries that were getting ready. Nothing like it. I just *loved* it!

"I watched every move of these Iranians. They don't know to this day that I studied Seyed-Abassy. [Shamseddin Seyed-Abassy won the 1970 World Championship at 136.5

pounds.] I watched him lose every ounce he lost. And then they carried him to the scale. . . . I watched the Russian matches. I watched the Americans. That tournament taught me that I could beat those guys. I could win. I could win the World Championships and the Olympic Games, because it's the same event, basically."

Gable knew he could be a horse with blinders and outtrain them all, and beat them all. "Because they just didn't put out. Didn't put out the effort to dominate and win—to be great. It was just more of a strategic type of match all the time. One point here. One point there. Cat and mouse. Instead of a damn dog eating them."

Gable learned his famous pinning hold, the double arm-bar, from Rich Sanders, a long-haired free spirit from Portland State. Gable learned the hard way, by losing to Sanders, 6–0, in the National AAU Freestyle Championships in 1967 in Lincoln, Nebraska. Gable vividly remembered his match against Sanders.

"He arm-barred me all during that match," Gable said. "Both arms behind my back, and he got them both. Just torched my face. It was all burnt. But he didn't turn me. But he had me in the arm-bars unbelievably tight. He didn't score any points on it, but I wanted to learn it. And basically I did.

"Those are really hard to learn, because they are potentially dangerous. A lot of people say, 'Well, the referees didn't call them potentially dangerous when you used them, and referees nowadays call them potentially dangerous.' That's not it. Nobody knows how to use the arm-bar. Very few people. Rich Sanders knew how to use them. I knew how to use them. And there's a way to use them where they're not potentially dangerous or illegal. But there's hardly anybody [who] gets the feel of them. I can't hardly ever teach it."

At Iowa State, Gable spent two hours in practice clamping on arm-bars. Teammates did not salivate for the opportunity to tangle with Gable during one of his arm-bar frenzies. "A guy would be in the wrestling room for five minutes, and he'd want to wrestle him," said former Cyclones national champion

Chuck Jean. "He'd get one of those double arm-bars on you, and he just *irritated* you with how he'd plant your face."

Gable pinned 25 of 64 opponents in high school and 83 of 118 in college. Over the last part of his junior year and first part of his senior year, he pinned twenty-four straight opponents; overall in his last two seasons he flattened fifty-six of sixty-four. Gable had thirteen falls in seventeen matches in the NCAA Championships. In his junior and senior seasons, Gable won the NCAA's Gorrarian Award for the most pins in the least time in the national tournament. In 1969, he pinned five opponents in a total of 20 minutes and 59 seconds; in 1970, he pinned five in 22:08. And, of course, he posted three pins in six matches in the Olympics. Many of his opponents stayed with him through one period, maybe two, but his manic, in-your-face style usually had them on their backs in the third period.

"It's an art to pin somebody," Gable said. "You've got to have all your weight exactly on them. You've got to be chest to chest. You've got to be able to knock their blocks out, and you've got to have their head out. Hardly anybody works at it enough in practice."

Gable also learned from the single match he lost, on a snowy March weekend in Evanston, Illinois, in 1970, in the NCAA 142-pound finals. "Bottom line is that match helped me. I needed to get beat. Because it not just helped me win the Olympics, but it helped me dominate the Olympics. But more than that, it helped me be a better coach. I would have a hundred times rather not have that happened, but I used it. I used it."

Larry Owings grew up in Oregon, the son of a carpenter, one of four boys in the family who wrestled and won state high-school titles. Owings won a pair, the unlikeliest champion of the bunch. Early in his teenage years, he weighed 170 pounds, and not much of it resembled granite. His nickname was "Porky." In the eighth grade, he shed twenty pounds and grew three inches—up, not out. He went out for wrestling in high school, and enjoyed the success and self-esteem it gave him.

As a high-school senior in 1968, he competed in the U.S. Olympic Trials in Ames. "I was a greenhorn in freestyle wrestling," said Owings, now forty-six, director of facilities in a school district in the state of Washington. "I had stars in my eyes for the Olympics. I thought this would be my best shot —until the first match."

In the first match, Dan Gable—an Iowa State sophomore who the previous spring had won his first NCAA title—defeated Owings, 13–4. After a second loss, Owings was eliminated. Gable hung around until he lost to Bobby Douglas, who attacked from angles and used Gable's gung-ho style against him in an 11–1 victory. In the match before that, Tom Huff of Air Force shocked Gable by pinning him in 1:10, the first and only time in freestyle competition that Gable would be counted out. Gable had other reasons besides Owings to remember the trials, but Owings would remember Gable as unfinished business.

Harold Nichols, the Iowa State coach, tried to recruit Owings, but Owings decided to stay closer to home and attend the University of Washington. (The school dropped wrestling in 1980.) As a freshman eligible to compete in the 1971 NCAA Championships, he was seeded fifth at 130 pounds but didn't place. In his sophomore season, he won the Pac-8 Conference's 158-pound title, but dropped to 142 for the NCAA meet. He wrestled up to 167, but 142 was his best weight— and besides, Gable was there. "I always wanted to come back and beat people who'd beaten me—even the score," he said.

The NCAA championships, held in McGaw Hall at Northwestern University, drew media from around the country, including ABC-TV's *Wide World of Sports* crew. Gable, the stoic redhead, held center stage, a senior capping off an unbeaten high school and collegiate career. Or so everyone assumed, except for a darkly handsome Washington sophomore named Larry Owings. He harbored the sort of swaggering confidence adopted by professional wrestlers and their acting coaches, and he made good copy.

Said Gable, "I didn't pay much attention, and then I was walking along, and all of a sudden there's a paper open, and it says something about Owings. I looked. And it had a quote from Owings. I looked. And the quote said, 'I'm not going to this tournament to be a national champion. I'm coming here to beat Gable. You might think I'm going to say I'm going to be national champion . . . but I know if I beat Dan Gable I'll be a national champion.'

"The funny thing was when the matches started, if I hadn't already wrestled, or if I had, I kept watching him wrestle. And he was making a lot of mistakes. The matches went back and forth, then all of a sudden he'd pin the guy. He'd catch him in an inside cradle, or he'd get some arm-bars on some guys, but he mostly cradled.

"And so I watched him almost every match, and by the time we got to the finals, I was thinking, 'God, don't get caught in his cradle. Don't get caught in his cradle.' "

Even before the match, Owings had done what no other wrestler had managed to do against Gable: ruffle him, shake his concentration. What's more, Owings thought he could beat Gable—"just by points, not a lopsided victory or anything"— by wearing down Gable the same way that Gable dulled his opponents' sharpness: with superior conditioning. In other words, he intended to out-Gable Gable.

"It was probably the stupidest strategy in the world, but I'm a big one on conditioning, and mental conditioning," Owings said. He ran three miles in the morning on the Washington indoor track, averaging a six-minute pace, sprinting the last quarter mile in under a minute. Owings wrestled two hours a day. He didn't fear a pin, although Gable had four falls in the tournament by the time they met. "I knew I could go the distance with him."

Owings, pinning all four of his NCAA opponents, entered the meet with a 30–1 record. His only loss was a 7–5 setback at 150 pounds to Oklahoma's two-time national champion, Mike Grant. Gable went up a weight to meet Grant during the season and beat him, 9–4, for a 29–0 record.

An hour before the 142-pound national final, Gable interrupted his warm-up and granted a *Wide World of Sports* request to deliver a short taped promotional teaser into the camera at the edge of the floor. It would be used during the week to herald the showing of the NCAA championships a week hence. Preoccupied and nervous, Gable held a microphone and stumbled several times over the reading.

"They came up to me, and they said all you've got to say is, 'Hi, I'm Dan Gable. Come watch me next week as I finish my college career one eighty-two and oh,' " Gable said. "And I said, 'I have not. I didn't win yet. After the match I'll do it. Can't do it.'

"They said, 'We gotta do it.' So being the good guy I am, I did it. And then I kept screwing up . . . Now I don't let my athletes do something like that. If [the media] want it, they can get them at the opportune time or don't get them. I've had people pissed off. I've had the NCAA threaten me. They didn't want my kids wrestling in the finals because I wasn't following all their protocol . . . Now I look out for my athletes."

The match took place on a mat on a platform. Every green wooden bleacher seat was filled, and then some, by a standing-room-only crowd of 8,500. It was the wrestling event of the season and, as it turned out, beyond. Ken Kraft, the ABC color analyst and longtime Northwestern coach, had a friend who canceled out of a North Shore society party to attend. "He said to his wife, 'I can't go to that thing. I've got to go to McGaw Hall.' And he jumped in his car and drove down and he couldn't find a ticket, and he walked over to a gate and he said, 'Here's twenty dollars,' and he was one of the standing-room-only guys."

The match held some of the ambience of a club fight, both wrestlers bathed in bright lights against a black backdrop, and the crowd noise rising and ebbing in tandem with the action. Owings wore a black singlet edged in white, and Gable wore cardinal and gold. Both had white headgear and wore leggings.

The referee was Pascal Perri, a veteran official from New York state. In the first thirty seconds, Gable scored a single-leg take-down. "My mistake," Owings said. "I made a move that didn't work, a leg trip, and he reached for my leg, and I gave it to him." Owings lashed back with a takedown and an escape, and led after the first period, 3–2. Gable was worried—though not because of the score. He had trailed this early before. It was how he felt.

"When we started, all I was thinking was, 'God, don't get caught in his cradle. Don't get caught in his cradle.' I was thinking so much about him that I didn't really get through my proper focus and concentration and warm-up. Within a minute I was dead tired. I'd never been that tired before. I wrestled so many matches when I was dead tired, but I never knew it until after the match. Now I knew it right away. Tired and weak."

Gable's teammates in the bleachers laughed off the early scores, but as the deficit mounted to 7–2 in the second period, a shared concern connected them. Ben Peterson, who finished fourth for the Cyclones at 190, looked over at a friend on leave from the Army who had come to support Peterson. "Gable's in trouble," the friend said, to which Peterson replied, "No problem."

"I laughed until there were 15 seconds left," Peterson said. "Owings made a fireman's carry, his second one on Gable, that put him on his back. I looked over at Phil, my friend, and I said, 'I've never seen him in this position before. It could be trouble.' I never told Dan about that for years, about me laughing at first. I had a guilty conscience. I had such confidence he'd find a way to come back."

Owings led, 8–6, at the end of the second period, but Gable tied it early in the third period with a reversal. A little later, Gable lost a contact lens, and Perri called time for Gable to retrieve it. The crowd began booing. Earlier, Gable, under siege, had scrambled out of bounds and been penalized for stalling. This was viewed as a smiliar gambit. Then the lens popped loose again and time was called and the booing re-sumed. Gable decided to go without either lens, and took the other out. The crowd's reaction stirred resentment in another of Gable's teammates, Jean.

"It was the hardest thing I've seen in sports," he said. "I don't see how anybody could wrestle under pressure like that."

Now Gable, in a burst of offense, was riding Owings, and grabbing Owings's left wrist with his hand. Gable thought, "I got to get going. Quit being a candyass." And: "I think I can pin the son-of-a-buck. I'm back in rhythm."

But Owings slipped the noose with his supple body, as he had escaped from Gable's clutches before. That gave Owings a 9–8 advantage on the scoreboard, but Gable actually led, 10–9, because under the rules at the time he had two points for riding time. Less than a minute remained. Gable could coast home on vapors, but conservatism did not come naturally to him. He attacked Owings's upper body, and Owings countered with a high single-leg takedown. The two hit the mat, with Gable rolling on his back. Perri signaled quickly—two and two—two points for Owings's takedown, two for exposing Gable's shoulders to the mat. Iowa State fans subsequently disputed the near-fall points, arguing that Owings hadn't exposed Gable's shoulders to the mat long enough. Kraft and other knowledgeable wrestling people thought it was a proper call, and Gable didn't complain. "I'm not saying it was a bad call," Gable said. "It just wasn't a call that you could really say was clear-cut, OK?"

Action continued for a short time before Perri called time and approached the official scorer to make sure the points had been tallied correctly. The flurry was so quick, and Perri's signals so swift, that many along the scorer's table and press row weren't sure about the scoring. Washington coach Jim Smith stood in Owings's corner and screamed for justice; Harold Nichols sat in Gable's corner and did the same. The crowd was in tumult. Matside, in front of his microphone, Kraft prayed for an 11–11 tie. "My mind was saying, 'Wow! We've got an overtime if he [Owings] doesn't get the back points. Let's see more of it. Let's not stop now.'" Perri walked back to the center of the mat to the wrestlers. Seventeen seconds remained. The public-address announcer recited the score—13–11, Owings—and Gable's expression dissolved into a look of deep and profound shock and dismay. He shook his head, then began swinging it back and forth, his eyes wide in disbelief.

"I heard some point signals, but I didn't hear no back ones, but that's beside the point," Gable said. "That's part of it. What it did is it taught me you don't put the matches in the referee's hands if you really want to [win]. Made me dominate from then on. Start getting that much tougher, so that I didn't have no referee determine my outcome."

With five seconds left, Owings tried a shot that missed. "I got to the finals by being offensive, and I wanted to stay offensive," Owings said. "Not once did I back up or slow up or stall. I made that shot, and it was probably stupid. If he'd known that, he could have spun around behind me." Gable tried to score but couldn't and time ran out. "I gave up. I was disgusted. It wasn't a good match from the beginning." Gable's voice broke. "I was crushed. I hurt."

Perri lifted Owings's left arm as the 142-pound champion shook hands with Gable, whose head was bowed and whose eyes seemed unfocused. Mack Gable left Katie and went to his son's side. Dan Gable, weeping, slumped to the floor behind the bleachers, his Iowa State warm-up robe drawn over his head. Eventually, he made his way down through the tunnels to the locker room. His teammates were crushed as well, but couldn't think of what to say. Jean went to the locker room and began to strip out of his uniform, even though he was scheduled to defend his 177-pound title a little later. For years afterward, the story circulated that Jean did not want to wrestle because he always followed Gable, his close friend, in a meet, and Gable had lost. And Gable convinced him to wrestle, for himself and the team, the defending Division I champion. What actually happened was that Jean was so disgusted with the crowd's behavior toward Gable that he wanted to pull out. That is, until an unidentified wrestler wandered in behind Jean and said, "I didn't think Iowa State was a bunch of quitters."

"My head about blew off after he said that," Jean said. "I got back up and decided to go out there. I thought, 'I'll get dressed, you worthless dog.'"

Before Jean wrestled, the top eight wrestlers from the 142-pound competition took their places on the awards stand. There are only live-witness accounts to document what happened when Gable's name was recited as the second-place finisher. While ABC-TV technicians scrambled unsuccessfully to change tapes in time, the crowd gave Gable a standing ovation. By some accounts, it lasted for five minutes. "Gable is standing up there, and tears are coming down," Kraft said. "I mean, and it wasn't like a thirty-second cheer coming down. He had to stand there for five minutes throughout this whole thing."

"They wouldn't stop clapping until I looked up," Gable said. "And I didn't know that's what they were waiting on."

Owings, meanwhile, sorted his own thoughts. "I'd finally won the NCAA. I was on the victory stand. I had time to think about it. The guy next to me had won every match, and it took a hell of an effort to beat him. I sensed the emotion in him. I saw the tears rolling down his cheeks. But instead of being a big baby, he stood up and took it. That's a heck of a mark of a man. I didn't talk to him. What could I say?"

On a backroad in Iowa, Dale Bahr was driving his 1966 Chevrolet with his wife, Nancy. A former NCAA champion and teammate of Gable's, Bahr coached high-school wrestling in Iowa. It was the night of March 28, 1970, and Bahr had the radio tuned to a broadcast of the Gable-Owings match.

"I remember the station, KRIT in Clarion," Bahr said. "It was a blow-by-blow thing. I'm driving from north of Iowa Falls to south of Iowa Falls, to my wife's parents' home. I remember exactly where I was when Kennedy was shot, and I remember exactly where I was when John Lennon was shot, and I remember exactly where I was when Gable got beat. I put it in that vein."

Gable returned immediately to Ames. The team had repeated as the NCAA Division I champion with six All-Americans, including three champions: Dave Martin (158), Jason Smith (167), and Jean (177). A day after the match, Gable intimated to Ben Peterson—his religious teammate and an All-American—that he might undertake serious beer-drinking, just for a while. Peterson remembered Gable saying, "I train all the time, and I still get beat. It doesn't make any difference."

Gable wasn't sure what he wanted. "I still couldn't get away from working out. But I did go right away to partying a little bit, and drinking some beer, and chasing some girls. I didn't wrestle as long as I normally do, but I still probably got an hour, an hour and a half in."

During the spring, Peterson was walking across a street on campus after a Saturday morning workout in the Cyclones wrestling room. It was informal, no coaches. Gable usually appeared, but not this time, and six teammates lifted and ran and wrestled without him. Gable pulled up on a motorcycle, and Peterson told him he missed seeing him at the workout.

"He hung his head. I knew something was bothering him," Peterson said. "He was at a party, and there was trouble, and he'd been sleeping all morning, trying to catch up. He said once or twice since he'd been back the cops had put him in jail to dry out.

"He was very open about it, very embarrassed about it. 'I'll be there next Saturday,' he said. 'I'll never miss again.' "

Peterson was raised on a dairy farm in Wisconsin, and was a devout Christian by the time he was in junior high. His Iowa State teammates ridiculed his religiosity, but Gable defended him. Now Peterson helped Gable. "I needed to be sensitive. I tried not to judge and lambaste. For one of the first times, I saw I could help Dan, that it wasn't just a one-way street. Let me quote scripture: 'Iron sharpeneth iron, so a man sharpeneth the countenance of a friend.' "

Katie Gable frequently called her son after his defeat, but he wouldn't take the call—or if he did, he wouldn't talk long. "It was really hard for me to talk to her on the phone," Gable said. "I'd choke up. It was like a death to me." Finally, within a week of Gable's loss, his parents drove to Ames to see him. No son of hers was going to be a Molly Putz.

"She cracked me across the face and said, 'Just wake up, kid! You know we love you,' " Gable said. " 'Just because you lost, that match isn't the end of the world.' "

Gable rebounded, aching for a rematch with Owings. After a couple of near-misses, they finally met in the 1972 Olympic trials in Anoka, Minnesota. Gable had moved back to his parents' home, and was working out with a rotating cast of partners including the Peterson brothers. Siddens let him use the Waterloo West training room, and every day Gable jumped in the whirlpool. It would have been idyllic, except that Gable had suffered a knee injury that kept him out of competition for six weeks, until the Olympic district qualifying meet in Iowa City.

By that time, he had adopted a new style, to compensate for his knee. Instead of smothering opponents with his offense, Gable laid back and countered with a front headlock, and snapped his man to the mat. He rummaged through the possibilities and also came up with whipovers and pancakes and snapdowns. "I just did them all the time. Because there's always some way to score, you just have to use your head." And then, as his knee improved, he kept what he had learned, and added it to his arsenal.

He sailed through Olympic district qualifying in Iowa City, pinning each of six opponents. Three weeks later, in the trials themselves, he pinned two opponents and scored 21–0 and 27–0 victories over two others, and stepped onto the mat against Owings. It was not the best year of Owings's life. He had remained a top wrestler, finishing second in the NCAA championships in 1971 and '72, at 142 pounds, but his personal life was falling apart. His wife was seven months pregnant, and they were having problems that would lead to a divorce. "She didn't want me wrestling. It took a lot out of my wrestling," he said. He wrestled best at 136.5, but he couldn't cut below 138, and so he went up to 149.5, Gable's weight. "He wanted another shot," Owings said. "I felt he deserved it."

Their match was anticlimactic. Gable, the defending World and Pan-American champion, burst to a 4–0 lead in the first period and handled Owings easily, 7–1. Kraft, who as a member of the U.S. Olympic Wrestling Committee helped train the team, witnessed a more aggressive Gable than the one he saw in Evanston. "I'll always remember the first move by

Owings in the match," Kraft said. "He tried a fireman's carry, and he penetrated so deeply, he went underneath Gable's legs —and so far that he lost him. It was a gutsy move, but he didn't score anything. He went right on through, about seven feet past him, and there went the arm and he got nothing. It was the last thing he was able to do." Then Gable began scoring. "When I got ahead of him, I just coasted," Gable said. "It'd been bothering me for so long—two years and three months—that it actually became a burden. I was carrying this burden that I just had to get off my back, and I didn't care [how]. . . . I didn't wrestle a good match against him, because I kept thinking, 'What if this guy beats me again? How am I ever going to explain the same guy beating me twice?' " The result was sweet relief for Owings as well. "It was hard to live with that," he said, speaking of his widely publicized victory. "I'm quiet and introverted. Every place I'd go, all anybody wanted to talk about was that."

From then until the moment that Gable stood atop the victory platform at the Olympics, his head bandaged and bleeding, he was unstoppable. In a ten-match span—counting four more to win an Olympics berth and six in Munich—he pinned four opponents and didn't allow a point in recording six decisions (compiling a 75–0 combined score). It was domination on a scale seldom if ever seen in international wrestling. Nevertheless, Gable will be forever remembered for a match he lost to a carpenter's son.

A quarter century later, Gable still had a tape of the match. He hadn't watched it in years—it was too painful. But at a friend's suggestion, in 1997 he brought it from home to the wrestling office and slipped it into the VCR. The picture appeared: grainy and in color, the Gable of nearly three decades ago came to life, with his cleft chin and stony expression, his last time in an Iowa State singlet. A couple of his Iowa wrestlers walked in, saw what he was watching, and immediately turned and left, shutting the door behind them.

There is something undefinably spellbinding about the match, almost eerie. The announcers' voices filter through like an overheard conversation, fragmented and distant. The cameras must have been set up in Joliet, so distant do the figures appear, lost in the black hole of McGaw Hall. The crowd noise begins as constant static, then escalates, then diminishes, gathering and spending itself. It remains transfixing, all these years later—the visual and historical equivalent of Bobby Thomson's home run, of Ali versus Frazier.

Once, the night before the Midlands Championships, coaches had gathered in a hotel suite and poured drinks and watched tapes of old matches, including the 1970 meeting between Gable and Owings. Halfway through, a hush fell over the room. A voice said, "I can't believe it. Gable's trying to crawl off the mat!"

This time, alone in the wrestling office, Gable watched grimly, pulling a chair up just to a couple of feet from the screen. He saw himself score the first points of the match with a takedown. "Should have pinned him right there. But he was double-jointed in the shoulders or something. Always got away." He saw himself try an arm-bar, and Owings slither out of it. "Got to get his arm back more." Gable sounded resigned. He knew it wouldn't happen just because he said it. He had four minutes of riding time, the announcers said. "Can you believe it? Half the match I've got in riding time—and I lose?" He watched himself search the mat twice for his left contact lens and then give up, and he heard the booing start. He watched himself scramble out of bounds, and return to the center circle a stride ahead of Owings, and Owings make a slight but detectable movement with his hand. "He's pushing me. Trying to psych me. I've done that, too." He watched himself be taken down by Owings, and roll, and Perri hold up two fingers, then two again. He watched himself, his full-head-of-reddish-hair self, gape when he realized he was losing, would lose, was beaten.

The tape ran out. Gable took it out and switched off the VCR. "Well, that's it," he said. He meant, "That's enough."

chapter **9**

BEGINNING THE LAST full week of January, Gable had much to do and not much time to do it in. He was scheduled for hip surgery on Thursday, leaving three days to regroup the team and review the mistakes made in Nebraska, and sound the bugle again for the nationals. He knew the team's No. 1 ranking was lost; he was now coaching the second-ranked Division I team in the country.

Jim Zalesky was put in charge of the Hawkeyes for their dual meet against Minnesota on Friday night at Carver-Hawkeye. Gable shrugged off the larger implications of the decision, that Zalesky had a firm grip on the head job if Gable retired at season's end. "It just means he's been there longer than anybody else," Gable said. "I think they [Zalesky and Tom Brands] both want to do well, and I think they're ready for this." Gable pointed out that Zalesky had taken the team on its eastern swing to Pennsylvania earlier in the season, and that "he thinks about things I don't think about."

"Bottom line, I still call the shots," Gable said.

Gable showed up at his office before ten on Monday morning, a departure from his floating schedule under which he conducted business from home or via his car phone. Oklahoma State had raised the stakes. "It's a different game now,"

Gable said, hobbling on his crutches across the parking lot toward the arena. "We got beat."

He felt rested. "The night I didn't sleep was Saturday night, when I learned Lincoln might not wrestle." For Gable, the McIlravy situation seemed to occupy a separate compartment, a mystery he couldn't solve. He couldn't let it go. His past and present wrestlers invariably described him as a master motivator who got inside their heads with just a word or a look —a different word or look for each wrestler—and switched on their engines. Joe Williams felt that way. "One day I got hurt in practice, and I was going to take the day off," Williams explained. "My ankle was pretty bad. And he came in the locker room—came in just normally, not doing anything—and he walked past me and he said, 'Oh, you're not going to practice today?' And I said, 'No, I just hurt my ankle, I'll probably just stay off it.' And he says, 'OK, well, that's OK. You already won nationals, so you don't have to work out today.'

"And this is my freshman year, and I hadn't done nothing. And that just pissed me off, to the point where it made me want to get up and work hard. And I went and got taped up, and I finished practice and never even noticed my ankle."

With a sentence or two, Gable could alter the mood and intentions of one of his wrestlers, make him forget pain and return to practice. But McIlravy was different—a fifth-year senior, a proven star, twenty-two years old, married and soon to be a father. Gable hadn't found the switch. Maybe there wasn't one.

Gable searched his own past for answers. He had never had a concussion—"I was too tough for that"—not that he didn't try.

"Kathy and I were going through some things, and I tried breaking a quart beer bottle over my head," Gable said. "Couldn't break it. Quart beer bottles are thick."

Practice was at 3:30 P.M. McIlravy walked somberly to the locker room to drop off his coat before a team meeting. Did he have a headache? He fluttered his hand in the air, indicating that the pain that came and went. "It's there," he said.

Gable herded the team and coaches into a third-floor conference room, the so-called Big Ten Room, where on a TV screen at the front of the room they would watch tapes of recent matches. Several wrestlers sat a few feet from the screen, in padded chairs, while the rest sat around a long table. McIl-ravy sat at a corner of the table. When Tom Brands entered the room, he placed a consoling hand on Ben Uker's shoulder from behind and moved on. Uker, out for the season with his shattered jaw, wanted to be part of the team.

The room was cold. Gable wore his cossack-style fur hat and swung and dipped on his crutches toward the front. He critiqued performances and made observations as the tape ran. There was a shot of Mike Mena, strutting and firing a baleful look at his opponent. "Look at that!" Gable piped. "You've got your game face on in the third period. I like it!"

Ironside was shown marshalling his forces on the bottom, gathering himself in the defensive position, and getting a rever-sal. "Look at that, Whitmer," Gable said to his 118-pounder. "See how Ironside built his base?"

In Kasey Gilliss's match, Gable seemed to be reminding himself of something as much as his wrestler. "We've got to keep working on your scoring ability, on the basic skills." Gable hauled Joe Williams up to the front to demonstrate technical points, and then told Williams to stop waiting and be more offensive-minded. He remonstrated with Mike Uker about his lack of movement—"your feet are stuck"—and then, in total exasperation, "You're behind and you get called for stalling. That's *ridiculous!*" All season Gable had been pushing Tony Ersland, trying to get him to forget about hus-banding his energy and let fly. Gable wanted more emotion. He watched a replay of the Cowboys' Mark Smith knotting Ersland's legs with his own. "How can he get his legs in on us like that?" Gable wondered. Ersland took his place on all fours in the middle of the mat. His head was bowed. "Is that the look of a fired-up man?" Gable said.

When the tape ended, Gable got to the punch line: "Two months from today is our first day of the national champion-ship. We've got a long ways to go. And we're no shoo-in right now. In fact, we're not even the No. 1–ranked team anymore.

Enough said. There's no doubt—I'm stingy when it comes to your being successful and winning. I don't like getting beat. We shouldn't have gotten beat. Bottom line. We've got some tough matches coming up, but we've also got to think about getting tougher and winning these meets.

"Anybody that says they want to be an All-American this year better retract that statement, because if you try to become an All-American, you set your sights too low. I just want you to know that. You try to become a national champion—you've got a good shot of being a national champion, or something close to it. You have any lesser goals, then we're going to have to talk with you.

"Every year you got left, that's how many national titles that you think you should win."

The team practiced for two hours, many of the wrestlers going "live"—match intensity—for half of it. McIlravy, in heavy warmups, rode an exercise bike impassively, looking past the wrestlers clashing in front of him. After showering, Ironside and others adjourned to the wrestling office to watch more tape. Tomorrow, Tuesday, the second semester would begin. Lee Fullhart, for one, eagerly anticipated the coming weeks. During winter break, he had met with academic advisors and received permission to cut his mechanical-engineering course load to two courses. The lighter load would help him determine if he could complete his engineering requirements in his remaining two and a half years—and still give adequate time to wrestling—or if he would have to switch to a finance and economics major to graduate.

Grades were not the problem, because Fullhart was a good and diligent student. The problem, as Fullhart saw it, was the stress from tough engineering courses that impinged on his wrestling—sapped him of energy and breath in matches.

"You've just got to do so much work [in engineering] that I'm just tired," Fullhart said. "Always having something on my mind. Never being able to just take a day and relax. Even if I take a day off and not do anything, I'm doing something— I'm thinking about how when I get back I've got to get this or that done. It wore me out."

A twenty-year-old redshirt sophomore, Fullhart, with his hulking shoulders and barrel chest, looked heavier than his 190 pounds. In a match or during a hard practice, running on empty, he seemed suddenly vulnerable, smaller than life. "All last week I practiced, but the thing is, they aren't effective, because I'll go out there and work hard, but I tighten up, and I can't breathe, and I've got to sit down so I can relax and go back out. I can't get enough air to keep going."

Mark Ironside, in contrast, dreaded returning to classes. He went because it was required, but it wouldn't make him a better wrestler. His major was health, leisure, and physical studies, and he wanted to manage a health club, or be a personal trainer or a coach.

"I like wrestling and I hate school, and I'm not quiet about it," he said. "I've always hated it. Ever since I was in kindergarten I've hated school. Because there's a million other things in this world that I'd rather be doing than going to school, but in order to wrestle I've got to go to school and pass my classes."

Before practices during the first semester, Gable usually began team meetings in the wrestling room by asking Steve Kennevan to come forward with any announcements. Kennevan, an academic coordinator specially assigned to wrestling, reminded wrestlers of appointments with tutors or advisors and gave updates on school and NCAA matters. Now, however, with the second semester beginning—and the national championships looming ever closer—Kennevan had to wait until Gable spoke before he was given the floor.

"This is how he gets in the last part of the season, when he really gets into wrestling," Kennevan said. "I said I'd talk first today, before he starts talking about wrestling, but he gets here and heads right into it.

"I think he's—and rightly so—more focused in the second semester on wrestling, and so it makes my position a little more difficult. He is less likely to enforce things the second semester than he is in the first semester. He wants them to get their grades and their degrees, but he doesn't really want that to occur at the expense of his time. And I can understand that."

Kennevan—lean, with thinning sandy hair, a former state high-school champion in Maryland—occupied a cubicle in the wrestling office, from which he kept track of how all thirty-seven wrestlers on the team were doing in the classroom, made sure they were advancing toward their degrees on schedule, and acted as liaison between the wrestling office and athletic student services. Kennevan's administrative tentacles reached into many parts of the university; on any given day, he could look at his records and tell Gable who had a test and when, which wrestlers had papers due and when, and who should leave practice early to make up an exam. Any wrestler whose grades fell below C-plus (2.4 on a 4.0-point scale) automatically received Kennevan's orders to attend "learning center," a euphemism for study hall. The sessions were held Monday through Thursday nights from 7:45 to 9:30, in the dining room of the Hillcrest Dormitory. Wrestlers and other athletes were required to go when a tutor in the appropriate academic area was on duty.

Gable was supportive of his work, Kennevan said, not only for self-serving reasons, but also for altruistic ones. Kennevan cited a reserve who was good enough to provide competition in practice for regulars, making them better. "He was on academic probation, and I talked to Gable about the situation, and he said, 'Well, let's hold him out of practice, because I just don't want him in here as a body,'" Kennevan said. "Gable gave him an opportunity to catch up with his academics. Even if the student isn't good academically or athletically, I've heard Gable say, 'Well, I don't know what this kid has in his life. And this program is important to him.' So he wants him to stay on the team, just because of that. Gable's got a big heart."

In a goals sheet he handed to the team before the start of every season, Gable mentioned academics prominently, and he backed it up by instituting in the wrestling room a place in the bleachers marked "the box." Wrestlers who failed to attend assigned study sessions were required to dress for practice, but were told to sit under the sign and watch, and risk losing their place at their weight. It was almost a wrestling-room pillory. Of course, some wrestlers who didn't feel like practicing would deliberately miss study sessions, in which case Gable ordered sprints.

Gable himself had been a serious student. Although his college days are more remembered for his torturous training and constant winning, he often left his roommates to their devices and went to another room or to the library to study. He pulled down a 2.83 grade-point average, and it took him only four years and a summer school to graduate. He majored in biology and physical education, both respectable areas of study at Iowa State. When friends asked him why he didn't take more Mickey Mouse courses, Gable had a stock answer: "If I wanted to learn about Mickey Mouse, I would take Mickey Mouse courses." Gable wasn't widely read, but he did read, mostly outdoor magazines about his favorite sports, hunting and fishing. When his father suffered a stroke and faltered, Gable began reading personal-finance articles and books, so that he could better manage his father's money.

As a coach, Gable also kept apprised of changing academic standards in the university and throughout the NCAA. In the early 1990s, when university presidents around the country called for a crackdown on athletes who slipped through academic cracks, Gable brought Kennevan on board. "As a coach," Gable explained, "you're supposed to keep up. If you don't, you fall behind, and then you buck the system and you've got problems. When academics became a big issue, I made it a bigger issue with me. I put it higher on my agenda."

Gable's 1995–96 national championship team compiled a 2.7 GPA, solid though hardly flashy. His athletes generally graduated. According to athletic student services figures, five of the six athletes officially recruited by Gable in 1992—wrestlers who probably but didn't necessarily receive athletic-scholarship money—were on track to graduate before 1998. In the decade from 1982–91, thirty-two of fifty recruited athletes graduated from Iowa. There may have been others who transferred to other schools and graduated, but figures were not kept for them.

Over winter break, Matt Hoover, a sophomore reserve behind Ersland at 177, approached Kennevan. Hoover was beaming. "This is one of the best days of my *life!*" he said. Hoover had not just come off academic ineligibility—he had flown off. From a 0.67 GPA in the previous spring semester, he had rung up a 3.3. He had stayed in shape, and through Gable's urging, remained on the team. He was going to classes for a change. And he was ready to compete again, first for Ersland's berth and then, he hoped, for Iowa in meets.

"I was really struggling," said Hoover, who looked studious enough behind black horn-rim glasses. "I wasn't sure if I wanted to be wrestling. I wasn't sure I wanted to be in school. And then I decided, hey, I can wrestle for the Hawks and go to school, and that's all there was to it. When I decided I was going to be both instead of one or the other, that's when things really started turning around. That and getting engaged. I just grew up."

Hoover, an elementary-education major, was still riding his academic high. "I never had that high a grade-point in high school. That was the first time in my life I got over a three-oh, and now I expect that of myself."

On Tuesday, Gable rewarded Hoover by giving him a stepping-stone to a starting berth. If Hoover could beat red-shirt freshman Lee Weber in a challenge match before practice, the road was virtually clear to moving into the 177-pound berth against Minnesota on Friday night. Ersland, the incumbent, had suffered a shoulder injury against Oklahoma State. The next day, he couldn't lift his left arm without pain. Kristen Payne had seen myriad injuries like this, a rotator cuff muscle strain. She gave him a set of exercises, which he did twice daily, and he was placed on a restricted practice schedule. Ersland didn't want to sit out the Minnesota dual; he was a senior, with a losing record, and missing any amount of time was too much. But his injury gave Gable no choice.

Meanwhile, Hoover and Weber shook hands in the middle of the mat in the wrestling room and began their seven-minute match to decide who would step into the lineup. Zalesky, in a T-shirt and sweats, shuffled around the wrestlers like any vigilant referee, calling points in a voice as calm as if he were calling home to see about his two young daughters. "Two," he intoned when Weber scored an early takedown. "One," when Hoover escaped. A wrestler kept time from the bleachers. Gable sat and watched in silence. It was 5–5 with ten seconds left. Fifteen wrestlers had gathered to watch. Five seconds . . . suddenly, with both men scrambling on the mat, Hoover reversed Weber for a 7–5 victory.

Hoover, more tired than elated, dragged himself to the locker room. Weber—tall and angular, like his older brother Daryl, a 1996 national champion—lay on his back briefly. *"Fuck!"* He jerked to his butt and then to his feet, spat in the general direction of the locker room and stalked off the mat.

Before he had found his 177-pound starter pro tem, Gable kept his final pre-surgery appointment with Dr. Marsh. After it, Gable returned to the wrestling office somber but determined. Surgery was forty-eight hours away. "He discussed everything," Gable said. "He talked about surgery, what he'll do at certain times, and reminded me of potential risks, and how he wants to handle the situation. We're going to have a three- or four-line statement after surgery [for the media]. My wife's going to say all the other stuff."

He felt "overwhelmed" by the choices presented him— general or epidural anesthetic? Darvon or Demerol for the pain? He had decided that he did not want the new hip cemented in place. Instead, he asked for a procedure whereby carefully monitored bone could form around the artificial hip and make activity a better possibility. All he wanted was to feel better, to begin healing and have his mind on coaching, not the pain. He admitted he was "a little bit scared" that everything go all right, and that he would have "a good damn leg" again.

"I just want to be able to work my body the way I used to, so I'm not so sore," Gable said. "I want to do stuff that doesn't beat me up—stuff that's probably normal for a normal person." He grew more pensive, the thin line of his lips as straight as a ruler. "No, I don't think I'll be able to do what normal people are doing. I'll probably place a little more emphasis on some other things, because a normal workout won't be good for me any more.

Gable loved to run, but he hadn't been able to do that for a decade, and now he wouldn't be able to again. Yet he hungered to sample pieces of an active lifestyle. "All I want to do is ride bikes, swim, play with tools." And even more basic activities—"walk, get up and move out of bed, and walk out and carry wood or shovel snow."

The conversation naturally turned to retirement. Gable had been typically evasive, or uncertain, in the month and a half since the season started. Now, however, he seriously entertained the idea of quitting coaching, although he would not name the exact time. As he spoke, he was seated across the desk from Wilkinson, his office helper, who occupied Gable's chair and had cleared the desk of clutter and was entering Gable's appointments into a computer. Slowly, Gable was giving up control.

"I still want to continue coaching the guys," he said. "I want to stay on and maybe coach the Olympic team, and have them make the team. And I'll still work with Iowa wrestlers, but it mostly depends on the rules. . . . I'm not averse to going out and raising money, speaking a little bit. I don't want to travel a lot, except to get in my car and drive fifty miles, a hundred."

That same day in January, Syracuse University announced that it was dropping its seventy-five-year-old wrestling program, along with men's gymnastics, and adding softball. Gable, irate, felt a sort of kinship with the program, because one of his former wrestlers, Chris Campbell, a two-time national champion and a bronze medalist in the 1992 Olympics at the age of thirty-seven, had been an assistant at Syracuse.

In a release, Syracuse athletic director Jake Crouthamel stated that the school "can't continue to meet the interests of our female population without reducing costs somewhere else." Again, the culprit, in the eyes of Crouthamel and Gable and others in the men's sports establishment, was Title IX, although clearly the wrestling program had done something to make itself expendable. Gable faulted the Syracuse wrestling coaches "for not having enough boosters that they can drop you."

"A lot of times it can be solved by simply making it an important enough situation where people say, 'We've got to keep that,' " Gable said.

(In fact, seven months later, Syracuse reinstated the wrestling program on a limited scale, after boosters presented a plan to raise $2 million to support the team past the 2000–2001 season. That put the number of Division I schools with wrestling programs at 95 out of 307. In Division II, 48 schools of 287 had wrestling, and in Division III, it was 107 of 397.)

Iowa's wrestling program ran on a $500,000 budget, twice that of some other Big Ten schools. Iowa wrestling, taking in $150,000–$200,000 a year, didn't come close to paying for itself, but it still could be considered a revenue sport. Season-ticket sales hung at around 4,500, with a top crowd of 12,000 or so turning out for the Iowa State dual.

Gable's value to the program was incalculable. Twenty-five years after he won an Olympic gold medal, his name resonated in the state beyond wrestling-room walls. Bob Bowlsby, the men's athletic director, filled Gable's calendar every spring with "I" Club speaking engagements, to raise money for the athletic department. Gable invariably spoke to packed houses and signed autographs long after his speech.

In a state where there were no pro teams, and college sports had top billing, Gable—a *wrestling* coach, for pity's sake —ranked as a top celebrity. The governor called to ask him to deliver the keynote speech in the spring at a so-called Family Summit. Gable's topic: what his family meant to him. He has hawked milk on television. And just that month, leaving University Hospitals after an appointment, he passed through a waiting room, and a man in a feed-store cap pointed at Gable and all but bellowed to the woman sitting next to him, "You know who that is, doncha?" Her face went blank. "That's Dan Gable! *Dan Gable!*" It could just as well have been Mr. Greenjeans. "You never heard of Dan Gable?" the man asked. He called to the back of the figure on crutches, whose cossack-style hat was clumsily tilted on his head. "Hey coach! Coach! Can you believe it? The wife never heard of Dan Gable."

Perhaps never in the history of intercollegiate athletics has a coach of a "minor" sport enjoyed such celebrity and clout, not only within the state but also in the highest echelons of a university athletic department. It went beyond the fact that Gable, in Bowlsby, had a homeboy in power. Or that Bowlsby's brother, John, was a heavyweight All-American on Gable's first two Iowa teams. It was more pragmatic than personal: Gable won.

"When he needs things, we try and get them for him," Bowlsby said. "If he comes in and says, 'Hey! My budget's getting a little short. I don't think I can do this without going over. Can you help me out?' I usually help him out.

"That's because he has such great credibility. I know if he asks, it's something that's important to him, and therefore it's in my best interest as well as his to get it done."

For two days leading up to surgery, Gable drove himself and his staff tirelessly. He seemed to be everywhere, conferring and coaching. Zalesky would report daily to Gable in the hospital, but until they actually sank the needle into Gable's back and put him out, the coach hovered over his work like a jeweler. Gable swung among the athletes arrayed in pairs around the wrestling room. He saw that Jessie Whitmer, practicing escapes, was trying a lame bridge. "Get your weight back! Get your weight back!" Gable shouted, gesturing with one of his crutches. "Move, Whitmer, move!" A few feet away, Kasey Gilliss kicked out and escaped. "Good job, Gilliss! Beautiful job!"

But practices generally were not as intense as they had been the week before. In team meetings, Gable told his wrestlers that they had to stay healthy, as if each was fighting the urge to snap a tendon. But he also did his part to clear the injury list by slowing the pace.

As his last two orders of business, Gable reiterated his concerns to Payne about how she was handling Wes Hand and his stinger, and the coach made peace with Payne—and vice versa. Gable and Payne were not used to this sort of scrimmaging. In happier days, she would tell him that the only reason he hired her was because he had a wife and four daughters himself, and what was the poor guy to do? And Gable would smile and say that was probably true.

"But now she's doing too much coaching," Gable said. "We're good friends. We want to make it work, but she doesn't understand how I think. Now, after I told her, she understood perfectly.

"It's like, this week, she already told me stuff she shouldn't have told me. She wants to get these guys ready and healthy, and I can understand—that's her job—and she wants them to do certain things to keep themselves fine tuned and not be put in any dangerous situations. And I can go along with that. But then she went and said the second thing. She said [that she told Hand], 'What we'll do this week is, I'll go to Gable and tell him to only use you if we need you for the matches.' Kristen! I've got to make progress on Hand mentally. If he's thinking that he's only going to be used if needed, he's going to waste the whole week mentally.

"Because you prepare every day for a match, when you know there's a match, and you know you're going to compete. . . . She almost started crying. I don't want to make her feel bad, either. But she's got to remember what's coaching and what's not coaching. And that's coaching."

With, say, Lee Fullhart, Payne had good rapport interwoven with the threads of a friendship. Fullhart often arrived early at the training room to chat with her. But Hand was more intractable; he had blown off one appointment, and his nerve injury defied easy understanding to a coach preparing his team for defense of its national title.

"Usually, if an athlete's being noncompliant, Gable will

help me out," Payne said during practice, after a shift of icing muscles and taping limbs. "He'll say, 'No! She said this. Don't do this.' With Wes, the situation hasn't been that way, and it's because of the nature of the injury. They're just not as easy to get a grasp on, and because it's a chronic situation, it's something that he'll always have just because of the way he's built."

Early in the week, Lincoln McIlravy called Payne and asked her to schedule a magnetic-resonance imaging test (MRI) at University Hospitals for his neck. Previous examinations and a history of his headaches did not indicate involvement of the arteries in his neck, but this would make certain. Payne's worry had been compounded because of what happened to him against Minnesota, when he became disoriented in the third period. His opponent had head-snapped him, so the headaches were understandable, but the dizziness was a new dimension.

McIlravy kept his 2 P.M. appointment and was not at the start of practice. Gable asked Payne about his whereabouts, and she filled him in, and they had what Payne called one of their best talks in a while. Assuming that the MRI was negative (it was), McIlravy would have passed a battery of neurological and physical examinations, and thus was medically cleared to wrestle. That alone would ease his mind and lower his stress, a key factor in attacking several forms of migraines and other chronic headaches. McIlravy wouldn't be pushed; Gable would let him give himself time to heal and return to wrestling when he was ready. No one expected him to wrestle in the second Minnesota match, but everyone expected that he would be ready for the Big Ten Championships in six weeks—the qualifier for the national tournament.

When he returned to the arena, McIlravy dropped off some medical literature on headaches he had copied for Gable. Slowly, doctors and Payne and McIlravy had documented for Gable the source and nature of McIlravy's headaches, and what could be done about them. As McIlravy walked into practice, Gable fell in step.

"I think there's a plan now. I feel better about that," the wrestler said.

"I wish I'd known about it before," Gable said, no blame in his voice.

"That was my fault. I waited . . . But I didn't know, either." McIlravy stopped and faced his coach. Gable, hanging over his crutches, pitched forward as if in a wind tunnel, nodded.

"I just thought you might be going to Chicago or somethin' to see a head guy to give you a new brain, so maybe you could think faster," Gable said, smiling.

McIlravy was determined to find out what was wrong. That was why he called Payne to set up an MRI, why he asked for medical literature. He even went to the football trainer, figuring that here was another contact sport with a high probability of concussions and headaches. "What he told me was that the players were more susceptible for a third concussion after they'd had a couple," McIlravy told Gable. "He said they take them out for the season after their third one."

A silence hung in the air. It was as if they both were counting concussions to themselves. There was the one McIlravy had suffered in practice in December, but apparently nothing as serious since, no incidents in which he lost or nearly lost consciousness.

"Anyway," McIlravy said, "the doctor said I should wait at least forty-eight hours before I wrestle again."

"I'd say wait longer if you want," Gable said.

"You never had a concussion?" McIlravy asked him.

"I never did, or if I did, I didn't know about it. We never had trouble like this here in wrestling before."

"Maybe I should get boxing headgear and wear it," McIlravy said, and Gable said he might grab the earflaps and fling McIlravy into a corner. McIlravy seemed to be seriously considering that possibility. "Naw, just kidding," Gable said, and turned his attention to practice.

He had his own health to worry about.

chapter **10**

On a bitterly cold and blustery Thursday in January, Gable signed in at University Hospitals and was prepped for surgery at seven A.M. on the sixth floor of orthopedics, in a complex of twenty-four operating rooms. Marsh and his team began the procedure at eight. They made an eight-inch incision in the left hip, and using a power saw, reamer, and more delicate instruments, they deliberately dislocated the femur, or thigh bone, and hollowed out a cavity, cleaving muscles and tissues as they went. The bony ball at the head of the femur—which fit into the original hip socket—was quickly removed with the whining saw. The socket was smoothed and filed and made ready to accept the artificial socket and ball. Next, a tunnel was made through the middle of the thigh bone, and into it was inserted an appliance made of cobalt chrome that connected the ball at one end to the femur at the other. Fifty stitches and they were done.

The surgery took more than two hours. Dr. Marsh reported to Kathy Gable, in the sixth-floor waiting room, that the operation was a success. He took personal pride in the result. "Sometimes you get that [hip-replacement] just right," he said two days later in his office. "Other times, well, it'll probably be OK, but it's not quite the way I wanted it. But this one looked very good. I was very pleased with it."

The rest was up to Gable. Reflexively, he would want to overdo and work the hip because it would feel much better. He wouldn't want to be, in his mother's phrase, a Molly Putz, a weakling. But Marsh said that because Gable's other hip had deteriorated to such an extent, it might force him to go slow. If Gable wanted a role model for what not to do, he could consider Bo Jackson, the former National Football League and major-league baseball player who was hit playing football and had to undergo hip-replacement surgery. He returned to play baseball, but the artificial hip didn't hold up, and he had to have it replaced a second time. Bo Jackson wasn't heard from on an athletic field again.

Gable was taken from the recovery area to 3RC West, a private corner room located near the busy nurses' station. Before he left the wrestling office on Wednesday, the Iowa coach uncharacteristically lapsed into gallows humor. Putting on his coat, he turned to address Bill Wilkinson, bent over Gable's desk. "See you soon unless I die," Gable said. "If I do, turn the office into a shrine."

Now, however, nothing about the experience was humorous. Gable suffered through the hallucinations he had feared from morphine-based pain-killers. "It's sad to go through that. I don't know why you have to go through that," he said. He hallucinated that someone was in his room, he didn't know who, and the apparition spoke, voicing the name "Molly." In another one, there was a shriveled, dying person in a concentration camp. In yet another, Gable found himself swimming in a test tube with his own blood particles, and suddenly thousands of pills came hurtling down upon him. He awoke and looked at the clock and went back to sleep and began hallucinating again. He called Kathy at seven in the morning, needing to be soothed.

But even more troubling was the pain in his right hip, the nonartificial hip, which certainly couldn't be called his "good" hip. Marsh speculated that the hip might have been placed in a painful position, out of necessity, in surgery, with Gable's full weight on it.

"It's a worrisome thing in two ways," Marsh said, shaking his head. "It's worrisome in that his post-operative protocol demands him being able to get himself around on his right hip for a period of time—from weeks to a couple of months.

"And, number two, he has a right hip, as I've said, that's very bad. It's not radiographically quite as bad as the left hip, but radiographically it meets all the criteria for hip replacement. I'm concerned that he may need other joints replaced. Or he may develop those kind of symptoms. And neither he nor I want that. It's not better to have two artificial hips than it is to have one. It's twice the possibility for problems."

Gable's surgery and recovery made it above the fold in most newspaper sports sections in Iowa—and sometimes on the front *news* page. State radio and television stations either led off with it or mentioned it early in their news programs. Dissemination of information fell to Kathy Gable, who spoke with reporters over the phone and gave the nurses a short list of people who would be allowed to see her husband. Ulysses and his mythical band of sailors had a better chance in the Straits of Messina against whirlpools and monsters than did the plucky fans and media members who tried to peek in on Gable without authorization.

"If you want to talk to me, Kathy's the one to see—she's handling it all," Gable said before surgery.

Jim Zalesky slipped over to see Gable not long after surgery, and reported that he looked ashen and complained of pain. "[Bob] Bowlsby tried to get in, but even he couldn't," Zalesky said.

Kathy's visibility wasn't surprising. All through his personal and professional life, Gable's wife and children had played important parts. "I couldn't be successful if my family weren't one hundred percent into wrestling," he averred. As a coach, he took them on road trips, and their suite became the focal, if not vocal, point of the Iowa delegation. Wrestlers clustered in the hallway near the Gables' room, killing time, and the Gable girls usually brought friends and kept the mood lively. In post-meet press conferences, Gable often referred to Kathy, depicting her as someone who breathed fire after a loss just like he did. After Iowa's defeat to Oklahoma State in the finals of the National Duals, Gable sighed and, apropos of nothing, said, "All I know is I'm going to have one hard time going home. My wife's going to be hard to live with. She takes these things a lot harder than I do, man. She could hardly sleep last night. I know I couldn't. And she was mad last night. I saw her a little while ago. *Steaming.* Oh, man!"

Gable also actively involved himself in bringing up his girls. He broke away from his work whenever he could to watch them participate in school activities. He read to them at home. One night, scooping up Mackie and taking her to the kitchen table, he opened her book about Jesse James. She asked who Jesse James was.

"Jesse James was an outlaw," Gable said.

"What's an outlaw?"

"An outlaw robs people and shoots them. He's a bad dude."

As the family grew, Gable occasionally fielded questions about the lack of gender diversity in the house. Wouldn't he, Dan Gable, coach of manly men with cauliflower ears, like to have a son? And Gable would give his fleeting, nervous smile and respond, "Wouldn't trade those girls for boys. They're great. Having girls was the best route, no doubt. With a boy, if he was in sports, like wrestling, I would have wanted to work with him. And I wouldn't have had the opportunity, because there wouldn't have been time, and that would have been frustrating." He took a breath. "Besides, it's not like I don't have boys. I've got Williams and Fullhart, the whole bunch. No, I've got boys."

Kathy believed her husband. "I've never been with him, like where he's sitting up in the stands watching boys wrestle or play baseball or something, where I've thought he's thinking, 'Gosh! I wish I would have had a son doing this.' "

The daughters grew up around wrestling and wrestlers.

When Jennifer was old enough to walk, Kathy dressed her in a short black Iowa cheerleading skirt and top, gave her yellow pompons, and took her to home meets, where she sometimes nested under the coach's folding chair. There Gable would be, exhorting, ranting, gesticulating, while under him a little girl in a short black skirt would be peering out, as if hatching. As the family grew, there would be more than one small girl in Iowa colors brandishing yellow pompons at Hawkeye meets, and their father was at least as proud of them as he was of the boys they cheered on.

On January 24, Iowa's wrestling team began the "LWG" phase of its season—Life Without Gable. The coach would be receiving daily reports from Zalesky, and once he got home, he would review videotapes of practices and matches, but he would be missing from the daily moil. McIlravy tended to discount his absence, declaring that Gable prepared his team daily for adversity and that the wrestlers would take his absence in stride. Ersland called it "business as usual," and felt comfortable with Zalesky in charge.

Fullhart, however, felt differently. "I miss not having him there," he said. "He's got such a high intensity that it really helps you. I know he'll review tapes and make suggestions—he'll do everything he can. And our own coaches [Zalesky and Brands] will step up and get us going. I mean, my best match was when Tom Brands was in my corner in the Midlands. But there's something about Gable. Sometimes when I'm tired, I'll hear him say, 'Let him up! Then take him down!' And I just keep going when I hear him like that."

Zalesky, ever the Hawkeye in a black V-neck sweater, yellow shirt, and beige slacks, sat on the bleachers in the wrestling room more than an hour before the match against Minnesota. Zalesky's face showed aging lines, and he had added a few pounds since his 158-pound heyday, but he otherwise looked the same as he did winning three national titles in the 1980s. And he still handled pressure inwardly, wrestling himself before he wrestled anyone else, his jaw clenched, his eyes narrowing. That's how he looked as he waited for the team to assemble so he could deliver a few reminders and remarks beforehand.

Once they had gathered, Zalesky proceeded to give the pre-meet talk that Gable usually gave, but without Gable's loosely hung sentences that gathered meaning and momentum and finally struck home. Stiffly, Zalesky worked through the weights, pointing to each wrestler, reminding him what to do. Without expression, Mike Mena heard that he was wasting the first period, that he needed to attack immediately.

Zalesky mentioned that Matt Hoover would be starting for Tony Ersland, who had a sore shoulder. Terry Brands, seated in the first row, flashed his temper. "What do you expect when a guy cranks on it like that Oklahoma State guy," said Brands, whose own postcollegiate career was being stalled by a shoulder injury. "He probably won't wrestle for a week."

Zalesky asked for questions, and Mena wondered when the bus left for Saturday night's dual at Wisconsin. It was not something to ask any coach, much less an acting coach who had to start two reserves, Hoover, and, for McIlravy, Eric Koble.

"Mena," Zalesky snapped, "we're not worrying about that right now."

A crowd of 4,614 convened in the arena to see if the Hawkeyes could improve on their 23–12 victory over the same opponent a week before in the National Dual semifinals. Annie Gable watched her younger sister Molly run up and down the aisle; the rest of the family stayed in the hospital with Gable. Lincoln McIlravy, that budding color analyst, clapped on a set of earphones and took his place beside Adams and helped the KXIC crew.

Jessie Whitmer began the evening by walking across the large mat, removing his headgear, and having his left arm raised by referee Mike Allen. Brandon Paulson, the Minnesota Olympian, couldn't wrestle because of his ankle injury, and the forfeit gave Iowa a 6–0 lead. Mike Mena followed, apparently with his mind still on bus departures instead of instant aggression. Against Pat Connors, whom he had beaten by nine points at the Duals, Mena needed a takedown in overtime to score a 6–4 victory. That set the stage for Kasey Gilliss to play giant-killer. During the week, Gable reminded the redshirt freshman that for all the basics the staff had worked on with him, it was important that he recognize his strengths, meaning big-move throws. In the first period, Gilliss carried the match to third-ranked Jason Davids, whose only loss in twenty-two matches this season had been to top-ranked Roger Chandler of Indiana. Gilliss, boring in on Davids, found the power and leverage he needed to throw Davids to the mat, a five-point move that produced a 5–0 lead heading into the second period. Gilliss, a .500 wrestler at 8–8, then dug in for what he knew was coming, desperation assaults from a dangerous opponent who had pinned nine opponents during the season. But it took a thrower to know one, and Gilliss held on for an 8–3 victory at 142 pounds. "It's the biggest win I've ever had," Gilliss said. "Nothing's much close." Coming on the heels of Ironside's eighth pin of the season, the victory extended Iowa's lead to 18–0.

Koble needed his confidence restored after a ten-point loss in the Oklahoma State match, but all he got was more of the same. Fourth-ranked Chad Kraft, with coach J Robinson's low, crackling exhortations in his ear, ran up a 7–2 lead before pinning Koble in the third period. After Koble hastened past the Iowa bench and ushers, and pounded up the cement steps to the locker room, he dropped to the bench, shaking with sobs.

Iowa's 29–12 victory was in hand when Hoover stepped in against Brandon Eggum at 177. Ersland sat in street clothes on the Iowa bench. To him, Hoover represented both competitor and teammate. Should Ersland cheer him on or hope he lost? "I didn't want him to lose—I wanted all the Hawks to win," Ersland said. "I also knew that if I met Hoover [in a challenge match], I wanted to beat him bad." It was Hoover's first varsity dual, and he meant to impress. He stormed after Eggum, the only freshman in the Gophers' lineup. But Eggum withstood the surge, and he applied pressure of his own, wearing down Hoover. Hoover's face flushed and he labored for breath; his limbs seemed to harden into concrete as he lost 14–

8. The match offered no-frills proof of how exhausting the sport can be, especially for someone like Hoover, a rural Iowan who had never wrestled before more than 300 people.

"I could tell I was tired," he said, caught in a whirlpool of youngsters holding up programs for him to autograph. "I mean, I could taste the blood in my stomach." He drew confidence from his late takedown, and from the fact that he had fought back from grade problems. "I came to Iowa with some goals. I thought for a while that they were flushed down the toilet, but not anymore."

Zalesky joked that he remained unbeaten as a head coach, but he knew that a victory in front of the home folks meant more than a cakewalk in Pennsylvania. He also knew that he might be auditioning as well as coaching. "I want to show I can do a good job," Zalesky said. "I want to be a head coach —and I want to show Gable that he doesn't have to hurry back."

Addressing the team, Zalesky expressed satisfaction with the way they had stormed back from the loss to Oklahoma State. "The only time we were really ridden was in Hoover's match, and that was because he was tired." Zalesky slapped his hands together. "We're back on track," he said. "Let's keep it going."

Jim Zalesky and Wisconsin coach Barry Davis were teammates at Prairie High School in Cedar Rapids, Iowa, and each won three national titles under Gable. They joined the army of assistants and head coaches who had wrestled, coached, or both under Gable, and introduced the Iowa system into their present jobs. In the eleven-team Big Ten alone, five head coaches had emerged from the Iowa wrestling room: Davis, Mark Johnson (Illinois), Duane Goldman (Indiana), Tim Cysewski (Northwestern), and Robinson (Minnesota). Four Big Ten assistants—Troy Steiner (Minnesota), his brother Terry and Bart Chelesvig (both of Wisconsin), and Jim Heffernan (Illinois)— all wrestled for Gable and moved on.

But an Iowa background also could work against a coach. Witness Wisconsin coach Barry Davis: As Iowa hit town on

Saturday for the dual against the Badgers, Davis was trying to quiet a few boosters who, four years after he took the job, still didn't like the fact that an interloper from much-reviled Iowa had been hired. He drew criticism when he put new black mats in the wrestling room; black was Iowa's color. It didn't help that the best the Badgers could muster for Davis was a ten-win season, and that this season they were 6–4–1, with a loss four days before to the University of Wisconsin–La Crosse, a Division II school. Injuries had poked holes in Wisconsin's lineup and morale had dropped lower than the temperature.

Already, Davis's voice was giving out. What remained sounded like a file brushed across the teeth of a saw. To get to his office in ancient Camp Randall Stadium, Davis had to walk past buckets set in the hall to catch the water from the leaky roof. But he wasn't giving up. He did what great Iowa wrestlers always did in hard times: He worked even harder.

Davis called a team meeting. "Gentlemen, this is the deal," he began. "It's a hard time right now. A lot of us are struggling with it. If I've got a problem with my marriage, I don't go out with the boys and start drinking. I spend more time with my wife and kids. It's the same with you guys right now. You're struggling too. So you've got to spend more time in this atmosphere. You gotta do it, see?"

It didn't help. Second-ranked Iowa won nine of ten matches and crushed Wisconsin 31–4. Uker was the only Hawkeye to lose, and he did it convincingly: Fourth-ranked Kevin Wilmot, one of the hottest wrestlers in the conference, had eight takedowns en route to a 20–6 major decision. It was Uker's worst defeat of the season and fourth in a row. Koble and Hoover both won in reserve roles, but they couldn't exult very much because of the caliber of the competition. The best match was at 126, where Mena, ranked third, defeated second-ranked Eric Jetton, in a tiebreaker. The previous night, Mena had wrestled just to the level of his competition; now he wrestled above it. Listening on the radio in University Hospitals, Gable must have awakened the floor with a whoop of joy when Mena scored a takedown in the last minute to tie the match, 2–2, at the end of three periods. It was the kind of get-tough situation in which Gable placed his wrestlers almost daily. "All right," he would say, "ten seconds left in the match, and you need a takedown to win . . . *Hit it!*" After a scoreless overtime, Jetton won the toss and took the defensive position, but Mena rode him through the thirty-second tiebreaker to win.

After Wes Hand had taken Wisconsin's heavyweight, Matt Schneider, to the mat six times for a 13–6 victory, the crowd of 1,777 headed home. Davis kept working long days, taking time off only to eat lunch with his pregnant wife, Nan, a former star distance runner at Iowa. Then back to his desk and the wrestling room.

Old Iowa habits die hard.

The Hawkeyes returned in time for Williams and Ironside to visit University Hospitals on Sunday and watch the Super Bowl with their coach. The resurgence of the Green Bay Packers sparked a thought in Gable, as it had when he was listening to them on the radio on the return trip from Michigan State. A team from a small town, the Lombardi-led Packers had unified their fans by winning. As he lay in a hospital bed, reading get-well cards, Gable began grasping the reach of his own team's accomplishments.

"I've gotten cards and letters from people I haven't heard from in a long time," he said. "It made me do a lot of thinking. It's like I never realized what we've done, or who or what I represented. I was doing my work, but I wasn't getting myself involved in the effect that it had on the support system.

"I want our guys to start realizing the lives they're touching with what they're doing—the way the Packers exemplified that. It's important. It won't be an easy challenge. I want to make great, great contributions. I want to focus more on that."

Hard on Gable's mind were the NCAA championships. Already, people from the Grout Museum in Waterloo had descended upon the Gables' home and carted off his old Waterloo West wrestling singlet, his Iowa State warm-up robe with its yellow sash, his medals and ribbons, and pictures from his childhood, even the huge bearskin coat he got in Russia for winning the prestigious Tblisi tournament in 1972. The bounty would be displayed during the week of the NCAA tournament, for all Gable and Iowa fans to see. Maybe, at another time in his career, it wouldn't mean this much, but now, on the cusp of possible retirement, it clearly did.

"It'll be emotional, just going to Cedar Falls," Gable said. "It's already sold out, and there will be so many people there from such a long time ago, like the Packers and their fans. I've got to get it into the heads of my wrestlers that they aren't just anybody.

"We have our own history. Not like in football or baseball, but our own. Our own names. Our own sport."

Gable also had other, more immediate worries. His right hip still hurt, and his left knee had filled with fluid and would have to be drained. His stomach, which had begun hurting in October, had not quieted. Doctors told him they weren't alarmed, Gable said, that it might be parasites. "Ironic," he said. "I had surgery and I still didn't get done what has to be done."

Gable received radiation twice in one day to retard or prevent the growth of unwanted bone. Marsh said that Gable's stomach problems precluded pills, another treatment option. But as he was positioned to receive radiation for his left hip, Gable again felt excruciating pain in his right hip. "It was a small table, and I did everything I could to keep from screaming."

On Friday, physical therapists worked on Gable's hip in his room, but on Monday, they took him to physical therapy and started him walking with assistance. He arrived in a wheelchair, wearing black gym shorts, a white T-shirt, long surgical socks. He looked ashen. "I'm disoriented, confused," he said as he was helped up by the physical therapist. Kathy kept one eye on her husband and the other on Mackenzie, who followed Gable and the physical therapist like a sleuth.

Three white-haired women, probably in their seventies or older, sat in wheelchairs, looking on. In short order, the physical therapist got behind Gable and helped lift and straighten him on a table on his back.

"How do you feel?" the physical therapist asked.

"A little tight. Not too bad," the coach answered, clasping his hands behind his head.

The physical therapist stood in front of Gable and tied a long red rubber tube around his left ankle and began slowly moving his left leg to the side.

"What he's doing is *not* lady-like," Mackenzie volunteered.

On Super Bowl Sunday, in snowy Ames, top-ranked Oklahoma State held on to beat No. 4 Iowa State, 18–15. OSU's wrestlers had to kill an evening and morning in a hotel near campus, and they looked stale and tired by the time they hit the mat. Only eight days before, the Cowboys had swamped Iowa State in the National Dual semifinals, 28–9. John Smith was glad just to win the second time around, and the closeness of the match finally gave him a chance to judge how his wrestlers in the heavier weights would fare under pressure. Mark Smith, John's brother, dropped a 6–3 decision to Iowa State's Barry Weldon, the newly installed No. 1 at 177. On the sidelines, the Cowboys' coach swung his fist in the air in disgust when Mark gave up two first-period takedowns.

OSU had come a long way under John Smith, through probation for infractions not of his doing, past two straight subpar years in the NCAA championships (seventh and sixth), to the top of the heap. He had depended on walk-ons in the lean years, and now three of the walk-ons were starting and had a combined record of 51–5: Steven Schmidt at 134 pounds, Scott Reyna at 142, and Hardell Moore at 158. Mark Branch (167) and Reyna were seniors, but 118-pound Teague Moore and 126-pound Eric Guerrero were sophomores with only two losses between them.

"Nobody expected this," Smith said. "It's good to be back in the midst of things. It's good to have Oklahoma State challenging Iowa again. It's not healthy for the sport to come out in the preseason saying, 'Can anyone catch Iowa? Is there anyone capable of challenging Iowa?'

"We're going to be competitive now and next year and so on. We're back to being a team that's going to be graduating seniors, having juniors and sophomores and freshman coming up and filling in. Whereas the last two years we've been just totally wiped out, and just had youth."

In his four years, Smith was 3–4 against Iowa, but all four losses had occurred in the last two seasons. Smith had to sit and watch debacles like 31–3 and 26–9.

"I've hated the last couple of years that we haven't been able to compete with him," Smith said, meaning Gable. "That's really motivated me, to develop teams that will challenge Iowa. Or compete—number one, compete. I don't think he was that motivating for me as a wrestler. But as a coach, there's no question."

Gable arrived home on Monday, January 27, after four days in the hospital. The following Friday, he said, he had his first good night's sleep. "You'd be surprised what a little sleep does," he said. "I wasn't only sleeping but a half-hour at a time. I'm knockin' on wood, but I do feel better with my joints." His stomach felt better as well, still queasy but without the diarrhea. He thought his health might be turning around.

Gable felt good enough to let Kathy drive him to the team meal at 12:30 on Saturday, after the Hawkeyes weighed in for the home meet that night against Northwestern. Lunch was at the Village Inn, which had charcoal drawings of Gable and other Iowa coaches on the walls. He ate soup and a sandwich and talked with McIlravy, which further brightened Gable's mood.

"He talked about wrestling today. He talked about waiting until Wednesday before he really wrestled hard in practice," Gable said. "I think he's still tentative. This thing must hit him hard when it hits, because I think he's scared."

Perhaps because retirement was on his mind, Gable increasingly tended to factor history and tradition into circumstances and situations. He was doubly disappointed with the Oklahoma State loss because he wanted to set an Iowa record with three straight unbeaten dual seasons. He planned to remind his wrestlers of their place in Iowa wrestling history. And now, with McIlravy, Gable chewed on the fact that his wrestler had a chance to become the best wrestler, by winning percentage, in Hawkeye history. McIlravy had an overall 88–3 college record, including 14–0 before he was hurt. He needed 12 wins to reach 100 and be eligible to take his place—perhaps even the top spot—among all-time Hawkeye winners. (Tom Brands led with 158–7–2, .952; Terry Brands was second with 137–7–0, .951.) But that meant that McIlravy would have to wrestle against Northwestern and in the final three duals—at home against Illinois and Arizona State on February 8, at Iowa State on February 16, and in the Big Ten championships leading to the NCAA championships.

There were many variables, of course, among them that McIlravy keep winning and that he have the opportunity to wrestle "pigtail" matches—extra matches in other weight classes to even out the bracket pairings—in conference and national meets. But McIlravy didn't have Gable's eye for history. "Records aren't a big deal to him," Gable said. "But it's fitting a guy with a wrestling percentage like that get the record."

McIlravy didn't wrestle against Northwestern, and Gable rested up. There wasn't much urgency as unranked Northwestern was 4–6 and had only five wrestlers with winning records. However, the Wildcats had managed to defeat sixth-ranked Michigan State, 17–16. Iowa made short work of Northwestern, literally: Whitmer, Ironside, and Hand were leading by fifteen points or more when they were declared winners under match-termination rules. Williams and Uker pinned their opponents in Iowa's 40–4 victory. Ersland returned at 177 and won, 4–3. He would keep his starting berth without having to wrestle Hoover, who hadn't impressed coaches in the wrestling room or in meets, and was injured besides.

All week, Zalesky worked with the team on completing moves—"going through" an opponent and taking him down. The result was that Iowa rolled up fifty-three takedowns to five for Northwestern. Koble, sinking fast as McIlravy's replacement, was the only Hawkeye loser, 9–0, to Drew Pariano.

At first, Gable had hoped to return as coach for Northwestern, but that was unrealistic. Now he aimed for Iowa's two home matches on Saturday, February 8, in the afternoon against No. 5 Illinois and at night against No. 9 Arizona State. The matches carved a significance undreamed-of until recently: They could mark the last time Gable would sit on the Iowa bench at Carver-Hawkeye Arena.

Gable had the staples removed from his left hip that week. He watched practice the same day that McIlravy returned to hard wrestling—without incident. He went to watch Molly in a swim meet, the only chance he had all year to watch her compete.

"It's a day-to-day thing, how I feel," Gable said. "I probably won't make a decision about getting back until the day of the Illinois and Arizona State meets."

And then the day came.

In the historic sweep of Iowa wrestling, begun with a one-match season in 1911, Gable's return had all the drama of Jim Zalesky chasing down the exercise bikes accidentally left behind in Lincoln after the National Duals. Gable, deciding he wanted to see his team in person no matter how he felt, simply clipped along on his crutches through the tunnel leading to the floor of Carver-Hawkeye and took his seat on a wooden stool beside the mat, his left leg stretched out. He had passed up the Illinois match—won by Iowa, 25–10—to save himself for Arizona State. He had missed three dual meets—five for the season—in the sixteen days since his hip surgery. Over the public-address system, Phil Haddy, Iowa's men's sports-information director, warmed up the crowd of 5,280 by asking if anyone wanted to see Dan Gable retire. *"Nooooo!"* the crowd responded.

Gable was touched and slightly embarrassed. He pumped his crutches in acknowledgement. "It was different just coming into Carver after being off like that," he said. "I didn't let myself think about how it might be my last time for that as coach."

In front of their head coach, the Hawkeyes (14–1) completed a successful day of wrestling by defeating Arizona State 28–12. Mena and Uker both lost in overtime, a signal to Gable that not everyone on the team was pointed in the right direction. The sprints and buddy-carries up the arena steps, the live wrestling in practice, the emphasis on scoring within a prescribed number of seconds—all of it was calculated to give his team the conditioining and confidence needed to win late in the match. "We've got to make more of our guys disciplined and dedicated," Gable said. "We've got to fight back and win the close ones. It'll make a difference in nationals. We might have quite a few two-a-day workouts now."

Five Hawkeyes won both their matches: Whitmer, Gilliss, Ironside, Williams, and Fullhart. Williams, top-ranked and unbeaten at 158, had the biggest victory in the Illinois match when he uncorked his specialty, the double-leg takedown, in the last ten seconds to beat second-ranked Ernest Benion, 5–4. Williams now was 4–0 against Benion, the 1995 national champion at 158. Benion, however, had scored the first takedown of the season on Williams, in the first period, when Williams admitted that he was laying back offensively.

Whitmer and Gilliss both beat top-ten opponents. Fifth-ranked Whitmer beat Illinois's sixth-rated Lindsey Durlacher 10–7. Gilliss upset Illinois's eighth-ranked Jon Vaughn with an immediate takedown in overtime, 6–4, for his fourth straight victory; he claimed his fifth straight in a 12–2 walk over unranked Adam Friedman of Arizona State. In the matches, Gilliss showed he was putting together not only what the Iowa staff was telling him, but also what he was learning in E-mail communication with Troy Steiner, the former Iowa national champion on the Minnesota staff who was from Gilliss's hometown of Bismarck, North Dakota. Steiner, who had won his NCAA title at Gilliss's weight, 142, helped the Iowa wrestler sharpen his technique, make his moves more economically. "It makes it awkward with the guys up here, a Minnesota coach helping an Iowa guy—and I'm sure Kasey finds it awkward at Iowa," Steiner said. "But he's been a friend for a long time, and just because we're at different schools, I don't know why I still can't help him out."

Ironside improved to 20–0 with his ninth and tenth pins of the season. He was, in wrestling argot, a "grinder," pressur-

ing opponents, rarely taking a backward step. He had confidence. "I should be beating everybody by at least eight points,"
he said. "I should never be going into overtime." Proof was in
the record: The junior from Cedar Rapids had posted bonus
points in eighteen of his twenty matches. He had become a
team leader who was never satisfied and didn't want anyone
else to be. "He's brawlin' and he's maulin'," Gable said, in
sound-bite English. "I got people like him who potentially can
do anything you ask."

Fullhart (17–3) was riding a streak himself. He had won
six straight matches since losing in overtime in the National
Duals semifinals, and seemed more assured and relaxed than he
had been at the start of the season. School was straightened
out. He had reinjured his neck, but it wasn't serious. A little
showman in him was emerging, too. "I want to be the most
impressive person on the mat," he said. "I want people thinking, 'Fullhart had an awesome match.' "

Gable decried that Illinois had nearly equalled Iowa's takedown total, 18–17. Takedowns indicated aggressiveness. If it
were earlier in the season, back at the time of the eastern road
trip, maybe he would not be as concerned. But now the national tournament loomed only six weeks away.

"We've got to get more serious," he told his team. "It's
not if we won, it's how we won. We lost those close matches,
and we've got to win them. It didn't go like I wanted it to. I
wanted perfect shutouts."

Gable felt that the team was vulnerable at 177. Tony Ersland had lost against Illinois and suffered a slight neck injury.
"He still hasn't turned the corner," Gable noted. "There's
trouble there." Matt Hoover was hurt and missing practices,
and had fallen from grace. Lee Weber started the first varsity
match of his career against Arizona State and was hammered
by Aaron Simpson, 10–3.

Eric Koble lost twice and continued to struggle at 150.
Illinois's Eric Siebert took him down thirteen times en route
to a 26–11 technical-fall victory, stopped with five seconds left
in the match. Koble was 1–5 filling in for McIlravy, and had
been outpointed 52–16. Gable was more exasperated than ag-

gravated, pointing out that, "He keeps making the same mistakes over and over." But McIlravy was ready to return. The only question was when. The Hawkeyes would end their regular season in eight days at Iowa State, where the Cyclones had Chris Bono on the launch pad. Bono led with his head and forced tie-ups to take advantage of his superior strength; it was even money that McIlravy would have a headache handed to him. Gable decided to save his 150-pound star for the Big Ten championships.

Wes Hand (15–6) was solid though injury-prone. Extremely agile for a 235-pound heavyweight, he made moves that surprised even coaches who watched him daily. Not for nothing was he the first Iowa freshman in four years, since two-time All-American John Oostendorp, to start at heavyweight.

Beginning with the post-weigh-in brunch, Gable put in a sixteen-and-a-half-hour day. It was not what doctors meant when they told him to return to work gradually, and he paid for it. His left knee was stiff and sore the next day, and he felt as if he himself had wrestled. But with the NCAAs on the horizon, the calendar seemed to do as much for Gable as medicine. He began to feel the best he had since November. His stomach was better, apparently rid of parasites, and his left hip hadn't hurt since the surgery.

Gable told his team he would shorten practices but make them more intense, with full-tilt live wrestling and fewer breaks. It was what he always did to prepare his teams for the national tournament. Iowa had its toughest practice of the year so far on Tuesday, and two practices on Thursday. The wrestling room seethed with emotion. Two reserves skirmished and had to be broken up.

"I saw intensity I hadn't seen for a long time," Gable said. "Right now, if things continue, we'll get a turnaround yet. I've preached and preached that this is the time to make a move.

"Lincoln is really looking tough. If he didn't get a headache the way he wrestled [today], he won't get one . . . It's critical I stay healthy. I've got to keep barkin' at 'em. I'm like a little puppy dog."

In such high spirits, Gable and the Hawkeyes arrived in Ames on Saturday afternoon to weigh in for Sunday's match against Iowa State. The weigh-in took place in the student recreation center. A heavy snow had begun to fall. Inside, Uker finished weighing in and slumped against a wall in the hallway outside the locker room. Whitmer sat next to him, but Uker stared straight ahead, exhausted from sweating off the last few ounces. Only the *pock . . . pock* from racquetball courts dented the silence. "It feels better out here—man, does it," he said. Whitmer only nodded curtly, lost in his own weariness.

Gable felt good enough to put on blue running shorts and take a sauna. He had started doing push-ups and sit-ups. Doctors had removed the dressing from his surgical wound, and now, sitting in the locker room, Gable dabbed medication on the eight-inch scar. Chris Bono entered the locker room, removed a towel from around his waist, and stepped on a digital scale and smiled. He weighed 149.8; he could weigh in for real now. He crossed the locker room and nodded to Gable.

The team ate at a restaurant on the way back to the motel. Around nine that evening, Gable and Zalesky slid into a rear booth in the motel bar and ordered. Two men in wide-brimmed cowboy hats hunched at the bar, while two college-age kids threw darts. The jukebox played George Jones, and the bartender brought over a cranberry juice for Gable and a Coke for Zalesky. Gable inspected his new crutches: space-age stuff, sleek with black heads and a yellow Hawkeye emblazoned on them. A Hawkeye fan had made them and dropped them off at the house. They were a toy that fascinated Gable. He picked one up in the booth and raised it to his shoulder, as if sighting a hunting rifle, and nearly bagged twenty-year-old Marisa Sulentic, the waitress bringing another round. Zalesky laughed and Gable apologized, while Sulentic smiled and didn't spill a drop.

Without introductions, she asked Gable how he was feeling and if the team would do well on Sunday. "I come from Mediapolis [Iowa]. They've got a good wrestling program there," she said at the bar. "A lot of guys there go to the Hawkeye wrestling camps and know Tom and Terry Brands.

And everybody has heard of Dan Gable. He's a legend—to me, anyway. I follow wrestling, and I remember all the stuff about him in the Olympics and everything. My husband, Tom, has been watching Gable since Tom was a kid. I'd like to get a ticket for Sunday. I don't know if Tom can go, he might have to work, but I want to. I want to see him [Gable] coach for the last time."

Gable and Zalesky talked shop. Rather, Gable talked and Zalesky listened. Like most of the other Iowa wrestlers over the last two decades, Zalesky called him "Gable" when he competed. As his top assistant, Zalesky still called him "Gable." To Gable, Zalesky remained "Jimmy," still a kid after all these years.

"Hoover still hasn't got it together," Gable stated. "We can use him, but he isn't there for us." Zalesky nodded and folded his hands around the cool glass. Gable shook his head. "You can see it in his face. He walks into the wrestling room and he doesn't look like he wants to be there. He's got moves nobody else in the wrestling room has, but . . ."

Then there was Kasey Gilliss (13–8), who would meet Iowa State sophomore David Maldonado (24–16). Maldonado had beaten Gilliss 3–2 on December 14. "Iowa State is big for Gilliss," Gable said. "He's got to keep it going. We need him to come through for us."

The Iowa coaches had occupied the booth for forty-five minutes when a short man in a blue uniform with a wide yellow stripe down the sides of the pants stopped by. Joe Campbell, head of motel security, handed Gable a pen and a piece of paper and informed him that Sulentic had dispatched him for an autograph. Gable signed in his stiff, formal hand, and studied Campbell.

"Say, you weren't the guy who arrested me here in this town twenty years ago, were you?" Gable queried, smiling.

"No, don't think so. I was on the Des Moines force then. You weren't in Des Moines, were you?" Campbell asked.

"Naw, I was here," Gable said. "I wasn't—what do you call it?—publicly intoxicated. I had an open beer is all. I wasn't underage. I was twenty-one."

The two briefly discussed crime fighting in Des Moines compared with Ames, and then Campbell handed the waitress Gable's autograph and resumed his rounds.

Gable looked toward the door and saw Tony Ersland wandering in, alone. He made a slight pivot in the direction of the bar.

"Hey, kid, got an ID?" Gable sang out.

Ersland whirled. "Oh, yeah, no." He turned to leave.

"Hey, it's OK, I was just kiddin'," Gable said, but Ersland was gone. "He hasn't made a breakthrough yet," Gable said.

The next morning, Kathy Gable left the room early and walked into the blinding white of a cold, sunny mid-February day. She was on a mission to lose the weight she had gained having four children. Her husband was no help: When he spotted her in the spring walking the narrow road back to their home, he honked and yelled out the window, "Want a ride, fatty?"

Later, the two Gables accompanied their daughters to breakfast in the dining room. Gable waited for his family to finish and then joined the team for their buffet: fruit, bacon and sausage and eggs, fried potatoes, and pastry. Gable was in a feisty, humorous mood. He obviously was feeling better. People would pay. He took on Kristen Payne, who sat at a long table with him and four ravenous wrestlers.

"Watch it if you go into the whirlpool, Kristen," Gable said. "Somebody's been peeing in it. Girls pee in whirlpools. Boys don't. Have you noticed that, Kristen? I never could understand why they—girls I'm talking about—why they can't stand and pee, anyway. Like guys. Why is that, Kristen?"

The trainer could handle most of Gable's many-pronged pontifications on issues other than strained quadriceps and migraines. She had even developed a dead-on imitation of Gable in his many moods: the serious coach, talking coach-speak, littering sentences with phrases like "point of view" and "bottom line"; the piqued administrator, pressing his thin lips together and then springing to the offensive with, "you're scaring me"; and the flippant forever-young redhead, awash in his amusement with, and appreciation of, women. But the direction of this conversation staggered even Payne. He had, in his expression, "broken" her.

She reddened. Gable persisted. He had found his groove. "So why can't girls just stand up and do it like boys?"

"Well, because it sprays too much, whaddaya think?" she said, cranking a sideways look at Gable that told him he had better graze in other conversational pastures. He turned to Lee Fullhart, cleaning bacon and eggs from his plate.

"You gonna eat any fruit?" the coach asked.

"No," Fullhart said expectantly, knowing more was coming.

"Where you gonna get your energy from? I was thinking, what about getting tomato juice from catsup? Can people do that? Is a tomato a fruit or vegetable?"

Two floors up, Ben Uker ran in the narrow hallways. Wires had been removed from his broken jaw. He didn't want to miss any more training time. A sophomore, he had been redshirted his first year. "Maybe I could get a medical [another year's eligibility granted for injury], but I want to give this my best shot. I want to know I've done everything I can before I throw it in. In high school, I lost in districts, and I had the feeling I didn't do everything I could. I don't want to feel that way anymore.

"I've had three 'scrapes' [arthroscopies] on my left knee since summer. Then this jaw. I was making a shot, and I hit the other guy's knee. I'm still at forty-two [142 pounds]. I don't know if I'll wrestle today. Jimmy says no, but maybe."

Jimmy said no, and Gable said no. Gilliss was hot. Gilliss would wrestle.

Gable waited in the lobby for Kathy and the girls to pack, and for the team to assemble for the ride to Hilton Coliseum. For Gable, the dual was doubly important. Not only was it a strong interstate rivalry—Iowa led the series, 41–14–2—but it was the last competition before the Big Ten and NCAA championships. Coaches were paid to worry, but Gable would do it for nothing.

"We had a pretty good Midlands, but we didn't wrestle

very good against Oklahoma State," he said. "Nobody else has really threatened us, but teams have scored a lot of points on us. I'm concerned about it. Penn State started off the year scoring a lot of points on us. Minnesota scored too many. Iowa State scored too many.

"Today, ideally, they're only going to be in the matches at fifty and seventy-seven. I'm not even going to say they're going to beat us there. Obviously, it's been pretty tough for us to win at those two weights, but somehow I've got to get my kids in the frame of mind that they've got to win.

"It'll be interesting. I think there's going to be a lot of topsy-turvy situations today. I'm kind of looking forward to learning something today. I'm going into this meet unsure. Usually, I'm more sure about our team."

As had been the case all season, the Hawkeyes were welcomed to town with media speculation that this might be Gable's last time through. ("DOUGLAS WILL MISS GABLE IF HE RETIRES," read a sports-page headline in the Saturday *Ames Daily Tribune*. "I think the sport would certainly miss him," Douglas, the Iowa State coach, was quoted as saying. "We may not know how much until after he leaves. . . . The support the University of Iowa got was pure Dan Gable.") Just as predictably, Gable wasn't revealing his plans.

"I think it would mean a lot to me if I knew it was my last time, but I'm not into that right now, even though I keep being reminded of it all the time. Like the paper yesterday. I'm surprised by that. There's so much focus on that."

A few miles from the motel, Ed and Kelly Banach were getting ready to attend the meet, along with their children, Riley, six, and Bailey, two. They lived in a two-story English Tudor home on a quiet, curling street in Ames. Ed was one of four three-time national champions who wrestled for Gable; the others were Tom Brands, Barry Davis, and Jim Zalesky. (In the history of the NCAA Championships, thirty-six wrestlers had won three titles each. Oklahoma State led with fourteen three-time winners. There has only been one four-time winner: Oklahoma State's Pat Smith, John's brother, who won 158-pound titles in 1990, '91, '92, and '94.)

Banach's hair had thinned since he won NCAA titles in the early 1980s, but the rest of him hadn't. "Put it this way, I could wrestle heavyweight now," said Banach, who wrestled at 177 and 190. Like many wrestlers and former wrestlers, he is accommodating and eager to share wrestling with the uninitiated. The day after he won his Olympic gold medal in Los Angeles in 1984, he answered a knock at the motel room and invited a reporter from the *Iowa City Press-Citizen* inside. The Banachs were packing. Ed plucked his gold medal from his carry-on luggage and encouraged the reporter to slip it around his neck. "I don't know. I didn't win it," the reporter said. Banach laughed. "Hey, it's OK. Try it on. Everybody should get a chance to wear one."

In the formal dining room, Banach held Bailey in his lap and prayed that Riley would keep napping upstairs. Banach wouldn't miss today's meet. Like Gable, he had ties to both schools. From 1985–89, he was an assistant wrestling coach at Iowa State, most of the time under Jim Gibbons, Nichols's successor, who preceded Douglas. Banach got out when he couldn't drill in the wrestling room without risking a migraine. He set Bailey down on the floor, and the little girl crawled and romped around the table. Banach's mind was elsewhere.

"I remember I was watching TV," he said. "And all of a sudden the TV just went up and to the left. I was seeing it that way, I mean. And I thought, that's not possible! There's something wrong with my head. I went to a doctor, and the doctor called in a neurologist, and he said, 'It sounds like you have post-concussion syndrome.'

"So I asked him, how many days or weeks does it take? And he said, 'Oh, it sometimes takes years to heal.' Eighteen months later I came to the conclusion that I could not coach wrestling, and I switched from that to counseling. So I'm coaching academically now."

Banach was a student-athlete counselor at Iowa State, working in several areas, including recruiting and sports psychology. He had suffered concussions in high-school sports, but the migraines didn't begin in earnest until 1983, his senior year at Iowa. Blows to the head brought on headaches, vomiting, and a visual aura. Gable never demanded that he wrestle when he was ill, Banach said.

Banach understood and accepted what Gable took years fighting and rejecting—that he was through with any kind of wrestling. "Physiologically, your body can't stand up to the punishment," Banach explained "I knew I'd have to stop wrestling, hard wrestling. With this injury, I don't even live drill, because the jostling nature and the potential for just getting a bump on the head is there. And if I get a bump on the head, I get a concussion. I mean, it doesn't take much.

"I play squash. I play racquetball. I play basketball. And sometimes I get bumped real hard. I've got to catch myself, because everything starts rolling in my head. I've tried to go into the Iowa State wrestling room and just drill, like with a dummy on the wall. But just moving quickly, just coming up from a crouch, that bothers me, and I can't do it."

Banach stood ready to help Gable and McIlravy in their misunderstanding over McIlravy's headaches, but he wouldn't intrude. "I talked to Kathy and said that if Dan wants to talk to me about it, if Lincoln wants to talk to someone about it, I'll make myself available."

Kelly came home from errands, woke Riley, dressed him in warm winter clothes, and helped her husband with Bailey. The four drove the five minutes to the Hilton Coliseum parking lot. They were in their seats by the time the crowd stood for the national anthem. Bailey broke from her parents, and Ed took after her. He wouldn't be seeing much of the Iowa State–Iowa wrestling meet.

As he had so often, Gable predicted exactly what kind of a dual it would be: topsy-turvy. First, Whitmer, fifth-ranked nationally at 118, pulled off an 11–9 victory over Cody Sanderson that was harder than it needed to be. Sanderson, a redshirt freshman and four-time high-school champion from Utah, had discovered the secret to wrestling Whitmer: weather his early rushes and peck away. Sanderson gave up three first-period takedowns and trailed, 6–2, but closed to within 9–8 with twenty seconds left in the match before Whitmer pulled off another takedown that offset the 1:11 Sanderson clocked in riding time.

At the end of the match, Gable rose without his crutches and stood frozen, his fingers laced across the top of his head and his elbows flapping to the side like a man ready to take flight. The victory brought relief. "I was pretty happy after winning eighteen," the coach said. "It looked like we were going to get beat."

Mena and Dwight Hinson—number two and three in the country at 126—continued their engaging rivalry. Hinson, a 2–1 double-overtime loser the first time around, thought he could pick Mena like a ripe peach if he could take him down three times. A showman and crowd favorite, Hinson tore into Mena and scored first on a takedown at 1:24 of the first period. Mena, meanwhile, staved off other takedown attempts but couldn't generate much offense himself. He lost two points for stalling, and trailed 5–4 with 1:18 left in the third period after Hinson's second escape. With the way the stalling calls were going, Gable figured that Mena could saddle Hinson with a penalty point by forcing the action. "Open it up! Open it up!" Gable yelled from the bench, but Mena was closing down. Both wrestlers were called for stalling as the match ended; Hinson, winning 6–5, went to 28–4, Mena to 18–4.

As applause rained down, Hinson quickly made quarter-turns in the center of the mat, pointing to the crowd in appreciation. Then he had his hand raised, slapped Mena on the butt, and ran to the edge of the mat and swan-dived into a cluster of ISU backers, several in Cyclones letter jackets, who were gracious enough to catch him.

McIlravy's absence at 150 might have created as much as a seven-point swing to Iowa State; Chris Bono's major decision over Eric Koble, 20–7, gave the Cyclones four points, whereas a victory by two-time national champion McIlravy would have produced three for Iowa. (He had beaten Bono, 8–2, in the first dual.) Even so, Iowa was not holding up in the areas targeted by Gable. "Weights like forty-two [Gilliss] and sixty-seven [Uker] were the matches that surprised me the most with the domination that Iowa State had over our kids," he said later.

Gilliss (13–9) looked tired and heavy-limbed, unable to fend off either David Maldonado, who took a 9–3 decision, or referee Chuck Yagla, who penalized Gilliss twice for stalling. The loss, which snapped his five-match winning streak, wouldn't help him in the seedings for the Big Ten championships. "He lost his power and strength, and that kid from Iowa State was not to be denied today," Gable said.

Even before he lost a major decision to Bart Horton, 13–2, at 167, Mike Uker (12–10) had wandered into Gable's doghouse. During intermission, while Gable talked to the team about stalling and made points to individual wrestlers, Uker was elsewhere, warming up. "Made me mad he wasn't in there," Gable said. "I didn't know where he was, so I wasn't going to get into it there, but maybe he needed to hear some of this stuff, because it sure as hell was one of his weaker matches by far." Before the match, Gable told Uker that in his 14–9 defeat to Horton in Iowa City, Horton had ridden him unmercifully. Don't let it happen again, Gable instructed. Uker had not permitted a succession of opponents since Horton to ride him that way. Uker nodded. But Horton made a five-point move at the end of the first period, scoring a takedown and near-fall, to take a 7–1 lead. It broke Uker's concentration and softened him up for Horton, who accumulated five minutes of riding time in the match, Gable's warning notwithstanding.

Meanwhile, no one on the Iowa staff was expecting miracles from Ersland, in and out of the lineup recently with injuries and struggling below .500 since the National Duals. Now Ersland (9–10) faced Barry Weldon (24–2), the top-ranked 177-pounder, who already owned a 15–4 decision over Ersland. Weldon had exhibited wrestling cool at weigh-ins, walking around in heavy gray sweats but not sweating much initially, skipping rope when the mood struck, pointing Iowa wrestlers in the direction of the saunas and scales. But now he wore his game face. An All-American last year at 167, he took down Ersland five times in the first two periods. He forced Ersland into stalls and retreats—and finally into a 13–4 loss.

Mark Ironside and Joe Williams had both gone to 21–0 with easy victories over sub-.500 opponents. Ironside handed Frank Kisley his seventeenth loss of the season, 20–6. "I needed a fall, I wanted a fall. Or a technical fall," Ironside said. "I had him pinned, but I let my arms slip out." Williams went into his match with explicit instructions from Gable to score a batch of team points, beyond a three-point decision. Williams nearly pinned John DeLeon in the first period and went on to register a technical fall, 23–7, in 5:50. It was Williams's fiftieth straight victory at 158.

Through 177 pounds, then, it looked as if Iowa State (7–6–1) would break Iowa's nineteen-match stranglehold in the series. The Cyclones led, 18–12, with two matches left. In the crowd of 6,180, Kathy Gable tensed forward in her seat, eyes riveted on the mat. On the sidelines, Royce Alger barked into Gable's ear that the dual was headed for an 18–18 tie, figuring that Fullhart and Hand would finish with decision victories. It had been twenty-seven years since Gable had turned conservative in a wrestling match, and he had lost because of it, in the NCAA final of his senior season at Iowa State. Gable listened to Alger repeat what the score would be. "And I kept thinking, eighteen-eighteen—I didn't come here to tie. I don't want to tie. Something snapped in my mind. I figured, if we don't go for the win, then maybe they win, but I don't want to wrestle eighteen-eighteen. I'm too old, too far along in my career not to see it end one way or the other."

Fullhart had stripped out of his warmups and started a sweat when Gable pulled him aside. Go for big points, not just a three-point decision, the coach ordered "We need it—the *team* needs it." Fullhart nodded and ran onto the mat, adjusting his headgear for the last time. Gable's goal fit perfectly into Fullhart's dream of running opponents off the mat and giving fans a performance that would leave them with the word *awesome* on their tongues. In their first meeting this season, Fullhart, now 17–3 and fifth-ranked at 190, had scored an 18–7 decision over Matt Mulvihill, eleventh ranked and 19–10. Gable wanted that and more from him again. Fullhart complied, overpowering Mulvihill and taking him down in the first thirty seconds: Fullhart up, 2–0. Fullhart let his opponent escape so that he could take him down again: Fullhart up, 4–1. Same thing again: Mulvihill escape, Fullhart takedown. It was 6–2 after the first period, and the only question was whether Fullhart's arms would give out before Mulvihill's tailbone did.

Throughout the season, Gable and the other coaches had worked with Fullhart to increase his arsenal of moves, to make him as dangerous on his feet as he was on the mat riding and turning his opponent. Mulvihill was seeing evidence of the transformation. With thirty seconds left in the match, Fullhart took Mulvihill to the mat for the ninth time and nearly pinned him. End of match: With riding time, Fullhart had a 23–7 lead and a technical fall with eleven seconds left in the third period. Iowa had crawled to within one point, 18–17. As Fullhart clomped off the mat, Gable rose on his crutches and swatted his wrestler across the butt. But it didn't mean anything unless Wes Hand won.

A heavyweight wrestler stands out on a team for reasons other than his size. For one thing, he usually doesn't have to cut weight. In the NCAA, heavyweights can weigh up to 275 pounds. For another, the heavyweight sits at the end of the line. Not infrequently in duals, he has a chance to win or lose the meet for his team. Iowa State heavyweight Trent Hynek had provided the points this season that beat Minnesota, Mankato State, and Pennsylvania. Hand had never experienced this part of wrestling, having the outcome in his hands—until now. "I always wanted something like this to happen," he said. "I thought about it my whole life." Alger gave Hand his mission statement before he stepped on the mat. Gable stayed out of it. "I knew Alger had been on him. I didn't want to get him all uptight."

Hand (15–6) and Hynek (19–9) had split this season; Hynek beat Hand in the dual meet, 9–4, but Hand won two weeks later in the Midlands, 10–6. Familiarity, and the closeness of the match, bred restraint. Both wrestlers were warned for stalling in the scoreless first period. In the second, Hynek, choosing down, escaped, and Hand picked up another stall warning with eight seconds left and was penalized a point.

Hynek led, 2–0. Gable had told his team during a break after five matches that stall warnings should benefit the normally aggressive Hawkeyes, but it wasn't working out that way. The chant built: "Let's go State! Let's go State!" Kathy Gable buried her face in her hands. She lifted her head in time to see Hand topple Hynek two seconds after the stalling call, the takedown tying the match at 2–2. Then, for the third period, Hand chose to start down. Hynek rode him, but not for long. The chanting resumed, and then Hand satisfied the screaming Iowa coaches by ripping clear for an escape point. Over the last minute, Hand repulsed Hynek's takedown attempts, and the wrestlers ended the match on their feet. Hand had won, 3–2, to put Iowa over the top, 20–18.

Teammates swarmed to Hand, but his happiness was not without reservation. "I just didn't wrestle as well as I could. I wanted to win better. That would have been the ideal, to come out and beat him bad. But I didn't. And I can't do nothing about it now. I can work for that in the future."

Still, Gable was upbeat. The Hawkeyes, finishing the dual season 15–1, had turned back an inspired Iowa State team and given Gable his twentieth straight victory over his alma mater. Gable, who at the start of the season jokingly upbraided a waitress for suggesting his team needed luck, took this fortunate victory with thanks.

"I won't sleep as good tonight as if the domination would have been there," he said. "But I'll sleep better than if I would have been looking at a loss right now."

chapter **11**

NOW CAME the most important part of Iowa's wrestling season: the final five weeks; three weeks to prepare for the Big Ten championships in Minneapolis, then two before the NCAA championships in Cedar Falls. Gable assumed that his Hawkeyes would win the conference title, which would be their twenty-fourth in a row and twenty-first under his direction. The only smile that Gable could manage after Iowa's narrow victory in Ames was when someone asked him which teams would contend with the Hawkeyes for the conference championship. He looked away and nearly shook with laughter. "Very simple," he said. "None. But there are some teams in there that are pretty good—Minnesota, Illinois, Penn State. But I don't expect any of them to challenge us. I expect at the national level we'll be challenged."

Gable's attention seemed always divided between Iowa City and Stillwater. Iowa's Big Ten championships and Oklahoma State's Big Twelve championships, in Columbia, Missouri, would both be held the weekend of March 8. The Big Ten, where all eleven schools fielded wrestling teams, was awarded sixty-nine qualifying places by the NCAA, the most of any conference in the country. The top six from each weight class would automatically qualify, with nine at-large berths.

The newly organized Big Twelve, in which only five schools had wrestling programs, won thirty-six qualifying spots, to be spread among the top three at each weight and six wild-cards.

No coach, in wrestling or any other sport, better prepared and peaked a team for major meets than Gable did. He had the ability, to use another Gableism, to "read" his teams, to know what kind of a workout was needed when, and to adjust day to day, hour by hour. "I don't know what my schedule'll be today, when we'll practice," he said during the long haul of training. "I don't know how coaches can say, 'We'll practice today and do this, and we'll practice tomorrow and do that.' You've got to see what the mood is. Every day isn't like every other day."

"He knows exactly when to push us and when to back off," Jessie Whitmer said. "You'll go in tired and expecting another tough workout, and he'll ease up a little, and come back the next day with a tough one."

Slowly, Gable pressed down on the accelerator. Practices were trimmed to an hour and a half, but they were more intense than the two-hour workouts of earlier in the season. Unending sprints, one end of the wrestling room to the other . . . the muffled thudding of bodies piling into wall mats, grunts, lining up to go the other way . . . a ragged chorus of labored breathing, a song of heat and sweat . . .

Gable needed to convince his team again, to make a big blinking neon sign, that once they had pushed themselves to the borders of their physical and psychological limits, they were ready to win individually and as a team. That when it came to the third period in a tight match, they had the advantage, because they were trained in the Iowa wrestling room by Dan Gable, and if they felt drained and used up, their opponents felt worse.

He pushed a little harder.

"You never hit the wall!" he yelled at them during sprints, meaning the figurative wall of exhaustion. "You always hit the wall *after* a match! When you sit down, *that's* when you hit the wall. You get tired *then!* OK, three to go. You don't hit the wall!

"C'mon, Uker. You do *not* hit the wall! Two to go. You muster it all. OK, we do another one."

Mike Uker kept trailing the pack while the team did sprints. Gable wouldn't stop until he saw Uker pick up the pace.

"Fuck him!" Lincoln McIlravy finally exclaimed, exhausted and exasperated.

"I can't help it. He's a member of the team," Gable fired back.

Wrestlers signed up for individual coaching sessions two or three times a week, during which Gable or an assistant would give them special attention in live wrestling against a reserve. Gable zeroed in on Tony Ersland's tendency to pull back during a match, reluctant to meet fatigue on its own terms. For a half hour or so, Gable put Ersland through "short go's," telling him that there were ten seconds left in the match and he had to score. "OK, hit it!" Gable would command, and Ersland would scramble for points. After ten seconds, Gable would call a halt and critique, and order another short go, and another.

Gable pushed every button he could, and sometimes some perhaps he shouldn't. After a dual match, he berated Ersland for his lethargic performance. He questioned Ersland's dependability, saying, "What if your family had to depend on you? Could they depend on you?" After the season had ended, Ersland hadn't forgotten the remark. "He did everything he could to get me ready," Ersland said. "He was hard on me. When he said that after the Iowa State match, I was thinking, what did he mean? What does he get out of saying something like that? But I know what he was trying to do."

Gable handled Whitmer differently, fluffing Whitmer's confidence like a pillow. Even this late in the season, Gable still quipped that his 118-pound wrestler was the "strongest man in the world." By the numbers, in almost Socratic questioning, Gable fixed in Whitmer's mind how to escape from the bottom.

"What was one of the main things we told you that you shouldn't do anymore? Especially from the bottom position?"

Gable asked in practice, moving close to Whitmer and his partner.

"Ummmm, go forward like this, get my head down," Whitmer said. "Ummmm, don't just put my hands in [back]. . . ."

"Like this?" Gable said.

"Yeah."

"That's the main one," Gable said. "That's where you're going to get your wrist caught. And you should be reaching with. . . ."

Different wrestlers, different approaches. It had been Gable's coaching style for two decades.

When Royce Alger was competing, he decided he needed a break. He asked Gable for a day or two off before the Big Ten championships. It was like a mail carrier requesting a vacation the week before Christmas. But Gable consented, knowing Alger would refuel and return with renewed vigor. Alger won three Big Ten championships in the late 1980s, and two national titles.

Then there was Ed Banach. He came to Gable with the idea that wrestling was all about attacking for seven minutes. The opponent was a door. Banach was a battering ram. Gable tailored special workouts for Banach, and he and J Robinson worked with Banach to develop his defensive skills, countermoves that would make him a complete wrestler.

"He designed workouts for me so I could at least stop someone from attacking me," Banach recalled. "He knew those things about me. He knows what all his teams need. You just have to put in the cooperation, put in the time.

"It's kind of like a mathematical equation. One plus two plus three equals six. You've done the one, you've done the two, you've done the three to equal six. There's no way to get around it. And if you haven't done those things, then you have no right to win. But if you have done all those things, you've got every right to expect to win."

Gable so immersed himself in his wrestlers' own abilities that he never tried to recreate them in his image. He fully separated Dan Gable, the competitor, from Dan Gable, the coach. Gable the competitor would never have taken a day off during the year, never mind during the season—and yet that is what Gable the coach had occasionally allowed his teams to do close to tournament time.

"I would never coach an athlete exactly how I was as an athlete," Gable explained. "He'd have to be just like me. He'd have to show every characteristic or every trait that I had. You have to treat them like they are. Individuals. You have to figure out what makes each one of them tick.

"I get letters, and somebody, like a coach, will say this guy's got this problem. Can you solve it? No, I can't solve it. I don't even know the kid. I can give you a general thing, but the only way I could solve it is if I know this kid inside out. Even then you don't know him a hundred percent, because they're them. And they don't think exactly the way you do."

Even so, Gable said, "I'm pushing my athletes through workouts that are harder than the ones of any other coach I've been associated with. So I've taken some of the stuff that I went through and tried to incorporate it into my people. But at the same time, the bottom line comes down to what they are willing to do. Are they dogging it and trying to survive? Or are they pushing hard through the time period?"

Each season, Gable fought, with varying success, for his wrestlers to understand that they were competing for themselves, yes, but also as part of a team. They had to realize why he might want them to turn a comfortable victory into a pin—because six points on the team total was better than three. The recent Iowa State meet, in which Gable ordered big points from Williams and Fullhart, served notice that the team score was not to be forgotten. The team, he knew, fed off individuals, and vice versa.

Sometimes, Gable asked for more than a few more points from his wrestlers. In Troy Steiner's case, Gable asked that he drop a weight class in 1993 so that McIlravy, who had been redshirting, could squeeze in at 142—where Steiner had won a national title. "We'd been struggling as a team," Steiner said.

"The only guy who could step in and help us win was Lincoln. I was in the wrestling room, I knew what was coming a month before Gable called me in.

"We had Northwestern the next week. Once Lincoln stepped on the mat for a match, he was out of redshirt. I told Gable I'd try one thirty-four, but I told him to have two guys weigh in at forty-two—Lincoln and somebody else. That way, if I didn't feel good wrestling at thirty-four, the other guy could wrestle and Lincoln could stay in redshirt and I could go back up.

"I didn't feel great the first time I went down [to 134]," Steiner said. "But I didn't expect to. I told him I'd do it."

Iowa won the 1993 NCAA title, but Steiner finished third at 134. McIlravy won his first national title, at 142.

"I expected to win it at 134," Steiner said. "Why I lost wasn't because of cutting weight. It was because I wasn't ready to score on the other guy."

The 1997 season had been even more disjointed than 1993. Gable, with his health problems, had been in and out of the wrestling room, as had McIlravy. But now, in February, Gable finally had everyone together for the final lunge at the tape.

"I don't have a team yet," Gable said. "Once I get a team, then I start working individuals. Seventy-seven [Ersland] was bothering me the most, but now those other two [Gilliss and Uker] are, too. Everybody should be a threat on my team. Everybody. I don't want any weak spots."

Mark Ironside and Joe Williams, not the most vocal of athletes, practiced hard and talked team. "We can't stand around," Williams said. "We're at a point in the season where we've got to put points on the scoreboard. We've got to pick it up, the whole bunch of us, for nationals. Some of our top guys have been beaten. We aren't wrestling at our best."

"I know we've got the talent to win [the national championship]," Ironside said. "We've got to peak as a team. We've got to start being dominant."

As February ended, the team was still operating on five or six cylinders, not ten. Ersland had fought off challenges and kept his 177-pound berth, but exhaustion made his performance problematical. Gable never let himself doubt that Ersland could qualify in the Big Ten championships for the NCAA meet. He would be unseeded, not the greatest vote of confidence, but Gable figured that Ersland could still wind up seventh or eighth, which would put him at the mercy of Big Ten coaches voting for nine wrestlers who didn't make the top-six cut at their weights. Gilliss had exhibited a rookie's inconsistency with strong performances in January but backsliding in February. He needed to use his legs more in his offense. And Uker, he had been an All-American at 150, but he wasn't wrestling like one at 167. He made a couple of good shots against Iowa State, but then his technique fell apart. He didn't keep his hips under him, and he hung on like a fighter in trouble instead of penetrating. Gable blamed conditioning. Wes Hand, and suddenly Mike Mena, needed to open up on offense, to concentrate on scoring. The shining light was McIlravy, wrestling so hard in practice that he needed stitches to close facial wounds. Gable was euphoric. "When he goes to practice, he gets more done in one day than a lot of people get done in one week. He's putting out. This week is the best he's looked. In two-a-days, he showed me something."

Gable floored the accelerator: timed miles on the Carver-Hawkeye concourse at 6:15 A.M., then sprints—nine of them. (Not coincidentally, against Iowa State, the Hawkeyes had had nine stalling calls.) Gable mixed in "red-flag days," as well, sessions even tougher than the normal practices, consisting of nonstop wrestling, running, and drilling, more than an hour's worth. Gable even threatened a "black-flag day." "That's extermination day," he said. "The tempo is increased higher than ever. Unbelievable intensity." It was the ultimate scare tactic. "Get going," Gable warned, "or we'll turn a red-flag day into a black-flag day."

If the wrestlers felt bad, Gable felt worse. His stomach had kicked up again. Doctors could find nothing alarming. His left knee swelled again, and he wrapped it. "I was sick before the season started, I'm sick now. It's been a trying time."

Stress snapped at him wherever he went. In his office, Gable had his administrative staff make calls, but no one could find a place in Cedar Falls for his wrestling entourage to stay during the NCAA meet. The meet had been sold out for months. Eleven rooms were located at a motel in nearby Waverly, but that wasn't enough. Finally, a block of rooms opened up at the motel, and Gable hoped he would have ten qualifiers to book there.

"Right now, we're behind other teams I've coached," he worried. "Even in conditioning."

Like their coach, Iowa wrestlers willingly placed the rest of their lives on hold to train for conference and national competition. The pace and pressure made it difficult to do otherwise. "I'm not saying you don't go to class. You do, or you try," Troy Steiner said. "But school comes second. Everything else is second."

Iowa wrestlers spent four or five hours a day at the arena, training or watching themselves on tape, talking with coaches or reporting to Payne for treatment. They were always going somewhere, doing something—Whitmer in his hooded yellow sweatshirt with "IOWA WRESTLING" in bold black letters on the front, Ironside in his two-sizes-too-big flannel shirt, Uker in the bright-green stretch pants he broke out for practice well ahead of St. Patrick's Day.

"I know I'm missing a few things about college life," Whitmer said. "But they're all the bad things, like going out. It's great to meet people, I guess, but some people you wouldn't want to meet. In some of those bars, the smoke kills your lungs.

"I feel like I've gotten more out of college life than some students. I travel, compete, let my ferocious side out."

While Whitmer's sort of single-mindedness undoubtedly helps stock the wrestling room with plaques and trophies, it necessarily limits the college experience. Dale Bahr, Gable's former Iowa State teammate and now coaching rival at Michigan, wonders about the trade-off the Iowa wrestlers make. Bahr sat in a hotel lobby one evening before a tournament and watched several Hawkeyes heading up to their rooms. "I tell my wrestlers that going to college is like walking down a hotel corridor, just like we have upstairs here," he said. "You can go

straight through to the exit sign at the end and not be involved
in anything but wrestling and get the classes you need and be
out, and you'll have a couple of experiences. Or you can open
every single door and get involved in this activity, that student
group, visit these hospitals. And I actually encourage my wrestlers to do that, because I like a well-rounded athlete.

"But your most successful athletes," Bahr continued,
"take that singleness of purpose, that *maleness,* and say, 'I'm
going to accomplish these things, and put everything else
aside.' "

During the last week in February, a week before the Big
Tens, Gable made two trips—one scheduled, one not—to the
Des Moines area. It had become both tradition and reward for
him to attend the Iowa high-school wrestling championships
at Veterans Memorial Auditorium in Des Moines. He and
Kathy took a downtown suite and he caught up on old friend-
ships with coaches and former coaches in the state's high
schools and colleges. It gave him one last chance to unwind.
Gable encouraged his wrestlers to attend; it would help under-
score Gable's theme for this season, that of the tradition Iowa
wrestlers had to uphold.

Two days before the tournament began, though, Gable
made a hurried trip to Ames. Harold Nichols, seventy-nine,
the former Iowa State wrestling coach under whom Gable
flourished, had died on Saturday night of stroke complications.
Gable paid his respects to Ruth Nichols, the pert, thin widow,
and then returned to Iowa City. He didn't attend the funeral
on Thursday; he had a doctor's appointment, and he thought
that someone should man the office and run practice while his
assistants were off recruiting.

Harold Nichols probably would have understood.

Nichols's funeral, held on a gray, brooding Thursday, at
the Evangelical Free Church in Ames, closed yet another chapter of Gable's past. More than 150 people gathered in the foyer
of the modern, low-slung building before the service, many
of them Nichols's former Iowa State wrestlers from the four
decades he coached (1954–85). They came from as far away as
California and New York, and they shared stories with one

another about the quiet man with the active and entrepreneurial mind.

Nichols was born on a farm near Cresco, Iowa, where the welcome sign outside of town still notes the years that the high-school wrestling team won the state championship. He was a solid, though not spectacular, wrestler in high school before he went on to win the NCAA 145-pound title for Michigan. He taught and developed physical-education programs in the Air Force during World War II, met Ruth on a blind date and married her ten months later, and started the wrestling program at Arkansas State before landing at Iowa State in 1954. He succeeded Hugo Otopalik, the longtime Cyclones coach and former U.S. Olympic coach who died in 1953.

Nichols changed both the face and fortunes of Iowa State wrestling. A reserved man whose hobby was collecting expensive vases, he stressed the flamboyancy of the pin to his wrestlers. ("It's the ultimate in wrestling. It makes the crowd stand up," he maintained.) He filled his wrestling room with quality wrestlers, and he was known among his coaching peers as a tough man to recruit against. Once, the story went, Nichols —or "Nick," as everyone called him—visited the home of a high-school wrestler. When he left, he saw a rival coach coming up the street. The Iowa State coach waited until the other coach left, and then knocked on the door, intending to have the last word. "Excuse me," he inquired of the wrestler when he answered, "did I leave a briefcase inside?"

Nichols won six national titles and fulfilled his promise to break the stranglehold that the Oklahoma schools had held on the NCAA championships. Gable, who arrived in 1966, appreciated the freedom that Nichols gave him to drill and wrestle independently. Like Doug Blubaugh, one of Gable's international-freestyle coaches, Nichols recognized that Gable was motivated and skilled enough to figure out most things himself. Gable also assimilated coaching skills from Nichols. Nichols planned each practice, taking notes on his intentions and conveying them to the team before the workout—exactly what Gable did as Iowa coach, every day. Working off a clipboard, sorting through scraps and full sheets of paper, Gable presented each day's schedule and announcements.

Gable was constantly writing down ideas for the team, new approaches to training, specialized workouts for certain wrestlers, reminders of what he wanted to tell a wrestler about his last match. Former Iowa wrestler Mark Trizzino stumbled upon Gable in the locker room before this year's NCAA championships in Cedar Falls; no one else was around. Handwritten notes lay all about, with Gable standing in the middle like a maypole. Trizzino finally put it together.

"He was breaking it all down, the nationals, what the team needed to do, who else was going to be tough, at what weights. People think that with wrestling, you only get better in the room. But he was working it out this way, too. Who else attacks it that way?"

Nichols regarded Gable, the wrestler, as someone who stood apart from the others he had coached, a phenomenon he could appreciate but not take full credit for. "I think he's the best there ever was, and we've had a lot of great wrestlers in this country," Nichols told the *Des Moines Register.* "He's reached that point where we just figure he's going to pin everybody. He's not particularly fast, but he just seems to have perfect feel and sense—plus the essential desire. He has no weaknesses now, is always in top shape, and his technique is beyond being perfect."

Through the years, Gable and Nichols publicly acknowledged their regard for each other, but neither man was particularly emotional, and they saw each other as if from across a chasm of unspoken sentiment. Nichols tried to keep Gable at Iowa State after Gable's Olympic triumph in 1972, but the Iowa State coach moved too slowly. For years afterward, Nichols held the University of Iowa responsible for an act of piracy, but he never held that against the best wrestler he ever coached.

"He was a good coach. At least, the kind I needed," Gable remembered. "He let me alone, and he used me to motivate other guys who didn't work as hard. I use Ironside like that."

It was a slightly cockeyed but talented group that paraded

before Nichols in Gable's day. Everyone had nicknames. Gable was "Weasel," because of the way he could weasel out from the underneath position. When weight-cutting time came, several ISU wrestlers, heavily layered and carrying flashlights, would lift a manhole cover on campus and follow Gable into the university's tunnel system. They would run in the hothouse climate for a while, then stop and play a few hands of poker in the dirt by flashlight. In ten-minute shifts, one after another would get up to exercise and then return to the game. "We were down there about an hour, cutting weight and playing cards," Dale Bahr remembered. "Then we found our way back to the manhole cover and crawled out. I'm sure somebody on campus wondered whether the zombies were coming out from under the manholes."

Gable's absence at the funeral caused whispers among a few mourners, but on the other hand, Gable was present in almost every other sense. In scrapbooks neatly arranged on a long table in the church foyer, newspaper stories chronicled Nichols's thirty-two-year career at Iowa State, and many contained pictures of and references to and separate articles on Gable. Kathy Gable sent flowers prominently displayed with other floral arrangements at the front of the sanctuary. Hers were tied with ribbons of cardinal and gold, and black and gold. In the five-minute film about Nichols's life and career that began the service, Gable was shown and mentioned often, both as an Iowa State wrestler and as the Iowa coach who came to honor the chesty Nichols at Hilton Coliseum. "The way he carried himself," Gable said in the film, "you had the feeling that the more his athletes won, the more his chest expanded."

Several speakers came to the pulpit to praise Nichols, who left behind a wife, two grown sons, and his highly profitable wrestling-products business. He was remembered by Bobby Douglas, an African American, as someone sensitive to color issues. Nichols once led his team out of an Oklahoma restaurant that wouldn't serve blacks, and he had hired Douglas as an assistant while Douglas took graduate classes.

His wrestlers appreciated Nichols's directness and honesty. Joe Galasso, a food broker from Des Moines who had a blocky build and black hair, told about going out for the team in post-Gable years.

"I wound up with a guy named Jones, who was a Bible-beater. Always saying verses, even in the wrestling room. He wrestled real funky. This one time I got him way up in the air, and he came down and got me in a cradle. He threw a forearm across me, and he said, 'I have strength from God.' I reared back and popped him in the nose. He let go.

"Nick heard the noise and came over and told me to get to the locker room. He came down a few minutes later and said he found out what happened and for me to get lost for a couple of days, not come to practice.

"Then he started walking away, and then he turned around and kind of smiled. And he said, 'I been waitin' to do what you did for three months.' "

While Harold Nichols's funeral took place, the second of six sessions of the seventy-first annual state high-school wrestling tournament was in progress in nearby Des Moines. What the state high-school basketball tournament is to Indiana, what the state high-school hockey tournament is to Minnesota, the state high-school wrestling tournament is to Iowa. More than 70,000 fans would pack Veterans Memorial Auditorium over the course of the three-day tournament. Located atop a hill near downtown, the auditorium seemed an impregnable fortress because of the heavy traffic and distant parking.

Morning, afternoon, and night the loyalists came, to watch wrestling in three classes: big (3-A), medium (2-A), and small (1-A). In the corridors and lobby, the air smelled of meat cooking and popcorn; people stood six deep at concession stands to buy $3 hamburgers and $1.25 small Cokes. In the vast arena, shrill-voiced girls in short pleated skirts and letter-sweaters camped by the mats and led cheers ("Turn him over! Pin him flat!"), and betrayed no disappointment when no one yelled with them.

Wrestlers came from towns like Wilton and Wapello, Columbus Junction and Clarinda, Chariton and Greene. They and their fans wore T-shirts proclaiming "REAL MEN WEAR SINGLETS," and sweatshirts sneering, "WE'D RATHER THROW YOU THAN KNOW YOU." Justin Waters, a sixteen-year-old wrestler from Jefferson, Iowa, near Ames, was eliminated in sectional competition, but he wouldn't miss the state meet. He had a spider-web design carved into the back of his blond head, the spoils of winning a bet with his father that Justin's school would send five to state. Waters already was cutting weight— up to seventeen pounds to wrestle at 119, he said. Five pounds went in one week. "It's OK. I just don't eat," he said, shrugging. "I skip supper once in a while, lunch maybe. My parents say do what it takes to make weight." Why did he sacrifice so much for wrestling? The stock answer: Wrestlers rely on themselves; they don't have to depend on teammates. "In, like, basketball, the best team always wins," Waters said. "But in wrestling, an upset can happen any time. You throw a headlock on the number-one kid in the state and you got a win."

Throughout the day and night on Thursday, even in more-lightly attended sessions, crowd noise rolled in waves across the eight mats as the public-address announcer rattled off mat assignments. Up in the balcony, row five, seat two, Janella Foster and her father-in-law, Dick Foster, settled in for a long day, a bag of caramel candy for sustenance in the seat between them. She had been coming to the state wrestling tournament for more than 20 years, since before she had white hair. Her husband, Dick Jr., was a longtime assistant coach at Norwalk, and Janella proudly claimed that she knew a sitout when she saw one. She pointed across the floor, toward section twelve. "One of the things I look forward to is finals night," she said. "Dan Gable comes and sits there. Everybody who comes tries to look to see him. Come the state tournament, he's on everybody's mind. He's still part of it."

But Gable, pride of Waterloo West, wasn't in section twelve during the tournament. Because of his hip, he had to sit at floor level, in the disabled section. People found him, anyway, and streamed to get his autograph. At the edge of the floor, Tony Ersland stood and watched matches. "I won two titles here," he said. "This gets me excited for the Big Tens next week. Practices were tough. Red-flag days were the worst. I think we're ready. I know I am."

chapter 12

DAN GABLE arrived in the Twin Cities for the Big Ten championships with a vigor that surprised everyone around him. If he wasn't a new man, he certainly felt better than the old one. "I feel great," he said. "It's been since November 15 that I've felt this good—and that's been three months." His hip was healing, and the pain in his left knee had subsided. He followed his team into a locker room in the Bierman Athletic Complex on the University of Minnesota campus, and while his wrestlers flung themselves into the final round of weight cutting, Gable escaped into the sauna.

When he emerged, baked rosy red, he ran into Jim Heffernan, the Illinois assistant coach who had been a four-time All-American under Gable and won the NCAA 150-pound title in 1986. Balding and quiet, Heffernan broke off his search for an Illinois wrestler to inquire about Gable's health. Gable gushed about how good he felt, and then told Heffernan about undergoing a complicated enema procedure recently at University Hospitals to determine the source of his abdominal pains. "If I get one more of those," Gable joked, "I'll have to join the gay liberation front."

The Iowa coach began discussing other parts of his aching anatomy, including his left knee: "That went bad when I went on a run in eighty-six. I had a twinge and had to stop. It never felt good after that." Only in a conversation between two wrestleholics like Gable and Heffernan would mention of a knee injured eleven years ago kindle talk about the NCAA championships. That was the year the tournament was held in Iowa City, Gable went on, and Heffernan and the Hawkeyes won. Heffernan recalled the next year, when he and the Hawkeyes finished second in Maryland. "Yeah, you lost in the finals, I remember," Gable said.

Heffernan moved on, and Gable started toweling off. As sometimes happened, he allowed an incident or conversation to fester before he brought it to the surface. Now was one of those times. Host officials at the University of Minnesota had requested that he appear with several other coaches at a press conference at 2:30 tomorrow afternoon, Friday, before the weekend tournament. "I told them I'd try to come, but it pisses me off," Gable fumed. "I hate that. Originally, it was scheduled for four-thirty. Now they want me there at two-thirty, which is when weigh-ins are, two to three.

"I told them if I had a wrestler who wasn't down [in weight], I wasn't coming. I need to help him cut. That's my job. I'm a coach. One thing you learn about a wrestling coach is not to make up schedules ahead of time."

The wrestler in question was Mike Mena, the same Mike Mena who earlier in the season had contemplated dropping back to 118 from 126. Now he was having trouble making 126. He was up near 140 pounds, by some accounts, before he began cutting. He had ridden an exercise bike in double layers of sweats, and now, with nineteen hours to go before the deadline, sat on a small couch in the locker room, brooding in silence. Not far away, on a bench in front of some lockers, Joe Williams, also in sweats, sat wordlessly. Thick lines of perspiration stretched across Williams's forehead. Tony Ersland appeared, smiling, from forty minutes on an exercise bike. He had stopped to weigh at the digital scale within sight of the door.

"Only two over," he said perkily. "Evidently I got a better

sweat than I thought." He turned to Williams. "How much you over?"

Williams stared at the maroon carpeting at his feet. It was 8 P.M., but the locker room bustled with wrestlers from several teams marching to and from the scale and the wrestling room.

"Nine-and-a-half," Williams replied.

"Well, it looks like you've got a good sweat going," Ersland said. Williams didn't look at him.

A row of lockers away, Jim Zalesky and Tom Brands stood talking with Gable and waiting for the Iowa wrestlers to finish their weight-cutting chores. Ersland wandered down and mentioned that he had seen the gritty film *Reservoir Dogs*.

Brands said, "I saw that in the theater, and I walked out." There was an angry snap in his voice.

"Yeah. That was a Tarantino movie," Ersland volunteered.

"I should have," declared Zalesky, meaning walked out. "Who'd make a movie like that? Like to run into the guy. 'You made that movie? Try this!' " Zalesky, unusually animated, swung a right uppercut in the air.

"So many 'f' words in that movie," Brands said.

"Mena likes that," Ersland said, pleased with having stirred up his coaches. "That's his favorite word."

Meanwhile, Gable had taken a quick shower and returned. He rubbed an antibiotic into the still-raw eight-inch scar on his left hip. The stitches had been removed, but one or two were infected. To protect the area, he would pull on a foot-to-hip white surgical stocking.

"Damn!" he said, sounding disappointed that the antibiotic didn't cause a jolt of pain. "I wanted to *feel* this. Well, maybe it's healed now."

In an interview room in Williams Arena on the Minnesota campus, three coaches of highly ranked Big Ten teams—J Robinson of Minnesota, John Fritz of Penn State, and Mark Johnson of Illinois—reported for a pre-tournament press conference. It was 2:30 Friday afternoon. Gable sent word that he would be late if he made it at all.

It was as if no one had gone home from the night before.

Gable, Brands, and Zalesky paced and conferred in the locker room. Mena slumped on the couch, unable to lock his eyes on anything, disoriented. It was as if he had sent part of himself elsewhere. He wore layers of sweats. He hung his head of black hair. He had thirty minutes to lose 2.8 pounds. Brands bent and leaned close to the senior three-time All-American.

"You made a deal," Brands said in a low rasp. "You made a deal. You made a *deal*."

The deal was that Mena would get two sips of water from a small cup if he returned to the sauna. He rose slowly and began a weaving walk to the showers and the sauna just to the right. Gable went with him. The Iowa coach, in his briefs, had removed his shirt and pants and left them in a locker. He placed his black "I" baseball cap on the bench in front of the locker, along with his glasses and gold wristwatch. He seldom took off the watch, which was a present from Kathy, inscribed on the back with "HAPPY 10TH ANNIVERSARY. LOVE FOREVER, KATHY." In the shower entryway, Gable and Mena passed a familiar figure in Duane Goldman, the Indiana coach. Goldman looked much the same as when he wrestled for Gable and finished second in the NCAAs three years running before winning the 190-pound title in 1986. He had massive arms and a back that looked like rounded rocks covered by a bedsheet; his waist wasn't a waist at all but a small connecting rod to his hips. He was escorting one of his own wrestlers through the private hell of weight cutting. The wrestler was pitched forward on an exercise bike a few feet from the sauna. His head rested on his hands, which were crossed in front of him on the handlebars; his feet were not moving the pedals. From behind, Goldman reached under the wrestler's arms and pulled him— limp and heavy with sodden sweatclothes—off the bike and dragged him like a battlefront casualty into the sauna.

Gable and Mena emerged a short time later, and Mena took two sips of water from a cup that Brands handed him. Gable and Zalesky took him back into the shower area, and he mounted the exercise bike that the Indiana wrestler had left. Gable put Mena's feet into the pedal straps. Mena started moving the pedals—*pedaling* is too strong a word for it. The reason might have been that resistance on the bike was set high, to force him to work harder in a shorter time, but there was no way to make certain. The heavy, slitted plastic curtain between the bicycle and the general locker room was closed, and Zalesky made sure it stayed that way.

While Mena slowly worked, Wisconsin coach Barry Davis came in with one of his own wrestlers. Davis stopped and glimpsed Mena through the slits.

"There's more to the sport than the wrestling room," Davis observed. "We're talking a lot of points there, with Mena."

The national title might well ride on how Mena held up for the next few minutes. He had scored heavily in the last three NCAAs, placing seventh, third, and fifth, and currently was top-ranked nationally at his weight. If he didn't even qualify for the Big Ten championships because of weight, and couldn't compete in Cedar Falls, the Hawkeyes' chances would be harmed considerably.

Davis knew all about the nightmare of weight cutting before the Big Ten championships, and the pressure and sacrifice it entailed. His own experience in 1982 had become part of Iowa wrestling lore. Davis had won the Big Ten's 118-pound title the year before and finished seventh in the national tournament, but now his weight soared out of control. It had gone as high as 146. On the day the team was to leave for Ann Arbor, Michigan, and the Big Ten championships, Davis tried to get into the wrestling room for an early round of weight cutting. It was 4 A.M. The door was locked.

"I was so tired and exhausted, and I said, 'That's it. I'm done,' " Davis said. "So I just started walking and ended up clear across town."

It was cold, so he ducked into an apartment building and fell asleep in the hallway. "And then the door of the building opens, and I look up, and I'm thinking, 'Oh, no! It's Gable!' And it's only this newspaper kid." Davis opened someone else's paper to the sports section. He read that the NCAA championships would be shown on tape delay on ABC-TV a week after the tournament. "I'm going, 'Geez! I blew it! The

team's going, and I'm not. I blew it!' So I walked to Hy-Vee
around the corner."

At the store, Davis bought doughnuts. No sense grieving
on an empty stomach. "I looked up and saw this blue van
coming up. I said, 'What are those guys doing here?' And
the next thing I know, the whole team is coming. I see my
roommates' car pull in. They're after me. And Gable is the first
one through the door. He goes, 'There he is!' Like I'm a crimi-
nal. 'There he is!' He grabs me and says, 'What do you think?
What are you doing?' So we walk out. And he says to me,
'What do you want to do? Do you want to wrestle or not?'

"I said, 'Yes, I do,' but I really didn't. I couldn't tell him
no. I've got a lot of respect for him. I went back and got my
gear. Made weight. Won the Big Ten."

An epiphany of sorts occurred in the following week,
when Davis was trying to cut weight for the national tournament, where as a sophomore he would win his first NCAA
title. Gable was leaving after practice. He asked Davis if he
needed help. "I said, 'No, I'll be all right,' " Davis recounted.
"He goes, 'You aren't going to take off are you?' I said, 'No,
I'm not.' He left, and all of a sudden in that locker room I
heard the door [behind him] go *c-l-l-l-ick*. As soon as it
clicked, I thought, 'Uh-oh.' Out the door. 'Gable! Hold on!
I'll be right with you!' We ran together and made weight.

"I knew as soon as the door went *click...boom!*...I
need him. *I need him.* I knew he was a guy to get me where I
wanted to go. And he knew. He asked me ahead of time. And
I told him no. But he knew. He knew what I knew."

Maybe the hard truth was that Mena also needed and
wanted what Gable was giving him, what he couldn't do himself. Or maybe Gable was pushing where no one should push.
Davis believed the former. "He's not a blood relative, but it's
another type of relationship, one of respect," Davis stated.
"He *cares* so much. That's what it is. You will do anything for
someone like that."

Zalesky and Gable, one on each side, led Mena to the
scale. Mena had stripped down and showered, and now he got
on. Gable watched the flashing red digits and ticked off the

amount Mena still needed to lose: "Two-point-one now. One-point-eight. Keep working." Gable sent Brands to get more sweats, and Mena piled them on. He looked like the Michelin Man. Now he boarded the bike. From a few feet away, outside the plastic curtain, Gable could be seen gripping Mena on either side of his neck, shaking him, talking to him in urgent, strident tones.

Once more, Mena marched to the scale. Once more, he stripped. Once more, he got on. He weighed . . . 127.1. Back in, the sauna this time. Back out. Strip. Back on . . . 125.8. Success.

"All right," Gable said to the assistant trainer, Jerod Gayer, who had been watching the drama and keeping track of time. "Get him over there," meaning to the weigh-in. By this time, Mena had pulled on dry sweatclothes and a black stocking cap and, in a sort of stupor, shambled away from the Iowa coaches and trainer.

He didn't get far.

"Get him!" Gable called out, in a tone of voice Davis probably heard after Gable had spotted him at the grocery. "Don't let him take a drink!" Gayer, a lean, soft-spoken senior, hurried after Mena, Gable's voice like the wind at his back. "Watch him! Get Tom to help!"

Water weight, as well as time, was the enemy.

The posse rounded up Mena. Gable looked him over. "Let's clean him up a little before the medical," the coach said. He explained later, "They disqualify you if you look too bad. But Mena looked pretty good."

Gable quickly dressed. "I feel good!" he declared. "The old man's got it yet! What this takes out of me, I couldn't do a month ago. Too sick. I would have cracked.

"Mena cracked. He didn't get a sweat going after he dropped to two pounds over. Mena ate too much when we were off. He had too much food clogging him, and it was hard to get a sweat going."

The Big Ten championships wouldn't start until the next day, but already Gable had won an important victory. "That was big, huge," he claimed. "That could mean the title—and not just the Big Ten."

Gable and his coaches and trainers loaded Mena into the van for the short trip to the weigh-in at Williams Arena. They asked how he felt, and he nodded. The only sounds he had made in the last hour were slurred protestations lost in the steady drum of his coaches' voices. As Mena was making weight, Gable hurried toward the press conference. Later, at the hotel a few blocks away, Gable held a team meeting. Royce Alger asked him how he managed to push Mena so hard so fast to get him down. Before he could answer, Alger said, "Only you coulda gotten him to lose. Gotten into his head like that."

Gable smiled, feeling better all the time. "Yeah? I even forgot what I did." He turned to Zalesky, who was standing with Brands. "How'd I do it?"

"Well, you kind of took him around the neck," Zalesky said.

"Yeah," Brands broke in. "This big ol' bicep just shot out there. Think Mena didn't see *that*? Every time he looked like he was going to quit, you'd squeeze."

Later, after the meeting, Mena was wandering down the hotel corridor. Gable stood at the door to his suite. Kathy and the girls were gone. He motioned to Mena. "Come in here," Gable said. "We gotta talk." The breaking down was past. It was time to build up again.

Williams Arena, with its raised floor, posed problems to coaches no matter what their sport. For basketball coaches, was it better to sit on the bench with the team and watch the game at sneaker level? Or stand and hear irate fans complain that they couldn't see? University of Minnesota men's basketball coach Clem Haskins chose to sit on a milking stool on the sidelines; the solution probably seemed natural to a Kentucky gentleman farmer like Haskins.

For most of the two-day tournament, Gable chose to sit with his team at one end of the arena rather than to attempt to navigate on crutches across an elevated floor already crowded with wrestling mats. Zalesky and Brands went to coach the individual matches and reported back to Gable.

The second-ranked Hawkeyes seemed to have shaken off

the Oklahoma State loss and Iowa State scare. After Saturday's first two rounds, Iowa led the meet with 136.5 points, followed by third-ranked Minnesota (121.5), fourth-ranked Illinois (111), and fifth-ranked Penn State (86.5)—all teams that the Hawkeyes had beaten during the dual season. Four Iowa wrestlers—Lincoln McIlravy, returning after a seven-week absence; Mark Ironside; Williams; and Mena—scored bonus points in all their matches and sailed into Sunday's finals. Nine Hawkeyes—all except Wes Hand at heavyweight—clinched NCAA berths.

McIlravy, saying his headaches were gone but mostly holding himself away from reporters who asked, easily handled two opponents by a combined score of 36–10. First he peppered Michigan State's Adam Elderkin with eight takedowns and rolled up a 22–6 match-termination victory in 4:35. Then as relentless and methodical as always, he posted a 14–4 major decision over Minnesota's Chad Kraft. After his 4–3 victory over Kraft in the National Duals, McIlravy had to take time off because of headaches. He hadn't changed his mind about Kraft. "The kid still is a headhunter," McIlravy stated, but added there was "nothing personal" when he wrestled him. As Gable predicted, McIlravy had kept himself honed for competition, even as he sat out. "I feel good. The conditioning is there," McIlravy said.

Mena didn't look like someone who had barely survived his battle with the scale. He began strong, swamping Jason Hayes of Purdue, 10–2. Gable clapped Mena on the back and then pointed to one of the mats, where Micah Hey of Northwestern—only 7–14 for the season—was handling Robbie Archer (21–12) of Ohio State. "That's who you got next," Gable said, meaning Hey. "He's upset two guys to get to you." Mena nodded and grunted but said nothing. Then Mena destroyed Hey, 22–8, and earned a finals berth opposite Wisconsin's Eric Jetton, who had handed Mena one of his four losses.

Williams and Ironside coasted and boosted their records to 24–0. With his two pins and a technical fall, Ironside picked up five bonus points for Iowa.

But the Hawkeye wrestler who brought the crowd to its

feet, and Gable out of the stands, was Mike Uker. Uker (12–9), seeded fifth, was involved in a tight second-round match with Minnesota's Zac Taylor (18–5), who was seeded fourth. In a wild, high-scoring match, Uker was penalized a point for what appeared to be an illegal hold but which Gable later said was roughing. Gable sat on the other side of the arena from the action, but he saw enough to rage at the official.

"Bullshit!" Gable yelled. "No way! No way was that a dangerous hold! I can't let that go!" He had loudly objected to other calls in the match, but this one jerked him to his feet. "Give me those crutches," he commanded Williams, who was sitting next to Gable with the crutches at his feet. The Iowa coach—forty-four days after hip-replacement surgery—climbed down four steps, more under his own power than with the help of his black-handled crutches. Jessie Whitmer, on the other side of Williams, began cackling at the sight of his coach heaving himself onto the raised floor and then skipping along, putting down his crutches every six or eight steps, and turning toward the Uker match and yelling and skipping again. The small crowd—2,949 in a venue that could hold more than 17,000—came to life. When Gable reached the Uker-Taylor mat, the principals were wrestling several feet away, with their backs turned. Uker led, 10–9, with 2:37 of riding time, so actually the score was 11–9. Gable leaned on his crutches for a brief time at the edge of the mat and then began pounding them into the mat, once, twice, three times, in rapid succession. The sound carried to the Iowa section across the floor. Gable and the referee exchanged words, and then Gable found a seat nearby in the stands. It was Gable's most visible display of temper at a match since the Midlands, where he objected when a referee warned Ironside about pushing an opponent when the two were out of bounds. (In a team meeting, Gable warned that the referee "had it in for Iowa wrestlers," and said he had asked Midlands officials to assign someone else to Iowa matches.)

But Gable's actions at the Midlands were mild compared with his outburst at the Big Tens. This sort of conduct by any other coach might have precipitated loss of a team point or other penalty. Through the season, it was not uncommon for officials to hand out team penalty points if, say, a wrestler threw his headgear or engaged in other blatant exhibitions of bad sportsmanship. But this was Dan Gable, in the final month of perhaps his final season, so there was no penalty—he suffered only slight damage to his crutch for his tirade. Uker—who ultimately won 15–13, avenging two previous losses to Taylor—knew only that there was a commotion before he turned around to see what it was.

"I heard this banging," Uker said. "He was going *bang! bang!* with his crutches. I haven't seen him that fired up in a long time. It sounded like the clash of the titans back there."

Robinson allowed events to unfold without intervening. He sat and watched, but he was not pleased. "That's all show-boat stuff," said Gable's former assistant, who was chosen as the Big Ten Wrestling Coach of the Year after the tournament. "Why does he do it? If he wants to coach, then sit and coach. It was grandstand. Kind of bush."

Back in his seat, Gable explained his motives to the incredulous. "He cost us five points—no, six—that referee did," Gable said. He was going hoarse. "He called a front suplex illegal. That's not illegal. The back suplex is. Six points. Six *points!* C'mon."

But that was just the beginning of Gable's irritation during the second round. Wes Hand (16–6), a redshirt freshman competing in his first Big Ten tournament, led Illinois's Seth Brady (19–5) 3–2 late in their match. Brady, seeded third, had beaten Hand, seeded sixth, 5–3 in a dual. Now, Hand appeared to fall victim to another stinger, and he took his third injury time-out. Gable immediately dispatched Brands to Hand's corner, with the caveat that the Iowa heavyweight would be disqualified after a fourth time-out.

For the final thirty seconds, Hand tried to hold off Brady without initiating offense of his own. Gable read his thoughts: "If he thinks he can win by stalling, he's crazy." He yelled at his wrestler, "Wes, you shoot! Wes, you shoot! Wes, you shoot!"

The two fell to the mat, scrambling. Hand began to roll over. Kasey Gilliss, unbeaten in two matches in the tournament, sat with Gable and caught the fever. "No, Wes, No!" Gilliss shouted. But Hand couldn't hear, and probably couldn't have stopped Brady's reversal in the last five seconds even if he had. Hand's 4–3 defeat was one of only eight defeats for the Hawkeyes in thirty-one first-day matches. "I had a mental lapse, and I lost an easy match," Hand said. "I let up."

Hand made no eye contact with his teammates when he returned to the Iowa section. Gable called him over. "After you scored, you had thirty seconds left, you started looking at the clock," Gable said. "You can't. You've got to stay mentally tough. You missed a takedown." Hand had ruddy cheeks naturally, but now the rest of his face was flushed from seven hard minutes of wrestling. "Cool down. Eat something," Gable told him. Gable turned to Payne, standing next to Hand. Either she or Gayer was always present, sitting matside, when a Hawkeye wrestled, ready to step in when an injury occurred. Hand's stinger issue was facing them again, and Payne had to know that Gable wouldn't let it rest.

"We have to talk about his care in the offseason," Gable said. "I have to do a better job." Payne nodded. Sending Hand off with a slap on the butt, Gable finished with Payne. "Mentally, he can't shoot hard, knowing he might get a stinger."

An hour later, Hand met Michigan State's Jason Peterson (11–11), who had lost badly to top-seeded Kerry McCoy of Penn State. This time, Hand came out more aggressively, although remnants of the stinger remained. "I felt a twinge in my left arm," he said later. "Initially, I didn't have any power." Hand's double-leg takedown in the second period gave him a 3–0 lead. "He made a move," Gable said derisively and to no one in particular. "Can you believe it? He made a move and he scored." With thirty seconds left, Hand stole a look at the clock, causing Gable to grump, "That's what killed him the last time." But Hand won convincingly, 7–3, setting up his evening match in the consolation bracket against Minnesota's Shelton Benjamin, whom Hand had beaten twice during the regular season. Hand was still alive for a top-six qualifying spot, but a second defeat before the consolation final would have dashed his chances for an automatic NCAA berth.

In a break between sessions, a dozen reporters encircled Gable, asking about his gallop on one good hip. "I've got my energy back, my spunk," he told them. "That's important. [If] we get beat, we get beat, but I won't take it lying down." It was mentioned that he had traveled some of the time without use of his crutches. "Did I? Instinct must have taken over. Dr. Marsh will not be a happy man."

Before the second round, Gable confided to Payne, "I better take it easy the rest of the time. I don't want to make any more enemies." So the Iowa coach stayed with his team, giving advice to his wrestlers and his assistants, and discussing the meet with members of his family when they visited from their section.

Gilliss, who started his five-match winning streak by up-setting Minnesota's Jason Davids in Iowa City, was preparing to meet him again. "Don't 'throw' if it's not there," said Gable to his big-move devotee. "Get the guy tired first. You're too big and strong for him." Not this time. Davids beat him in the 142-pound semifinals, 7–2, while in the 190-pound semifinals another Minnesota wrestler, Tim Hartung, seeded second, took out Fullhart, seeded third, 7–1. Fullhart fired his headgear across the mat, as he was wont to do.

"That's embarrassing. What's the matter with Fullhart?" Gable asked Brands, fearing a team point would be subtracted. Gable answered his own question: "Psychologically, Fullhart broke."

Another concern distracted Gable. Hand was locked in a tight match with Benjamin, who had accidentally slapped Hand's neck and caused another stinger. Injury timeout. Gable nearly went back on his vow to Payne by rushing over to his wrestler.

"There's nothing wrong with his neck," Gable said. "God, we got to get him a new neck."

Hand said before the match that he had not had a stinger in two weeks, but now his good fortune had ended.

Another stalling call against Hand. Benjamin led, 3–2.

"He quit! He quit!" Gable yelled of his own wrestler.

Four times, Gable repeated, "Shoot the move, Hand!" Finally, Hand did. His takedown with twenty-five seconds left gave him a 4–3 lead. Hand rubbed his left shoulder, attempting to soothe the stinger, but kept wrestling. Then, confident he could score another takedown, Hand let Benjamin escape. Benjamin, however, held him off, and the match went into overtime, tied 4–4. Hand pressed the attack, but Benjamin got control and began to topple him.

"He's beat! He's beat! Hand is beat!" Gable called out. Benjamin finished the takedown for a 6–4 victory.

Gable, unable to sit and watch, pushed off on his crutches to the floor, but didn't leave the Iowa area. "The mentality, the mentality," he muttered. He cornered Zalesky. The subject now was Fullhart, who had fallen behind Hartung, 6–0, before losing. "Fullhart told me he quit. Just *quit*," Gable ranted. "Too many times our 190-pounder and our heavyweight haven't come to practice, or can't practice, and it shows up here. No mental toughness!"

Gable had spent most of his life ignoring his own pain. It was simple: You didn't break, you overcame. Like many coaches, he considered today's athletes soft compared with his day. The courage and commitment it took to be a Division I wrestler, Gable thought, winnowed the list of potentials. Fullhart and Hand hadn't done much to change his mind.

"These guys got to be at practice," Gable told Payne. "They've got to compete. Understand what I mean?"

Kathy Gable appeared by Gable's side after Hand's and Fullhart's losses. In speeches during the spring and summer to come, Gable would repeat the conversation he had with his wife, and the audience would roar. What was the matter with Iowa? she wondered.

"What do you want me to do?" Gable said.

"Try winning some matches," she replied.

In truth, there was nothing the matter with Iowa. The Hawkeyes rolled into Sunday's finals and consolations with a fifteen-point lead over Minnesota—and four finalists to the Gophers' two. But Minnesota had enough numerical leverage in the consolations to worry Gable, and it did little for his peace of mind when two people from the Iowa athletic department—Phil Haddy, from sports information, and Les Steenlage, from Bob Bowlsby's office—informed him separately before the matches that because of a computer error, the team points might be closer than announced. Nobody knew how much closer.

"Fine time to tell me," Gable snorted. Later he told Steenlage, "It doesn't matter. It's all in our hands in matches like this."

Iowa split in the finals, with McIlravy and Ironside winning, and Mena and Williams losing. After McIlravy had completed his annihilation of the 150-pound class with a nine-takedown, 19–7 romp over Bill Lacure of Michigan State, the Hawkeyes were on their way to their twenty-first Big Ten title under Gable. Halfway through the weights, they had outscored Minnesota, 60–41, and they would win the title with 140.5 points to Minnesota's 116.5 and third-place Illinois's 105.5. It hardly mattered by the time Steenlage told Gable that the computer error wouldn't make much difference in the team scores after all—"and not hurt anybody who was ahead."

Ken McIlravy watched intently as his son plowed through three opponents and scored bonus points in each match. The father seemed relieved to be talking about wrestling and not headaches. "Lincoln's probably at eighty-five percent," he said. "He could be in better condition. I thought he was a hair sluggish."

Ironside also rang up bonus points through the finals, where he beat second-seeded Jeff Bucher of Ohio State, 18–5. Bucher, reeling and wilting under Ironside's pressure, took two injury time-outs and twice was called for stalling. "I hate stalling," Ironside spat. "It takes away what you're supposed to do —go hard. That pisses me off. I want to bury them." As Uker raised the first-place team trophy over his head after the matches, the announcement was made that Ironside had been the media's choice for Big Ten Wrestler of the Year for the second straight year. An Iowa wrestler had won or shared the award in nine of the eleven years it had been given. Gable, smiling, glanced at Ironside. "All he eats is roadkill," the coach said.

Like Whitmer and Gillis, both fourth, Mena didn't wrestle up to his seeding. He groped for offense in the 126-pound final, but couldn't find it, and lost 2–0 to Wisconsin's third-seeded Eric Jetton. When Mena chose the down position in the second period, Jetton wore him down with a leg lock and scored a point of riding time.

Gable took Mena aside after his loss. "You can't let an opponent have an ankle like that," he said. "You've got to get out from under." Mena had survived a numbing siege of weight cutting only to wear Jetton like a suit on his back. Mena stared straight ahead, never blinking, never speaking.

Joe Williams had beaten Illinois's Ernest Benion five times without a loss in college—last year's NCAA championship match included—but this time Benion pulled off a 2–1 victory in double overtime. They had so much respect for each other that neither took a chance with a daring offensive move. All points were scored defensively, on escapes. Benion chose the down position in the final overtime and escaped with eighteen seconds left in the thirty-second period, ending Williams's two-season fifty three match winning streak. Gable anticipated trouble, having properly "read" Williams before the match: What he read said that Williams had little enthusiasm to wrestle someone he had competed against so often. But that was no excuse. Gable let Williams catch his breath and then approached him. "You've wrestled him so much maybe you're tired of it, but you should never get tired of winning," Gable said. "You've got to move more. You didn't do anything in the two-minute overtime." Williams, stone-faced, didn't answer. "Maybe you can win wrestling that way," Gable continued, "but that leaves it up to the referee's calls, and you can't count on that."

Earlier, Hand sat in front of Gable, who massaged his

neck and talked to the wrestler's parents. Gable thought that if Hand could win the match for seventh place over Purdue's David Pierce (14–9), the Iowa heavyweight would be dealt a wild-card for the the NCAA tournament. "He [Hand] can beat this guy," Gable told the parents. "He hasn't met him, but it doesn't matter. Of the bouts today, this is a big one."

Hand hung on for a 6–4 victory and, as Gable predicted, received an NCAA berth. Sulking, Hand gathered his belongings. "I'm not pleased with anything. It hasn't been my weekend. I want to get the heck out of here."

Whitmer, seeded second, did not have a good tournament either. Several times he had come to the sidelines after matches, choking back tears and anger, with a cowlick rising roosterlike from the back of his head. His power had become his curse. It would produce an early lead, but would ebb through the match until he lost. Whitmer opened with a 20–4 technical-fall victory over Indiana's Derek Moscovic in 6:22, but in two matches he threw away leads in the last thirteen seconds and lost. Third-seeded Lindsey Durlacher of Illinois rallied to drop Whitmer out of the winner's bracket with a 5–4 semifinal victory, avenging two earlier defeats. Whitmer beat Purdue's Tim Demlan 6–1 to earn a spot in Sunday's 118-pound third-place match against sixth-seeded Jeremy Hunter of Penn State. There, again, Whitmer led until the last, when he tired and faltered, giving up a reversal to lose 9–8. Gable sat with Brands and despaired. "The same darn thing," Gable moaned when he saw Whitmer hanging on Hunter. "Unbelievable. Like a nightmare. Stalling again. Not aggressive."

"Same exact thing he did against Durlacher," Brands said. "Same exact thing."

Whitmer made the long walk back to his teammates. And Gable. "Got to score in the third period, Jess," Gable said. "Might have cost you a seeding place, we'll see. You should've killed him."

"I'm not happy at all," Whitmer said, packing away his gear. "Iowa wrestlers are expected to get first. They don't want less than first. I just shut down too early. I do great things in the first couple of periods, but then . . ."

Gilliss, seeded third at 142, placed fourth after a 4–2 loss to fourth-seeded Clint Musser of Penn State. He won three of five matches, picking up a bloody lip on his first day for his efforts. But he was a freshman, like Hand, and Gable noted that that should be taken into account.

During Whitmer's and Gilliss's third-place matches against Penn State opponents, Gable became enraged by a fan sitting across the aisle from him in a cluster of Penn State partisans, including wrestlers. The fan apparently was a student, dressed in a flannel shirt and jeans. During Whitmer's match, the fan yelled loudly for Penn State's Hunter. Gable turned toward the booming voice and shouted the vilest insult he could think of: "Nikita Khrushchev!" As a young wrestler, Gable had cut out magazine photographs of great Russian amateur wrestlers, but he admired them only for their abilities, not for their politics. Gable fired again: "Communism!" Later, as Gilliss bobbed and weaved and searched for an opening against Penn State's Musser, the fan sang out, "Hey! Green's stalling! Green's stalling!," referring to Gilliss's green ankle bands. Gable looked across the aisle: "Shut up!" The fan didn't act as if he had heard. Gable nudged Alger. "I may have to send someone over there." Alger, in training for an ultimate-boxing contest, didn't need to hear more. "I'll go," he said. "I haven't been pissed off in a while." But the mood blew over. There was a championship to win.

Uker completed his turnaround from losing a major decision at Iowa State. Seeded fifth in the conference meet, he won four of five matches, helped derail Minnesota's chances on the first day, and finished third. He pinned Purdue's sixth-seeded Davion Peterson in the consolation semifinals and scored two major decisions, the last one in the 167-pound third-place match, where he again defeated Minnesota's Zac Taylor, 14–6. This time, Gable didn't fly from the stands brandishing his crutches. He didn't have to: Uker was in control all the way. "After Iowa State, I was sick—weak and sick," said Uker, receiving a hug from his twelve-year-old sister, Hannah. "I went to the wrestling room on red-flag days and drilled and took saunas, and then Gable gave me a mental break, and I started feeling better. Now I feel strong, in my body and mind."

Tony Ersland, unseeded, finished sixth at 177, while Lee Fullhart took third at 190. Gable gave the whole meet a mixed review. His team had won, but several wrestlers—namely, Whitmer, Fullhart, and Hand—lost tight matches. Williams slept through his final. Mena might as well have. "I'm worried," Gable declared. "I think we have to be ten, twelve days better than we are right now. Not so much physical, but mentally. This performance just will not cut it in the NCAAs."

Gable, like many another coach, has blown his share of smoke and worn a worried look while his insides were chortling. But his anxiety seemed well placed, and it was shared by the team. As the Hawkeyes gathered on the floor of Williams Arena for the winning-team picture, the photographer poked his nose out from behind the lens.

"Hey, can't you guys look happy?" he prodded the Hawkeyes. "You *won* again."

chapter 13

NIKITA KHRUSHCHEV didn't impose state rule as swiftly and surely as Gable did after the Big Ten championships. Originally, he planned to ride home with Kathy. But after what he had seen for two days in Minneapolis, he vowed to take the bus back with the team. "Don't have time to take five or six hours off," he said. "Try to help these guys get turned around a little bit. Got to make certain decisions, and you can't just think and hope things happen. There's got to be something done between now and then." The NCAA championships would begin in eleven days in Cedar Falls, and Gable knew well from the team's nose dive a decade earlier what could happen in the wake of inattentiveness and overconfidence.

Before the 1986–87 season, Gable had 10,000 small buttons made with a large yellow roman-numeral "X" on a black background and also branded Iowa singlets with an X to signify that the Iowa wrestling team stood ready, willing, and able to capture its tenth consecutive Division I wrestling title, which at the time would have set an intercollegiate record. In 1982, Gable had recruited what wrestling experts called the best freshman class in the country. Two of them, Rico Chiapparelli and Jim Heffernan, took redshirt years and were seniors on the 1987 team. Gable's 1987 team finished seventh in the Mid-lands, was beaten soundly by Iowa State and Penn State in duals, but defeated Oklahoma and Oklahoma State. Wrecked by injuries and the attitudes of a few of its wrestlers, Iowa finished second to Iowa State in the NCAA meet at the University of Maryland. The Hawkeyes had two national champions, Royce Alger and Chiapparelli; Iowa State had four. But the streak had ended.

For the decade he had been Iowa coach, Gable showed up for work after the national championships, recruiting and catching up on paperwork. Vacations were what losers took. But before the 1987 tournament, Gable decided to plan a Hawaiian vacation with his family, to celebrate the anticipated breaking of the NCAA record. What was supposed to be a celebration, however, turned into a wake capped by an epiphany.

"I was one miserable S.O.B.," Gable said. "I hadn't lost in ten years! And my wife was miserable, too, for a little bit, but she got over it. So after about the second full day on Maui, I'm still working my butt off, taking notes and stuff and being ornery.

"My wife read me the riot act for about a half hour. And it made me think a little bit. And all of a sudden, instead of just moping around, bitching and moaning and not having a good time, I said, 'I'm going to have a good time. But I'm going to turn my study time around toward how I can change things from a positive point of view. What needs to be done in the program. I'm going to do some analyzing and evaluating instead of just complaining.' "

Gable decided that a change was needed, a reordering of priorities; less time playing and more time working, more control of a program whirling out of control. The talent ran deep on the 1987 team, but often natural skills were not nurtured by practice. Several wrestlers wound up in court for public drunkenness and disorderly conduct. One reason Gable had lasted two decades in the bureaucracy of a state university was that he could anticipate brush fires and extinguish them. This one, though, was turning into an four-alarm blaze. The fault belonged to all, not just the class of '82 who were seniors in '87; Gable accepted blame for not keeping closer watch. This dereliction of duty gnawed at him, and became a cautionary tale he related to audiences in the offseason. "After we'd won three or four [NCAA titles] in a row, I'd go to work, and I wasn't observant," he related during a paid speech after the 1996–97 season. "I got to work and it was like I had champagne in my desk and I was ready to celebrate. Things on the team I needed to clean up, I didn't. Why? We won. I was old-time. I didn't change my ways. Then I thought, bull. If there's a better way I better find it.

"Some guys would be in bars at eleven-thirty at night, and I cleaned that up. I'd go in the front door, and they'd have somebody stationed there, and they'd say, 'Gable's here,' and they went out the back door."

Gable called it the New Era. Wrestling posters came out before the 1988 season showing Gable wearing a professor's robe and carrying books and a chalk board, and three of his wrestlers standing with him in suits. A garbage can held old newspapers with headlines of past troubles visible. "NEW ERA" was in bold lettering. One of the wrestlers on the poster, Brad Penrith, typified the problems Gable was having with what he called the "old school."

Penrith won the NCAA's 126-pound title in 1986 as a redshirt sophomore. He came from a broken home in Windsor, New York, the son of an alcoholic father and a mother who supported them with custodial work. He received $200 for books to walk-on at Iowa. Penrith wanted to be one of the boys, and many of the boys drank, so he drank. "I didn't want to go out and have a couple—why go out and have a only a couple?" he remembered. "I wouldn't get an effect off just two. What was the point? I'd get out of the bar at twelve-thirty, go party and get in at two, and go work out in the morning." In the spring of 1986, Penrith was arrested for drunk driving, put on probation, and fined. The university placed him on academic probation, and Gable had long talks with him. "I laughed it off," Penrith said. "They were picking on me. I'm twenty, twenty-one years old, I can't have a drinking problem." He finished second in the 1987 NCAA tournament in Maryland. That summer, he made the papers again when he was involved in a bar fight. Gable, under administrative pressure to drop Penrith, convinced his wrestler to enter a twenty-six-day in-patient treatment program at a center in Waterloo. Gable called and visited, and brought him back after twenty-six days to a gathering at the Gables' house. Penrith—black-haired, with a brisk efficiency about him—finished second again in the 1988 NCAA tournament as a senior and graduated, after Gable told him to pick up the two hours he needed, with a liberal-arts degree the next year. Penrith won a gold medal in the 1991 Pan-American Games and a silver the same year in the World Championships. After that, he became an assistant coach at Nebraska. He also stopped drinking on June 23, 1987. "I owe Gable a lot, for giving me a chance," he said. "Sometimes coaches get bit in the rear when they stick their neck out like that. I'm glad I didn't do something foolish that would bite him."

The conversion from old school to New Era took a while to run through the pipeline. "What happened was, the recruits of eighty-three took on the work ethic of the recruits of eighty-two," Gable said. "But eighty-three wasn't as good as the recruiting class before it. They worked as hard as eighty-two, because those guys were winning. Eighty-four worked as hard as eighty-three and eighty-two. But the trouble was that the eighty-two class didn't have as good a work ethic as eighty-one, eighty, seventy-nine. So we were starting to get worse as early as eighty-three."

Then came the 1989 national tournament, Gable's low point in coaching. The Hawkeyes had lost duals to Penn State and Michigan, but finished the season with a flourish, earning victories over powerhouses Oklahoma State, Arizona State, and Iowa State. In the Big Ten championships, however, the winning Hawkeyes had only one champion, Tom Brands. It bore faint resemblance to the 1983 team that crowned nine champions. In the NCAAs, seven Hawkeyes advanced to the quarterfinals on Friday, but one after another they began losing. Gable still calls it Black Friday. No Iowa wrestler made it to the finals. Only four made All-America, none above 158, and the highest individual finish was fourth. The team finished sixth, when previously the worst any Gable team had placed was third. Worse still for the Hawkeyes, the championships were hosted by Oklahoma and Oklahoma State, and won by Oklahoma State.

Gable watched the finals as a spectator, with friends. It was a new experience, not having a wrestler in the finals. No one was happy. "They looked at me, and I looked at them, and they said, 'This can never happen again. We'll help you out. Get a game plan.' But I'd already started rehabilitating the team and the program. We had a huge bad day. But I'd been a head coach for thirteen years, and a bad day every thirteen years isn't too bad."

To make sure there wouldn't be another huge bad day, in Cedar Falls in 1997, Gable and his staff worked the team as a unit and individually. They kept close track of Mike Mena's weight; there would not be another close call this time. Jessie Whitmer would need more than just work to keep him pressing when he had an early lead; he also needed a shot of confidence after his fourth place in the Big Tens. Gable continued to point out his strength in front of the team until one of his teammates sighed, "Uh-oh. Here we go again." It was not the first time Gable had used the ploy: When Penrith and Alger roomed together, he stroked Alger. "Gable goes, 'Royce Alger is the toughest man pound-for-pound on this campus,'" Penrith recalled. "The very next day I go into the office, and I see Gable, and I start laughing. I go, 'Ha! Ha! I remember what you said about your boy.' And he goes, 'My boy? He's your boy! He's your roommate.' And I said, 'No, he's your boy.' We went back and forth, must have been ten times. Then finally he goes, 'You don't understand. I had to say that. That's how I motivate Royce.' Royce was the greatest. Royce was the best. And Royce believed him."

But to snap Fullhart out of his funk, Gable needed help. For an hour on the bus returning from the Big Ten meet, Gable huddled with his 190 pounder, framing his 7–1 defeat to

Hartung as symptomatic of a larger problem. Gable told Full-hart that he had allowed his opponent to dictate the match: "You took a back seat," Gable said; Fullhart mumbled something back, and the two, in Gable's words, "kept babbling to each other." The conversation continued when Gable, on his way home from dropping off Fullhart at his apartment, called him from his car phone at 2:30 in the morning. Then they resumed their discussion the next day in the sauna. Mena overheard and took Fullhart aside, bringing Gable's message through another door. Said Gable later, "Mena told him he wasn't working hard enough in a match—which was the same thing I was telling Fullhart, but this way, he could keep his pride. Mena taught me a lesson in coaching, that you've sometimes got to change around what you're saying to fit the athlete. The mind is so important. People think wrestling is all physical, but everything—the physical stuff, the tactical stuff—comes after you get to the mind."

Initially, Gable plotted a series of tough two-a-days to prime the team for the national tournament. One week before weigh-ins, he scheduled two half-hour individual sessions on each of two days, and one on the third day heading into a weekend of rest. Gable and his two assistants each watched a mat as the wrestlers dragged themselves through the first day, lifeless. Gable arose the next morning feeling weary; he admitted to himself that if he felt this bad, his wrestlers—under pressure to make weight and win nothing less than a national title—probably felt worse. So he called Zalesky and Brands with a radical new plan: All workouts were cancelled in favor of easy sweats and rubdowns. First thing Thursday morning, just one week before the tournament, Gable encountered Ironside—top-ranked, unbeaten, a glittering star who had scored bonus points in 23 of 25 matches—in the wrestling room, sweating and relaxing with a sheet wrapped around him.

"Well, whatdya think?" the coach asked.

"Coach," Ironside said, "I'm really glad you canceled practice. You know, you made the right decision."

Later, Gable would say, "It was a huge relief to me. If a leader like Ironside says that, you feel good."

Gable even dabbled in group psychology. He wanted his wrestlers to believe that everyone—or at least everyone in Oklahoma—was laughing off their chances. Ostensibly, it would be a hard sell; Iowa had been ranked No. 1 through the first half of the season, had lost only one dual, and had three top-ranked wrestlers (Mark Ironside, Lincoln McIlravy and Joe Williams), one of whom had won two national titles (McIlravy) and another who was a defending champion (Williams). Also, the tournament would be held about an hour-and-a-half from Iowa City, in the Hawkeye coach's backyard, and, finally, Iowa was going for its third straight NCAA title. Still, top-ranked Oklahoma State, the slight favorite, also had qualified all ten wrestlers in its relatively small conference tournament; two of them—Mark Branch at 167 and Mark Smith at 177— were top rated, and Branch had won an NCAA title and twice was runner-up.

Nevertheless, against impressive odds, Gable managed to convince his wrestlers that they were disparaged underdogs who had to prove the world wrong. He was sent ammunition from friends in Oklahoma, newspaper clippings of what the opposition was saying. He quoted the scurrilous prose at practice, particularly the remarks of Oklahoma coach Jack Spates during a Big Twelve coaches' teleconference: "Iowa's got some serious question marks. They've got a lot of holes. I think Iowa is coming back to the pack now."

Gable also paraphrased, from *Amateur Wrestling News* and with little concern for accuracy the musings of respected wrestling analyst Ron Good on the NCAA tournament. Good, the longtime editor of the magazine, wrote, "On paper, no team is within forty points of the Hawks and Cowboys. The next two teams, Iowa State and Minnesota, have similar strengths, yet Minnesota is long on balance while the Cyclones have excellent individual strength." Iowa wrestlers were told that Oklahoma State *alone* was given a forty-point edge on the field, including the Hawkeyes. Later, Good said he heard that Ironside also had a hand in Gable's translation. "It's a ridiculous statement, that Oklahoma State was forty points better than Iowa going in," Good said. "Iowa used it for fuel. We got a lot of publicity. Whether that's good or bad, I don't know."

Publicly and to the media, Gable tended to talk about the NCAA tournament in terms of the team race, but all season he had been gauging individuals in his lineup against what he wanted to see from each in Cedar Falls. Two months before the tournament, around the time of the National Duals, Gable had determined who on his team could hold up under three tough days of wrestling and win his weight. "We can win at eighteen [Whitmer]," Gable told a friend after practice. "And twenty-six [Mena], thirty-four [Ironside], fifty [McIlravy], fifty-eight [Williams], and ninety [Fullhart]. Five of the first six. But I can't tell my team that. I don't want forty-two [Gilliss] to think he can't win. And I still want ten championships." (Gable has had as many as five champions, in 1986, when the Hawkeyes scored an NCAA record 158 points and won by the widest margin in NCAA history, 73.25 points.)

This team, however, was different in many respects from that of 1986's. It had four newcomers in the lineup, two freshmen (Kasey Gilliss and Wes Hand) and two seniors (Whitmer and Tony Ersland). It had been wildly inconsistent failing to keep the dual-match winning streak alive but increasing its nine-year winning streak at Carver-Hawkeye to forty-five matches. There was not one time all season when Gable felt everyone had wrestled well. The four new starters were up and down, and even Williams had now lost to an opponent he had regularly beaten.

Unlike any other team in Gable's twenty-one years, this group had to bear up under stresses that rode with them to Lake Okoboji in November and hadn't left. The coach himself was injured and had missed practices and meets. For two years, he had delayed his decision about quitting, and now, finally, there was no more cushion. His left hip had seen to that. Rarely did he mention his situation to the team, except offhandedly. "Well," he said, hunkered over his crutches at practice, "some

guy from the media today was asking me about what I was
going to do, so it's another distraction, but we can't let stuff
like that get in our way."

Gable told everyone—friends, media, countrymen—that
he would announce his decision after the season ended. But
the speculation wouldn't and couldn't end there. He was returning to his hometown, the national title and his coaching
career in the balance. Pink call-back slips from reporters
gathered dust. But Gable couldn't escape. On the final day
of the Big Ten meet, a six- or seven-year-old blond boy
sheepishly handed Gable a slip of paper and ran away. Gable
opened it:

> Mr. Gable,
> Please stay at Iowa. I'm coming in 2008.

Gable folded the paper and tucked it into his wallet and
said nothing. People, he said, were pushing from both sides.
His family was nearly unanimous: *Get out.* Only Mackie
wanted him to stay, because of her affection for Lee Fullhart
and Ironside. Bob Bowlsby, the AD, wanted Gable to stay
in some capacity and coach. They were not warring factions,
Bowlsby and Kathy Gable, only competing parties. Gable's
delay complicated recruiting; he had to know that coaches
would be doing what was called "negative recruiting," telling
prospects that Gable was on his way out, so why consider
Iowa? Gable told recruits that he would be around the program
no matter what and that Iowa wrestling was bigger than a
single coach.

He felt pressure from fans who wanted him to stay and
keep Iowa winning, but he knew he also had obligations to his
family and to himself. "This one guy said, 'If you lose, you
can't quit—not if John Smith wins it,'" Gable allowed one
night after practice, heading toward the parking lot. "Well,
what difference does that make? It's all about competition.
How you do when you have to do it, not about quitting. That's
what it's about." Gable would make up his own mind in his
own time. He would not be pressured, and he could not be

predicted. "Nobody knows me," he had said the year before, over a lunch of sandwich and chips at his desk. "If anybody knows me, it's my wife, and she doesn't know me."

The coaching situation took on a life of its own. Marc Hansen, a news and sports columnist for the *Des Moines Register*, was visiting Gable in Iowa City, taking notes for a four-part front-page series on the Iowa coach to run during NCAA tournament week. In the wrestling room, Hansen began talking with Tom Brands, who divulged that at age twenty-eight he was leaving behind his wrestling career to concentrate on coaching. Like Gable, he had been a world and Olympic champion, and now he was a candidate for Gable's job. The *Register* bannered the story on its front news page.

But any such speculation would keep. More immediately, Brands had three days in Cedar Falls to worry about.

It had been an unusually hard winter across Iowa. Snow had accumulated in amounts not seen in nearly two decades. But as March wore on, the snow melted and the rich, dark soil surfaced and surrendered its fragrance to the spring winds. In Cedar Falls and neighboring Waterloo, the combined citizenry of 100,000 welcomed back the NCAA Division I Wrestling Championships. The tournament, which began in 1928 in Ames, Iowa, last was held in Waterloo–Cedar Falls in 1950. The host school—Iowa State Teachers College, now the University of Northern Iowa (UNI)—won it that year, and now was playing host again, Thursday through Saturday. The sixty-seventh championships would be held on campus at the UNI-Dome. Seating 16,400, the structure looked like an open parachute that had fluttered to the flattest earth this side of North Dakota.

The Hawkeyes stayed a few miles north of Cedar Falls, in Waverly, at the Red Fox Inn. Gable liked the idea of ferrying his wrestlers in and out of the UNI-Dome and avoiding the tournament hubbub. It would be a challenge. Some hotels had been booked for two years. Hawkeye fans in their black-and-gold caps and sweaters and bib overalls would descend on the UNI-Dome and help set NCAA records for single-session attendance (a standing-room-only throng of 17,436 for Saturday night's finals) and total attendance (90,064), breaking marks set at the 1995 championships in Iowa City.

The Hawkeye delegation arrived at the Red Fox on Wednesday and settled into their second-floor digs. Gable joined other coaches for an afternoon press conference at the UNI-Dome. He had taped the crutch he damaged in the Big Ten tournament, and he seemed less effusive and upbeat than he had been at the start of the conference championships. But this was the meet that he focused on all year, the only one that mattered, the one that might be his last. Gable waded through the forty-five-minute press conference, giving little of himself, staring off as if something in another room was vying for his attention. Once there was a sound like a gunshot. "Hope nobody is trying to kill me," Gable joked with a weak smile.

The five coaches sat hunched at a long table before microphones and tape recorders, like a doo-wop group ready to record. Smith and Gable sat separated by Bobby Douglas of Iowa State and Penn State coach John Fritz. Gable, Smith, and Fritz each had ten qualifiers, which conferred instant contender status on their squads. Don Briggs, on his way out as coach of Northern Iowa, sat on the extreme left, next to Smith, and bade all welcome. "The University of Northern Iowa, as well as Cedar Falls, are just bending over backwards for this tournament," said Briggs, who had been a tough lightweight wrestler in Cedar Rapids and later at the University of Iowa. "Everywhere you go, people are talking about it." He turned over the floor to the other coaches. Fritz and Douglas installed Iowa and Oklahoma State as their favorites, and then they sat back and listened to Gable squirm.

"I think it's been a rather, uh, I don't really call it interesting, but it's been kind of a unique situation this season for me," Gable said. "I think a lot of people coming into this season felt that Iowa's pretty much the team to beat this year.

But I've also made the announcement that this is possibly my last season, and with those two things, things have kind of turned around a little bit.

"All of a sudden, we're really not the team to beat right now as far as being ranked number one and getting knocked off by Oklahoma State, and myself saying I'm not sure what my situation is right now."

Gable did not mention any of his wrestlers unless asked. Twice he was asked about McIlravy, the two-time NCAA champion with a 91–3 career record. Was he healthy and at full strength? Based on his Big Ten performance, he's ready, Gable said, and no more. But didn't his absence make a huge difference in the Iowa-Oklahoma State match at the National Duals, and won't his presence make a huge difference in the NCAAs? "Oh, it's not a dual meet," Gable said. "It's hard to say . . . There's a lot of other factors, but obviously Lincoln McIlravy is a big difference in our lineup, whether it's a dual meet or a tournament."

The smoke screen was just clearing when Smith jumped in. "As far as the tournament, he's number one," the Oklahoma State coach said of McIlravy. "Could be the best wrestler in the country. And I've got a kid [Jimmy Arias] ranked number ten. I believe that's about twenty points or so. So obviously it's a big lift getting Lincoln McIlravy back. Any time you take the stud out of your lineup, there's a possibility of it affecting the other nine. Put him back in and they come back together. One individual you wouldn't think could do that, but in some situations it will affect your team."

Nevertheless, Smith accepted the mantle of favorite and tolled the names of Cowboys wrestlers who had made a difference, including sophomores Teague Moore (118) and Eric Guerrero (126); three-time NCAA finalist Mark Branch (167), who "has been a leader ever since he stepped into our program"; and his own brother Mark Smith (177), "who I don't know if he was even ranked before the season, and currently he's number one." Although the Cowboys started four sophomores, their coach said, the team had acquired the maturity to wrestle well in big tournaments. "This is a squad that, if they wrestle well and up to their capabilities, we'll have a good opportunity to possibly win this championship," Smith asserted.

Douglas, who had taken Iowa State to second place a year ago with only five qualifiers, had nine this time around—including Chris Bono, defending champion at 150, and top-ranked Dwight Hinson at 126—and could not be ignored. Even in his mid-fifties, with white-tinged hair, Douglas moved with the assured grace of a world-class athlete. He took fourth in the 138.5-pound freestyle competiton in the 1964 Olympics, becoming the first African American to wrestle in the Games. Over the next thirty years he knocked down other color barriers: He was the first African American to coach a major-college wrestling team (the University of California–Santa Barbara, 1973), the first to take a team to the NCAA wrestling championship (Arizona State, 1988), and the first to coach an Olympic wrestling team (1992). His Iowa State team had nearly upset Iowa in Ames and finished second behind Oklahoma State in the Big Twelve tournament. No, Bobby Douglas could not be ignored.

"I'm not letting Bobby off the hook here," Smith said, shooting a smile toward Douglas. "I watched him at the Big [Twelve] Championships. Obviously, a fine team. It takes all ten to win it, and that's what we had. But he has a very talented squad, and you definitely have to include Iowa State in there. They may not have numbers, but they definitely have the quality."

Penn State, fourth in both the National Duals and the Big Ten championships, finished with a 16–4 record, but came within seven points of Iowa when the two met. Top-ranked heavyweight Kerry McCoy (36–0) had won the 1994 national championship and was a two-time All-American, but six of his teammates had lost ten or more matches. "I figure you probably have me out here to talk about the other guys and their chances," Fritz said.

Even with Brandon Paulson, the Olympian, hampered by an injured ankle, Minnesota was a consensus high finisher that some thought could possibly even prevail if the leaders sputtered. Minnesota's ten qualifers included two All-Americans from a year ago, Jason Davids (142) and Chad Kraft (150). There were no seniors in the lineup, leading Smith to aver that J Robinson would have the best team in the country returning in the fall. Later in the day, Robinson gave his team a chance to win its first national title. "It'll depend on the seeds and some luck. Who gets hot at the right time. We can't worry about the other guys. We just have to go out and dominate."

John Smith looked and felt tired. Weather-related travel delays kept the Cowboys from arriving until early morning. He had seen the size of the venue and knew the tournament had long been sold out, and he was worried. "We step onto the mat, probably eighty-five to ninety percent of the fans up there are going to be rooting for our opponent," Smith said. "But one thing about this team that I've been impressed with all year long is that they've wrestled well on the road."

Douglas reckoned that the team with seven All-Americans —seven wrestlers with top-eight finishes—would win the tournament. "We've got to have at least three in the finals— and that's providing the points are split up," he said. In winning last season, Iowa had just those numbers, seven All-Americans and three finalists, all of whom won.

Traditionally, though, the tournament trafficked in the unexpected, in favorites losing and surprises winning. Daryl Weber came from the pack in 1996 to win the 167-pound title for Iowa. And back in 1970, in Evanston, Illinois, a wrestler from Iowa State named Dan Gable, with 181 straight victories, was upset on a night he'll never forget. Smith needed no reminders. "I think the first two rounds are going to be the crucial rounds of the tournament," he said. "There's going to be some upsets, and those upsets will pretty much dictate the winner."

That night, in the lobby of the Red Fox, Iowa's wrestlers waited for the final team meeting before the tournament. McIlravy, in his Sherlock Holmes coat, whisked through with his wife, Lisa, and they started upstairs toward their room. Ken

McIlravy spotted Lisa before she reached the stairs. "Is Lincoln lying low tonight?" the father asked.

She looked quizzically at her father-in-law. "I don't know. What does that mean?"

Ken smiled. "He's lying low."

Hand, Ersland, and Gillis sat around a coffee table reading newspapers, bored. Hand didn't like his draw. He would meet eighth-seeded Jason Gleason of Syracuse in the first round. Hand, unseeded, had upset Gleason—had "Grecoed the Greco"—at the Midlands, but this was early in the national tournament to meet a 1996 Olympian. One good thing, Hand said, was that his neck didn't hurt. "And it won't. This is *the* one. It can't."

Gable ate a steak with his family and presided over the team meeting at 9:30 P.M. in Payne's room. He leaned forward on one crutch, pairings sheets in his left hand. The wrestlers were strewn on beds and on the floor, and, except for Ironside, who had on plaid pajama bottoms, wore jeans and shorts.

Gable informed his team that none of them had preliminary matches, or "rat-tails," on the first day. They would begin wrestling at 11 A.M., conclude at about 2:30, return to the motel and rest, and return for the night session. Gable went around the room, commenting on what each Iowa wrestler had to do to win. The coach didn't know about many of his wrestlers' first-round opponents, but he would investigate. He got to Gilliss, slated to begin his NCAA tournament experience by wrestling Iowa State's David Maldonado, who had won both meetings with Gilliss this season, 3–2 and 9–3. Gable jabbed his finger at the 142-pound Gilliss, who was sitting attentively on the edge of the bed. "I think it's time you kick this guy's butt," Gable averred. "I really do. That's a real important match for us. Now, the one thing that we did notice about this guy: He somehow likes to get fired up for you. You're an Iowa guy. He takes it personal." Gable continued, stressing techniques at length to Gilliss such as how to frustrate his opponent by underhooking his arm on a side that Maldonado didn't like underhooked.

Gable hadn't looked to see who McIlravy was wrestling. Now he looked. It was Jason Peters of East Stroudsburg (Pennsylvania) University. "Chances are he's got some wrestling background from that kind of school, but I'm not worried about him," Gable said. "But I am worried about getting some bonus points at 18, 26, and 34. And I'm looking for [them] right now. I mean, pin, that's great. But let's beat him good. Beat him solid the whole match." To Williams: "I already told you a little bit about your guy. I don't know him. Somebody told me—I can't remember—but they said he was a 'legger.' [A wrestler who extensively rode his opponent's legs.] Anyway, I'll find out right away what that loss [in the Big Ten finals] meant to you, or if I'm going to have to do something else to get you going. But I'm thinking the loss is going to . . . Inner peace? You know? You know some things make you feel better than others. Most of us, we don't like ourselves unless we wrestle well."

Gable told Hand to react quicker than he usually did when the referee warned him for stalling, because a penalty point might be close behind. He reminded Whitmer that if his opponent was riding him with a deep-waist lock—one arm cinched tightly around Whitmer's middle—the Iowa wrestler couldn't give in and be taken to his stomach on the mat. Whitmer had to build his base and fight out of it. "But that's not going to happen," Gable said, meaning that Whitmer would not let himself be forced to his stomach. "We've been too long, too many hours preparing to make those kinds of mistakes."

Gable's eyes swept the room. He saw Lee Fullhart staring into his folded hands, listening but thinking ahead to tomorrow. It still bothered Gable that his 190-pound All-American —counted on for bonus points and a title in the NCAA tournament—raised surrender flags in his 7–1 loss to Minnesota's Tim Hartung in the conference meet. "You don't put your head down [in a match]," Gable snapped. "You just don't do that. You just don't give up. You represent yourself. Sometimes our legs are tired and fatigue overtakes us. But it should not overtake us. No matter what. Ever."

And, lest anyone forget how low Iowa registered on some

people's respect-o-meters, Gable told of two encounters. "Main writer today. I couldn't believe it. Standing right there beside me at the social, and he, *Amateur Wrestling News*'s main writer, just goes, 'You can't beat Oklahoma State.' Just looked right at me and said that. I kind of looked at him, and he said, 'But I'm not so sure that [Oklahoma State 134-pounder] Steven Schmidt is going to be wrestling that well. I'm not so sure Hardell Moore is going to be wrestling that well. I'm not so sure [Mark] Smith is going to be wrestling well.' Is what he said. And he said, 'If they're wrestling like they're capable, you probably can't beat them.' "

Sneering sounds emanated from the audience, little nasal huffs of vitriol. Gable pressed on, the great motivator at work. "I was pissed about that. I'm still pissed about that." And who else should Gable run into today but Oklahoma coach Jack Spates, who in Gable's mind had diminished the Hawkeyes in his remarks. "Not that I confronted him. He confronted me," Gable recounted. "He saw me on my crutches, and he yelled some derogatory term to me, kiddingly. And I looked at him, and I didn't want to see him anyway, and I said, I just told him, 'Spates, you've been all over the papers here, and it hasn't been good.' "

Gable told his team to eat an early breakfast—he had food in his room, if they wanted—and then go back to bed and be ready to leave at 9:30 A.M. There would be a short meeting before they left. The meeting broke up at ten. The corridor was quiet, and so were ten Iowa wrestlers. Their real season had finally arrived.

chapter **14**

THE UNI-DOME ATMOSPHERE was everything
Dan Gable hoped for, and everything John Smith dreaded. The
first session on Thursday morning drew 14,520, an NCAA
opening-day record, remarkable because the field—330 wrestlers from 73 schools—was just starting to sort out. It was
such a vociferous, black-and-gold crowd that it started its own
cheers before the wrestling even began. From one side of the
arena to the other, fans volleyed and echoed, "*I! O! W! A!*"

The fans didn't need any more encouragement, but they
got it anyway. Ed Aliverti, the ubiquitous collegiate-wrestling
announcer with vocal cords as strong as elevator cable, began
his basso profundo examination of the subject at hand. "The
sport of wrestling had its origins fifteen thousand years ago, in
the dawn of man . . ." Aliverti, a dark and vibrant man who
probably wouldn't have to cut to make 126, then forged
through the wrestling careers of George Washington and Abra-
ham Lincoln and others, arriving, finally, at the present. Then
after the national anthem, Aliverti and his veteran announcing
sidekick Sandy Stevens—a UNI graduate married to a former
UNI heavyweight wrestler nicknamed "Bear"—called wrestlers to eight mats to begin the sixty-seventh NCAA tournament.

When the preliminary "rat-tails" were completed, Jessie Whitmer started the Iowa drive toward its third-straight national title. The 118-pound senior, seeded sixth, pressed the attack against unseeded José Enriquez of Brigham Young. Unlike the strong starts and weak finishes of his recent matches, Whitmer kept up the pressure throughout and took an easy 17-7 victory. When the match ended, Whitmer received a thunderous—and for the most part standing—ovation. It was so loud and sustained that late-arriving Iowa fans outside the UNI-Dome sensed immediately that Whitmer had won. Tom Brands and Jim Zalesky sat in his corner; Gable remained with the team in the end bleachers, three rows from the top.

From that high up, still on crutches, Gable hadn't planned to visit the arena floor unless the building—or Oklahoma State—caught fire. For a different reason, Kasey Gilliss managed to bring Gable down in thirty-seven seconds—that's how long it took for the redshirt freshman to execute a leg sweep on David Maldonado and pin him. Gilliss, following orders, locked up Maldonado with an arm underhook, and then delivered the leg sweep that had Maldonado dancing in air and crashing to the mat. The fastest pin in NCAA history is nine seconds, but Gilliss's first pin of the season had a sudden sweetness all its own. Brands pounded the seat of a chair in unabashed joy. Gable pointed to the crowd, rising and cheering wildly. TV minicams encircled Gilliss and moved with him, holy televison lights upon him. "Gable talked to us a lot about bonus points, and how we needed pins and big wins," Gilliss said. Gable, proud architect of the fall, had worked with Gilliss to uncork the leg sweep. "He's had it, he just hasn't used it," Gable said. "We told him it's there, use it. This is a big one."

Bob Siddens, Gable's high-school coach, came up and shook his old charge's hand, the former West Waterloo coach with his prized athlete. Everywhere Gable turned, he found old friends and family. Mack Gable was here, interrupting his routine of going to a fitness club and lifting weights. An old friend, Mike Narey, left his local business, where he made and reconditioned wrestling mats, to watch Gable and the Hawkeyes. Narey, plump and balding, had never wrestled, but was a wrestling fan. He knew Gable from Gable's Iowa State days, when the two lived in the same house with other wrestlers and paid twenty-five dollars a week in rent to Harold Nichols. Narey, who was Molly's godfather, was one of a handful of free spirits who counted themselves as Gable's friends. While he was never much of a reveler, Gable admitted a weakness for people who entertained him, made him laugh. Gable still told the story of the time that Narey, under the influence, took a cab to his mother's house and opened an unlocked door and fell asleep on the couch. He awoke to discover he had missed his mother's house by half a block.

On the dome floor, Gable went over to see Lincoln McIlravy, who scored a 24–8 technical fall over East Stroudsburg's Jason Peters. McIlravy needed stitches afterward over his left eye. Kristen Payne, watching from the entrance of the medical area, said he had not suffered a concussion. McIlravy and Joe Williams told reporters they needed to pull themselves away from distractions and wouldn't comment until after they were finished. Gable moved to another mat to watch Tony Ersland win a squeaker, 3–1, with a takedown in overtime. Craning over his crutches to see still elsewhere, Gable watched Lee Fullhart, seeded fifth and losing 2–0, rally to pin his unseeded opponent.

The session wrapped up with Wes Hand versus Jason Gleason. It was scoreless in the second period. Gable waved for the crowd to become involved in the match, but the response wasn't strong. After the two thrashed and stumbled out of bounds, Hand lay supine on the mat, injured. Trainers came out. Another stinger. Gleason didn't know what happened. "I saw him rubbing his arm, but I didn't make sense of it. We kind of got into a flurry, and next I know, he's calling time out." Hand continued and gave up a point. Gable shouted at Hand and motioned to the crowd again. More reaction this time. The match ended: Gleason 1, Hand 0. Hand walked off dejectedly, rubbing his aching right arm. The wrestler who couldn't let himself be injured was.

Hand was the only Hawkeye to drop into the consolation bracket after the first round. He would have company after the second round, when Gilliss, Mike Uker, and Ersland lost matches, by a total of four points, making four Hawkeyes losers by a combined total of five points. Gilliss had been tied 2–2 with Minnesota's Jason Davids with one minute left in the final period of their 142-pound match. Davids, seeded third, had beaten Gilliss two out of three times during the season, and was waltzing with Gilliss with twenty seconds left. Then Gilliss tried going out of bounds—a mistake, Gable said later. "When he jumped toward out of bounds, it created an opening for both legs. If he had stayed in, he could have possibly countered the takedown. Out of bounds seems like safety sometimes, but it's not, really." Whatever the case, Davids grabbed Gilliss's foot and hung on. "I saw a piece of his heel," Davids said. "And something in my mind kept saying I better not let go." He kept Gilliss in bounds and took him down, claiming a 4–2 victory. In the end bleachers, peering out from under his black Iowa cap, Gable slammed his fist down onto his right thigh. Davids was surprised that the crowd hadn't been as vocal in support of Gilliss as he thought it would be. The Minnesota wrestler thought that Gilliss's restraint on offense—he didn't dash off anything like the leg sweep that won him the first match—kept the crowd quiet. "Watch, when [Mark] Ironside and McIlravy go, there's a big contrast," Davids pointed out. "With those guys, the fall's the law. Crowds really like that. I was wrestling at the other end from those guys, and I could feel the vibrations from the crowd through the mat."

It was true. McIlravy and Ironside, along with Williams and Fullhart, were winning with big moves and scoring big points. After Thursday night's second round, they had four pins among them, two, by Williams, in the first period. Ironside and Fullhart each had a pin and a ten-point major decision. McIlravy won by sixteen and fifteen points for match-termination victories. The Hawkeyes sent six into Friday's quarterfinals, Oklahoma State seven. But Iowa led with 40.5 points, including 20 from bonus points. Half of those came from Iowa's five pins (including Gilliss's). Oklahoma State, scoring only one pin and 12 bonus points, held second with 27.5, while Minnesota, with four quarterfinalists, was third with 24.5. It was Gable's domination theory paying off, off-setting his team's fewer quarterfinalists with victories by pins or eight or more points.

John Smith asked how many Hawkeyes made the quarter-finals, and then was probably sorry he had. "Six? And we had seven. And we're behind by ten points. They got pins today. We didn't. There's quite a few bonus points—physical points —that can make a big difference. But they got them, you know? Maybe if we got them I would say it's the greatest thing in the world."

Smith suggested that Iowa had an easier draw than the Cowboys, a circumstance that paved the way for the Hawk-eyes' bonus victories. "There were some tough battles for us today, some very tough early matchups," Smith said. "We weren't put in a position to pick up many bonuses." It would have been a handy alibi for the top-ranked team in the country, trailing No. 2 in the national tournament, but there was more than a trace of truth in it: Oklahoma State wrestlers faced five seeded opponents in the first two rounds; Iowa wrestlers met three. Smith also discounted the meaning of the first two rounds. "The meet hasn't even started yet. These are just 'play' points. They're very important, obviously, but . . ."

Gable accepted the bonus points with thanks, but be-moaned the close losses that dropped four Hawkeyes into the consolations, or wrestle-backs. He had expected seven quarter-finalists, figuring that although Hand lost, at least one among Uker, Gilliss, and Ersland would advance. Uker's 12–11 loss to sixth-seeded Brandon Slay of the University of Pennsylvania particularly nettled Gable. In what J Robinson—and anyone with two eyes—called the best match of the evening, Uker bolted to a 5–0 lead, but Slay rallied to tie 8–8 in the third period, then 10–10 with forty-four seconds left. Slay got a takedown, then was penalized a point for locking his hands as the match ended. Earlier, Uker had nearly pinned Slay; Gable thought he had, and loudly proclaimed as much to the referee. Angrily walking without his crutches away from the mat, Gable fumed, "That one sixty-seven match was huge. He was pinned, I guarantee you." Later, leaving a press conference,

Gable passed the official in the corridor. "That was a big call. You missed it," Gable accused, and walked on.

In the van that returned the Iowa wrestlers to Waverly on Thursday night, Ironside turned to Whitmer, the fifth-year senior and quarterfinalist. "This is your last shot," Ironside said. "Balls to the wall. Leave everything out there on the mat."

Whitmer was warming up before his match on Friday morning when an anxious Gable supplied the plot line for the day. "Just from the seedings, we should win five of six," he said. "But we've got to win six of six." He nodded toward the mat where in a few minutes the sixth-seeded Whitmer would meet third-seeded David Morgan of Michigan State—the only quarterfinal in which a Hawkeye had a lower seeding than his opponent. Whitmer was 0–2 against Morgan, losing two entirely different matches within two weeks of each other around the start of the year. In the 118-pound finals at the Midlands, Morgan had ridden Whitmer like a stable pony but only won 1–0. Later, in a dual at East Lansing, Michigan, Morgan had opened up and rolled to an 18–7 major decision. This, their third meeting, would decide who would advance to Friday night's NCAA semifinals. Gable expected a tight contest. "[John] Smith likes his position," Gable said. "We've got to start winning one-point matches."

Aliverti's charged voice came over the public-address system. "Gentlemen, would you clear the mats, please." Another big crowd started the "I-O-W-A" chant. There was a moment of silence for Harold Nichols. The final note of the national anthem was still hanging in the air when the cry "Go Hawks!" flew toward the glowing white top of the UNI-Dome, chased by a cannonball of a cheer. Gable took his seat with his team in the stands. Whitmer clapped himself on each arm, shook hands with Morgan, and began the biggest match of his life.

Early on, Whitmer got a takedown, and led, 2–1, at the end of the first period. Suddenly, Gable appeared on the other side of ropes cordoning off the mats, and both he and Brands, jackknifed forward in a folding chair in Whitmer's corner, were yelling instructions at the Iowa wrestler. "When I saw him

[Gable], I knew I'd better pick it up," Whitmer said. "He doesn't come down for every match unless it's an important one." Presto: Whitmer got another takedown and led, 4–1. Gable gleefully pounded his crutches four times into the floor, but Morgan escaped twice and got a stalling call on Whitmer to tie it, 4–4, in the third period. Brands yelled through cupped hands, "Go, dang it!" With five seconds left in the period, Whitmer—who with more than a minute of riding time advantage actually led, 5–4—did what he had been unable to do in the Big Ten Championships: He finished as strong as he started, muscling Morgan to the mat. "He was moving from side to side," Whitmer recounted. "He must have been getting tired, because spit was flying out of his mouth, and I was loving it." Whitmer, finishing with a 7–4 victory, danced at the edge of the circle, his mouth open, his arms spread. Morgan knelt without moving, huddled into himself. Whitmer ran into Brands's arms and broke away, only to be ambushed by a cluster of reporters. Weary and out of breath, Whitmer drank deeply from a water bottle and gasped for words. It looked as if someone had turned a hose on him. Whitmer beamed. "Pretty good feeling, least so far," he said. "Just to get the team started off for the day—it's an important round. I felt I could do it. Give them a little fire."

And Whitmer did ignite something. The Hawkeyes began to win close matches. With seventeen seconds left in the tied third period of a 126-pound quarterfinal, Mike Mena scored a takedown on unseeded Terry Showalter of Lock Haven and was clamping on an arm bar and turning Showalter when time expired; Mena won, 3–1. Ironside, meanwhile, was having trouble against eighth-seeded Jeff Bucher of Ohio State. Ironside had pasted an 18–5 decision on Bucher in the finals of the Big Ten Championships, but this was an altogether different match. Ironside led, 8–1, with riding time, but then he began forcing outside shots, and Bucher worked his way back into the match. Bucher pulled off a takedown and near-fall, a five-point move that brought him to within 8–5 going into the third period of their 134-pound quarterfinal match. With momentum on his side, Bucher chose down and escaped to pull to within 8–6, then engineered a takedown to tie it, 8–8. Ironside escaped for a 9–8 lead, and Bucher called an injury timeout in the last minute. Gable hauled Ironside aside and slapped him, the first time he had done that to the wrestler. "He was shaking and muttering to me—hyper," Gable said. "He was wrestling the same way—way off. I just wanted to slow him down." In the final thirty seconds, Ironside steadied himself and nearly nailed a takedown as time expired in his 9–8 victory.

Good news continued winging Iowa's way. Gilliss, showing more offense, got a reversal and took a 6–2 lead into the second period en route to a 17–7 victory in the 142-pound consolations. Aliverti announced that after the 150-pound matches, Iowa led with 57.5 points, followed by Oklahoma State (43.5), Minnesota (35.3), and Iowa State (31). Slowly, the Hawkeyes were inching away. Then, an unheralded wrestler from Lehigh (Pennsylvania) University named John Van Doren pulled the upset of the tournament, hastening the Cowboys' demise: With the UNI-Dome erupting, Van Doren, a sophomore, executed a takedown in the final twenty seconds and beat Oklahoma State's top-seeded Mark Smith, 10–9, in the 177-pound quarterfinals. It was 12:45 P.M. on March 21, but for Iowa fans, it felt like New Year's Eve. Van Doren left Smith kneeling on the mat and in shock, received a standing ovation from people who would be hardpressed to name the state in which his school was located. Even during the match, Van Doren recognized he was becoming as popular in Iowa as pickup trucks. "It was like fifteen or twenty thousand people yelling—yeah, it felt good. It was enjoyable. It helped."

As Friday wore on, it was becoming apparent that Iowa had arrived at a familiar place, when coaches conceded a title a day ahead of the finals. "It's a battle for third, fourth, and fifth now," J Robinson said. "Oklahoma State has really been hurt by tough draws. Then it's hard to lose a couple like they did that they didn't expect to lose." Robinson had seen it before, been part of it before: Iowa would catch a spark and ignite, and it always happened in tournaments, and always because of Gable.

Iowa's momentum carried into the consolation bracket. Uker won, 5–4, after getting a pin in his previous match. The crowd chanted, "Uke! Uke! Uke!" as he waved. On an adjoining mat, Ersland polished off an 8–4 victory, which Gable lingered to watch. Meanwhile, Royce Alger stood and watched Hand's match, shouting, "re-shot, re-shot," explaining that, "Hand is real good shooting when people shoot at him." Hand, shaking off his stinger, won 8–4. Forty-five minutes later, Hand trailed, 5–0, in another consolation bout. He slapped himself in the face, although any Iowa coach would happily have obliged. A takedown in the second period brought him to within 6–5. Entering the third period, Hand had the choice of which position he wanted to start from. Zalesky signaled him to start on his feet. Fifteen seconds later, Hand took Pat Schuster of Edinboro (Pennsylvania) University to the mat and pinned him. "No way! No way!" Schuster groaned and began swearing, convinced he had fought it off. But his words were drowned in the wave of cheering. Gable, playing to the crowd again, flashed ten fingers, then four. Iowa had reeled off fourteen straight victories and was in control heading into the evening's semifinals. "First time I realized how many we'd won in a row. Right now," he said.

And it wasn't over yet.

Up stepped Whitmer again, this time in the semifinals. He had never been a starter at Iowa before this season, and he never would be again. This was his first NCAA tournament. Yet in this, his senior year, he had turned into a leader. He believed in himself as much as Gable always had. "They could throw anybody in there, and I'd be comfortable," Whitmer declared. The match was doubly important because Whitmer would have a chance to knock an Oklahoma State Cowboy— second-seeded Teague Moore—out of the championship round.

Thirty seconds into the match, Whitmer scored a takedown, then another and a third. The last one came when he wrapped up Moore in a bear hug and dropped him, in the Greco style. It was 6–3, Whitmer. But then Moore, who had beaten Whitmer 8–5 in the National Duals, stormed back to within 8–7. Gable, in the bleachers, twitched and worried. The crowd noise grew like an approaching locomotive. Whitmer responded with a takedown in the final two seconds to earn a 10–7 victory and a finals berth. Now the UNI-Dome was as loud as two locomotives, as Whitmer joyfully flung his arms open, the huge arms that had encircled Moore and carried the Cowboy to his doom, and acknowledged the cheers. "I swear," Whitmer said, "I didn't want to go back to the corner if I'd lost, because the [coaches] would rip my arms off. They'll love me to death, but still I think they'd rip my arms off just because I was going real good, and if I had ended up losing they would have been upset."

Ironside and Fullhart and the other Hawkeyes, loosening up on the warm-up mat behind curtains on the UNI-Dome floor, stated that they heard the outburst and knew Whitmer had won and felt an extra spurt of adrenalin. *Fifteen straight, and counting* . . . Mena, who had lost twice in the NCAA semifinals, squeezed through this time with a 4–3 victory over Iowa State's top-ranked Dwight Hinson. "It's just about time is all I can say," Mena said. "I mean, I should have won a couple [championships] already, you know?" *Sixteen and counting* . . . Ironside, composed and resolute again, advanced, winning 8–4. "Tons of people have doubted us all along. That Ron Good of *Amateur Wrestling News* says we're going to lose by forty points. I guess that's their prerogative. But they're not in the room. They're not under Coach Gable." *Seventeen and counting* . . .

Gable slipped over to watch Gilliss, who was coming off his second pin in the tournament, recorded in his previous consolation match. "He wins this, he's an All-American," Gable said. "But he's got to control the 'ties' [tie-ups], and get his hands on him. This guy can shoot." Gilliss and eighth-seeded Brett Matter of Penn headed into sudden-death overtime tied at 2. Gilliss shot from the outside and decked Matter to take a 4–2 victory. Gable raised a crutch jubilantly. *Eighteen and counting* . . . McIlravy defeated Minnesota's Chad Kraft 9–3 and advanced into the finals for the fourth time in his career, as did Oklahoma State's Branch at 167. It was the first time since McIlravy returned to the lineup—a string of six matches —that he had not scored a bonus-point victory. Kraft, who in the Big Ten Championships had offered himself up as a bonus-point sacrifice to McIlravy, marveled at the two-time national champion. "The thing about him, he's hard to set up and shoot against," Kraft observed after their 150-pound semifinal. "He's moving around so much. Always moving his hands. So tough. His technique isn't great, but he knows how to move and set up a shot. At this level, it's hard to handle his pace of wrestling." *Nineteen and counting . . .*

Joe Williams followed at 158 and, like Whitmer, sent a Cowboy semifinalist into the sunset. The top-seeded and once-beaten Williams stopped fifth-seeded Hardell Moore, 8–3. Gable was stupefied. "I can't believe this," he said, weaving in and out of pedestrian traffic to watch matches and accept congratulations. "Williams is so quick he's unbelievable." Just as Gable had hoped, the team was wrestling consistently, 118 through heavyweight, the best saved for last. "I was rounding a corner, and the guy that was wrestling the Iowa guy was flying through the air somewhere," Gable said, awestruck. "We've hit some really big moves that have put people—*boom!* I don't know where they come up with those all of a sudden." *Twenty and counting . . .*

Uker, who along with Ersland had been a different wrestler since the Big Ten Championships, defeated eighth-seeded John Dattalo of Virginia Tech, 6–4, to reach the consolation quarterfinals. For the second straight year, Uker was an All-American, guaranteed.

Twenty-one . . .

Now Mark Smith, the former top seed at 177, the coach's kid brother, began his consolation match against Ersland, un-seeded, a victory away from an All-American certificate in his senior season. Ersland knew a secret to his success, besides the long hours of individual sessions in the wrestling room. "I wrestle well in tournaments, like the Midlands, the Big Tens, nationals," he said. "The deal is, when I have just one match, in a dual meet, I think too much. I spend too much time burning energy, worrying. I'm a nervous wreck. I end up in the third period feeling like my legs are gone. No way should a guy who trains in the Iowa room feel that tired. But in tournaments I feel comfortable. 'Cause I'm on the mat every hour or every other hour. I'm wrestling, eating, resting, getting back on the mat again. I don't have time to get worried." Against Smith, Ersland's outstanding wrestling continued, but the streak didn't. Smith won in sudden-death overtime, 5–3. The crowd stilled. Ersland was crestfallen. "People say I did better than I did all year. But I'm not happy I fell short." Gable gathered both his crutches in his left hand and swung his right arm around Ersland. A few weeks before, Ersland took personally the Oklahoma coach's remark that there were holes in the Iowa lineup. Gable would suggest at a press conference after the Friday session that, to the contrary, Ersland wasn't a hole in anybody's lineup.

Lee Fullhart completed the Hawkeyes' parade of six into Saturday night's finals by beating Edinboro's Jason Robison, 10–3. The crowd rose as one. Gable turned to his adoring public and flexed a bicep. Fullhart hugged Payne as he left the mat, and said, in effect, take *that, Amateur Wrestling News.* "They said we couldn't make it. That's why we did it," Fullhart panted.

By winning their first twenty-one matches Friday, the Hawkeyes had clinched the NCAA Division I wrestling title for the third straight season, sixth of the last seven and fifteenth in Gable's twenty-one years as coach. Through the quarterfinals and semifinals, they had expanded their lead over Oklahoma State from 25.5 to 60.5 points. With one day remaining, the Hawkeyes, with 148 points, were threatening to smash their own NCAA records for team points (158) and margin of victory (73.25), both set in 1986. The six finalists— Whitmer, Mena, Ironside, McIlravy, Williams, and Fullhart— tied Iowa's NCAA record set in 1986 and 1991. If all six won titles on Saturday night, it would break the tournament record of five set by Iowa in 1986. One record beyond reach was the number of All-Americans: Iowa had eight—Hand, still struggling with injuries, and Ersland each wound up a victory short—but the most was nine, which Iowa had in six different years.

Gable couldn't remember a better day for Iowa at an NCAA tournament—fourteen straight in one stretch, twenty-one for the day, twenty-three over two days, another tournament record. "It's amazing that we could do something like this—to surprise the coach and everybody else—because we've done so much in our history the last two or three decades," Gable said. "Not only winning, but how we won. Dominating a lot of scores, and pinning and majoring and just creating upsets that people would never imagine." He thanked his coaches—Brands and Zalesky and Alger—who filled in for him during the season. He thanked the good people of Cedar Falls and Waterloo for bringing off the tournament in the structure where the University of Northern Iowa plays football. "You kind of look at my history. It's Waterloo, Ames, and Iowa City. And I think that's real crucial, the whole environment, because that's where all the fans are and this is my home. It's very special. Very special."

But Gable wouldn't release all his feelings. As usual, he held something back, hoarding some of himself for the job ahead. Eight Iowa wrestlers were still wrestling in the national tournament, six in the finals. He had to make sure they had every chance to win. For Gable, one of the worst parts of the job was remembering the Iowa wrestlers who fell just short of an NCAA title as he sat during their matches just a few feet away, unable to do anything about it. It was no accident that Gable vividly recalled Jim Heffernan's loss in the 1987 semifinals, no accident because it had never left his mind. He remembered Mike DeAnna, too: An Ohioan of immense ability, DeAnna twice failed in the finals at the beginning of the 1980s —once, Gable was convinced, because he popped too many M&Ms, became hyperglycemic, and lost stamina. ("I still hurt because of that. He pooped out. It shouldn't have happened.") Maybe Gable had taken one final lesson from the Owings match of 1970—knowledge of how it felt to lose the biggest, most public match of your life.

"The tournament isn't over," Gable said. "I've got a lot

of kids that want to do a lot of things, so I've got to stay focused. I can't, as a coach, sit back and feel comfortable, even if we won the tournament. It's something that a lot of kids' individual goals are still on the line, and that's a big thing to me. The thing is, a defeat sometimes can overtake even a championship."

Oklahoma State coach John Smith, virtually assured of second place, had three wrestlers in the finals: Eric Guerrero, who would meet Mena for the 126-pound title; Steven Schmidt, set to face Ironside at 134; and Mark Branch, who would take on Penn's Brandon Slayer—who knocked Uker out of the championship bracket—for the 167-pound crown. Oklahoma State, with a few exceptions, had wrestled well enough to remain within striking distance in most national tournaments. But not now, not in Iowa, with the Hawkeyes charged not only by newspaper clippings but by Gable's possible retirement.

Smith had done all he could to prepare his team for the noise levels of the UNI-Dome, and still it wasn't enough. "Two full days of that support out there definitely got them on a roll," he said. "But you've got to give credit to their team, to their effort, to coach Gable. Had them well prepared. Won some big matches . . . It was really an outstanding performance by that squad."

Gable put in a twenty-hour day on Saturday. At 11 A.M., in the consolation semifinals, he watched Gilliss lose for the second time in the tournament and the fourth time this season to Minnesota's Jason Davids, 7–3. Unseeded, Gilliss finished sixth in the country at 142, with a 5–2 record and two pins in the tournament. Like most Iowa wrestlers, Gilliss wanted more, felt short-changed. Gable watched him stalk off the mat and throw his headgear against a wall. When Gilliss's frustration and anger dissipated, Gable talked quietly with the redshirt freshman, telling him that he had made good progress and outlining what could be in store the next three years. "He's sixth in the nation, but if he wants to go up from there, he's still got things to learn," Gable explained, striking a familiar theme with Gilliss. "He's got big moves and great skills, but not some basic skills you need to catch people. If he had all the skills he needed, he'd be first, not sixth. It's just [a question of] if he heard me, what I was saying. I don't know."

Iowa's finalists quietly filed through a rear curtain, warmed up, and left. The crowd of 15,000 fired up its "Uke! Uke! Uke!" chant one last time for Uker, who finished his collegiate career as a two-time All-American with a 6–2 victory over Arizona State's Casey Strand for fifth place at 167. Gable quoted the result to his finalists, building a fire for Saturday night.

At 5 P.M., several Iowa wrestlers stood in the second-floor hallway of the Red Fox Inn, waiting for the team meeting. Gilliss stood against one wall, bouncing a racquetball against the other wall. Uker, walking past, intercepted and hurled the ball down the distant stairs. He turned to Gilliss and smiled. "Yours?" he innocently asked.

Gable, in a suit, white shirt, and brown-print tie, called the meeting to order. The entire team was present, except for the late-arriving Mena. It was like most of Gable's speeches to the team during the season—and then again, it wasn't. He gave the scouting reports, described which of the three positions the Iowa wrestler should choose, and summarized how each of his athletes had wrestled. But this time it wasn't business as usual; there were national titles in the balance. In the dimming afternoon light filtering through thin, half-open curtains, a sense of tension and anticipation spread through the room.

Gable started with Whitmer, sitting in a chair near the window. "I just want you to know, this guy isn't [David] Morgan on top," Gable said. "He isn't even the last guy [Moore]. If I remember right, you escaped from him at the Midlands." Whitmer had beaten Illinois's Durlacher twice but lost to him in the conference championships. Gable reminded Whitmer that he had had Durlacher in deep trouble, on his back, three or four times. And Gable remembered something else: "He's been bad-mouthing you pretty bad. I don't know if you saw it. Did you hear about it? He just said that you did real bad at the Big Tens, so that means you're not good enough to be here, to beat him, basically." And finally, "You've been the spark plug for us the last couple of nights. These guys are going to do whatever they're going to do anyway, but you've helped a lot, so let's continue that way."

Mena finally slipped in, nearly ten minutes late for the most important team meeting of the year. He was inscrutable to the end. He arrived just in time to hear Gable say: "OK. Twenty-six. Your game plan was good yesterday, and you're the one that came up with it. Pretty much controlled him, but then you started going defensive ... I don't think this guy [Oklahoma State's Eric Guerrero] can beat you. Can beat you at all. Stay tough and stay in there taking your shots, riding tough."

To Ironside, facing the Cowboys' Steven Schmidt: "He's not that physical. He shoots, but he's not been looking very good. But he's been winning. He's a roller. He can scramble pretty good. But you're a better scrambler. You've got to be on him and don't ever let him shoot. You've got to be on him when you're setting up your stuff. You've got to have him so ragged that he can't stand up—not even in the first period. Then he'll be yours, yours for the picking."

McIlravy would face Iowa State's Chris Bono, against whom he was 4–0 in his career. Watch his go-behind after he shoots for a leg, Gable instructed. Don't let up at the edge of the mat. McIlravy and Bono hadn't met in the last Iowa–Iowa State dual, when McIlravy was still out of the lineup. "Got to show him you're for real," Gable said. "See, he's coming out, hoping to win, and he's hoping that you're not quite as tough, but you're going to show him that you're tougher than ever." Gable surveyed the room. "All of you guys. You're going to show them you're tougher than ever."

Williams's turn. The defending 158-pound champion sat propped against a headboard, in yellow warmups, next to McIlravy. Usually, Joe Williams's expression betrayed no emotion. Now he plainly looked stressed, even worried. He would face Edinboro's Tony Robie in about three hours. Williams had beaten Robie, 6–2, in the 1994 Midlands. "I already told you a little bit about him," Gable said. "Try to use power. He's scared of you, but he'd love to slow you down and just have a one-move match or something . . . I really like it when you create emotion. I mean, Hardell Moore didn't know where you were coming from. You really were quick and you exploded and you knew you had to be, and that's the same way you've got to be tonight."

Fullhart sat on the floor between the beds, his legs apart, easing out the kinks. He would face Oklahoma senior John Kading (24–1), the defending NCAA champion at 190. Kading had missed a month with a bruised hip, and in February he suffered a torn anterior cruciate ligament in his right knee during a match. He wore a knee brace and wrestled five days later; he was scheduled for reconstructive surgery on the knee forty-eight hours after the tournament. His only loss was to Michigan State's Brian Picklo, in a double-overtime tiebreaker. Kading had never wrestled Fullhart (25–4), and Gable did not want Fullhart to be a Molly Putz. "Don't let that brace be a factor," Gable said. "That may be the lead leg, the right leg. You shoot to that leg quite a bit. That's OK. Take it even if it does hurt him. He's been faking a little bit. We've talked about it. We think he kind of wants the referee and his [teammates] to kind of feel sorry for him a little bit. I saw him practicing and warming up. He's moving, moving, moving. He mostly just steps in with that leg and both hands. He likes to stay in." Gable stressed the importance of positioning, of Fullhart imposing his offense on Kading—injured knee or not. "Don't let that leg slow you down in any way. If he gets in there and starts yelling stuff, that's his tough luck."

Class was dismissed. The graduate exam would begin at seven P.M.

chapter **15**

O<small>N</small> S<small>ATURDAY</small> <small>NIGHT</small> a roaring, NCAA-record crowd of 17,436 jammed the UNI-Dome one last time. Dan Gable lined up at one end of the floor—and not because he couldn't find a seat. He would take a brief part in the grand march of former NCAA champions, a group of well over 100 that ranged from Verne Gagne, the former University of Minnesota heavyweight who was one of the first "good guys" of big-time professional wrestling, to the tournament's only four-time champion, Pat Smith. Every year was represented, except for the years during World War II when the tournament was suspended. The All-Americans from this year's tournament marched and took their places on the elevated mat that would be used for the finals. There they were, all eighty of them, some in street clothes, the finalists in their warm-up suits. Two heads popped above the rest, appearing and disappearing, appearing and disappearing: Mike Mena and Mark Ironside were doing jumping jacks.

Then it was time for Jessie Whitmer to face Lindsey Durlacher on a platform under bright lights that made them performers as well as athletes. Tom Brands gave Whitmer his final instructions, Gable shook his hand, and Whitmer ran to the center of the mat, flapping his arms like a barnyard chicken. In the first thirty seconds, Whitmer took Durlacher down. Gable stripped out of his coat and yelled encouragement. Durlacher escaped, but Whitmer got another takedown as the first period closed. Whitmer 4, Durlacher 1. In the second period, after Durlacher took him down, Whitmer escaped to lead, 5–3. Gable was right: Durlacher couldn't hold him on top. Durlacher, choosing down in the third period, closed to 5–4. Gable raised his fists. "C'mon! C'mon!" he yelled, as Whitmer held on for a 5–4 victory. A senior first-time starter had won the 118-pound national title. Deafening crowd noise crashed like a boulder down at Whitmer. He danced and pranced and blew kisses to his parents and brother and sister in section E, row twenty. Gable shot his right arm in the air. "Strongest man in the world!" he bellowed toward the crowd. Whitmer embraced Tom Brands and then, on the way to the media interview room, hugged Terry Brands.

Each day of the tournament, Whitmer had won and started an avalanche of Iowa victories. But tonight it was different, as Mike Mena stepped in against Eric Guerrero. The team race was settled, but there was still pressure on Mena to beat an Oklahoma State wrestler.

The match was tied 2–2 at the end of regulation, a defensive struggle in which Guerrero had an escape and a stalling point, and Mena riding time and a stalling point. A two-minute, sudden-death overtime ended scoreless. Before the thirty-second, sudden-death tiebreaker, Mena won the flip and chose top. He already had earned a point for riding Guerrero for 1:11 in the second period. What were thirty more seconds? If neither wrestler scored in the overtime, the offensive wrestler—Mena—would be declared the winner. Gable let Mena make his own choice, figuring that he had earned the right in a match this big. "And I didn't want him carrying a chip on his shoulder if he lost," Gable said. In fact, Gable was leaning toward having Mena, or any Iowa wrestler, take the bottom position. "In a thirty-second period, nobody should hold you in a national championship," Gable said. "Which doesn't mean they wouldn't."

Guerrero dropped to all fours, and Mena dropped to one

knee and put his near arm around his opponent. The referee
blew his whistle. Guerrero bucked away from Mena and stood
and turned toward him for an escape and a 3–2 victory. Mena
had made an uncharacteristic error for an Iowa wrestler in a
championship final: Instead of staying glued to Guerrero's side,
he allowed Guerrero to jump in front of him, and he lost him.
Lost the match.

Without expression, Mena stood beside the referee, who
raised Guerrero's arm. Gable slapped Mena on the back as he
left the mat and gave him a long look. Mena joined ten other
Hawkeyes who were four-time All-Americans; only one other
—Mike DeAnna—had never won a title. In the corridor leading to the locker room, Mena threw an elbow, hard, into the
pop machine and slapped his headgear against the wall before
he disappeared.

Ironside knew what happened to Mena, and he used it for
motivation. He wouldn't let a loss happen to him. Besides, he
explained, "I wasn't going to let another Okie win out there."
Ironside's grandfather lay ill with cancer in a hospital bed in
Cedar Rapids. KXIC technicians from Iowa City rigged a radio
so that he could hear Adams's broadcast of his grandson's
134-pound final. Ironside, the unbeaten junior, had four takedowns and 3:08 in riding time en route to a 10–4 victory that
wasn't quite perfect: He wanted at least a 12–4 margin, a major
decision. But he'd take this. With one year left, Ironside was a
three-time All-American. On his bedroom wall, Ironside had
hung a picture from his loss last year in the NCAA semifinals.
Now the picture could come down. "I might bring it out some-
time if I get in a slump—and not just in wrestling," he said.

After the 150 final, it was Lincoln McIlravy's turn. Feeling
pressure and "wrestling tight," McIlravy scored a takedown
with thirty-seven seconds left in the two-minute overtime to
reclaim his title from Bono, 5–3. McIlravy, who finished his
second unbeaten season, ran his career record to 96–3 and
was named the meet's outstanding wrestler. Afterward, the
father-to-be lobbied for an assistant's job at Iowa, citing
Zalesky and Brands: "Seems like they like the three-time champions to stick around and coach. . . . I'd like to stick around in

some capacity." McIlravy spoke of Gable as if Gable had already resigned, as if their differences had never happened—or if they had, as if he was sorry about it. "He's got the pressure of ten guys," McIlravy said. "I'm just one. I try my best not to pressure him anymore. But he wants us to win probably as much or more than we want to win, if you can believe it. And that just takes an unbelievable toll on you. He just cares so much . . . He's given an unbelievable amount of his life to our athletes, and I'm just really appreciative of that."

Like McIlravy, Joe Williams wrestled cautiously, but still pulled off two takedowns and successfully defended his title with a 5–3 victory over Edinboro's Tony Robie. After all but explicitly saying he was dedicating the match to Gable, Williams stood on the top step of the awards platform; when his name was announced and the applause grew, Williams, imperturbable to the end, raised his right fist to chin level, shook it twice, and lowered it.

Fullhart, in his 190-pound final, saw immediately that he didn't have to shoot on Kading's right knee to weaken it. As he attempted to throw Fullhart in the first period, Kading felt the knee buckle and he backed off. Despite that, Kading, a barrel-chested blond, held a 3–1 lead at the end of the second period. Fullhart's escape late in the third period pulled him to 3–2, and constant pressure by the Iowan, combined with Kading's injuries and conditioning, brought a stalling call against the Oklahoma wrestler with ten seconds left in the third period. They went 3–3 through the first overtime. In the second sudden-death overtime, Fullhart won the flip, chose down, and quickly escaped for a 4–3 victory, dethroning the defending champion and giving the Hawkeyes their fifth individual champion—two won in overtime—and a record NCAA total of 170 points. Oklahoma State finished second with 113.5 points—18.75 more points than when the Cowboys last won the title three years before—and two champions. Minnesota placed third with 71 points and no champions, while Iowa State was fourth with 70 and one champion.

Gable had ridden a roller coaster such as he had seldom seen in his twenty-one years of coaching. Up and down. Winning the Midlands but losing a family friend in a highway accident. Undergoing hip surgery but feeling good enough to traverse the floor of Williams Arena sans crutches. Losing to Oklahoma State but beating the Cowboys when it mattered. All within a few miles of his boyhood home. All with a team that jelled precisely when it had to.

Crutchless, Gable took his team onto the mat for the last time, to accept the winner's trophy before the screaming Iowa fans. Siddens, silver-maned mentor of Gable and several other NCAA All-Americans and national champions from Waterloo West, was the presenter. The two men embraced. "You're the best I ever had, and Iowa is still the best," Siddens told Gable "Now the whole world knows it."

When he had limped down the stairs to the arena floor, Gable was engulfed by reporters and fans wanting autographs. Six-deep they stood. Eventually, Gable found a chair and table and sat for forty-five minutes answering questions and signing his name.

"It'll make my decision harder, what took place here," he admitted. "I'd said this meet wouldn't have a big influence, but I don't know, when you win like this . . . And it'll be tough not to come back and coach three national champions." (Actually, four: Ironside, Williams, and Fullhart, plus the redshirted Jeff McGinness, who had won at 126 in 1995.)

Twenty feet away, Mackie Gable kicked a crumpled paper cup, waiting for her father to finish so that they could return to the motel and celebrate with fans and the team. She did a small, playful, private pirouette, and allowed her father to savor what might be his last official act as coach of the University of Iowa wrestling team.

Afterword

GABLE SPENT a well ordered and busy spring and summer. He and his family went on a ten-day Florida vacation after the national tournament. Upon his return, Gable helped coach Lincoln McIlravy, Terry Brands, and others in the Hawkeye Wrestling Club who were training for the big freestyle meets that establish the top world and national rankings. He hit the I-Club circuit and worked his camps. He met three times with Bob Bowlsby about his future. The Iowa men's athletic director had expressed confidence at the NCAA tournament that he could convince Gable to stay as coach: "I'd be shocked if he wasn't back—just from what I'm hearing from people around him," Bowlsby then maintained.

But Gable listens more than he talks, and some may misinterpret his quiet for consent. He was a wolf, after all, watching, watching. And thinking. The more time that separated him from the NCAA tournament, the more he favored quitting. Gable compared his situation to that of a recruited athlete, who in the first heady days of talking with the coach and visting the school thought that he had found the ideal situation, but then realized that he was viewing a dream world that existed only in his mind.

To be sure, many aspects of coaching—even apart from

winning—touched and tantalized him. He remembered talking with Tony Ersland halfway through the season. Ersland had been upset. Everything else was going so well in his life; his grades were good, and he planned to get married in the summer to his high-school sweetheart. Why couldn't he bring his wrestling under control and finish his career with a flourish? he asked achingly, tearfully. Gable helped him, worked with him, and at the end, while Ersland fell short of his All-American goal, Ersland knew he had done all he could to try to make it come true. And, in a different tone, there was Jessie Whitmer. Gable saw him padding around before the NCAA final without shoes or socks, and noticed he had red toenails. Whitmer explained that his girlfriend had painted them, at his request: "I look at them, and I get fired up looking at red," Whitmer said.

But coaching also meant watching Mike Mena, like Sisyphus, nearly push the boulder to the top of the hill, only to have it roll back down. It also meant time away from Kathy and the four girls. One of them, Annie, was about to leave home for college, headed to the University of Kansas in the fall to study journalism. Of the girls, she was the one who most resembled Diane Gable in appearance and mien, with her short brownish hair and vibrancy and independence. Gable and his wife were protective parents, doubly so because of memories of Diane. They warned their girls to be wary of strangers and never to hitchhike; through the years, they put them on the school bus each morning in front of their mailbox and sat in the old wooden porch swing and watched until the bus lurched out of sight. Dan and Kathy Gable did everything and went everywhere with them. Just before Annie's graduation from City High, Gable interrupted a heavy speaking schedule in Cedar Rapids to drive forty-five minutes back to Iowa City to attend an all-school assembly honoring Annie and other seniors. "I worry about her. She's fearless," Gable said, sitting behind the wheel. "But I've got to let her go away. I won't try to stop her. It's not fair to hold her back."

Kathy didn't think that her husband was getting the enjoyment he once did from coaching. Gratification, yes; fun, no. Gable disagreed. "That's not true. But maybe it's the other factors in my life, the things that happened that put things in perspective. Like going back to the death of my sister—so many deaths. Like the Mitchell family getting in a car wreck and losing a mom. I mean, the pain of losing is nowhere near the pain of losing someone."

Gable's mother died a hard death three years before, from cancer that spread through her body to her face. She received chemotherapy treatments at University Hospitals. After Mack had a stroke and couldn't bring her, she drove to Iowa City and back by herself. She seldom complained of pain. Bowlsby once visited her at University Hospitals after she had undergone throat and jaw surgery. He saw her standing in the doorway of her room, attached to an IV pole on wheels. She held a washcloth to her wounded mouth. She removed the washcloth, and she was . . . *smiling.*

Katie was the one who convinced her son to retire from competitive wrestling although he was drifting in that direction anyway. In 1975, when he was an assistant coach at Iowa, Gable entered the Northern Open in Madison, Wisconsin, and lost 7–6 to Lee Kemp, a future three-time national and five-time world champion. Gable had a neck injury and little strength in his right arm, but he wrestled anyway. Narey, his friend from Iowa State, sat with Kathy. Gable asked Narey what he thought, and Narey said, "You sure didn't look like the same guy that I used to see." To which Gable replied, "You know, I can deal with getting beat. What I don't like dealing with is what everybody is going to say to me." To himself, Gable thought, "This don't feel right."

But it was Katie who had had enough. The loss didn't do it; the injuries and surgeries did. She told her son to quit wrestling, that every time he got hurt it hurt her as well. And so he left behind his gold medal and his 181 straight victories in high school and college, and plunged into coaching. He was never sorry. It was all-consuming, coaching was, because it wasn't just himself he was responsible for, it was an entire team, a challenge worth undertaking for someone with Gable's competitive nature. When he replaced Gary Kurdelmeier in 1977 and Iowa subsequently lost two straight years to Iowa State,

Gable felt just as mortified as he would have if the Hawkeyes had lost to Oklahoma State. As he told Barry Davis when Davis wondered how he would handle coaching against Gable and the University of Iowa, a true coach immersed himself so deeply in his job and in his wrestlers that all such questions became unimportant.

Nevertheless, Gable's health and family, plus the near-misses of wrestlers like Mena, led Gable in June to decide to step down. He knew that Katie would have approved. As a gesture to Bowlsby, Gable agreed to call his departure a leave of absence, and to work as an adviser in the men's athletic department, on call as a speaker or a consultant to athletes and coaches. Jim Zalesky would become the interim head coach, Tom Brands would move up to top assistant, Terry Brands would take over as second assistant, and Lincoln McIlravy would slip into the volunteer-coaching slot; Gable might only work part-time. Bowlsby asked Gable to devote more time and attention to taking care of himself, so that he could heal and think about coaching again. And at the end of one year, if he felt well enough, had the itch badly enough, Gable had only to tell Bowlsby and the director would happily, thankfully, put him back in charge.

But Gable wasn't thinking along those lines. "Somewhere I got to make a break," he said one evening in a small country restaurant outside Iowa City. "I don't know how, but I've got to do it." Not that it would be easy. "It hit me hard in our last [home] dual, the Arizona State dual. I walked out on my crutches, and I was thinking this would be it. And [at the NCAAs] when my high-school coach gave me the trophy, it [coaching] crossed my mind again. And I have to change those thoughts. I get too emotional too easy. This [stepping down] is something I need to do, for my health and for my family."

The formal announcement of the changes came in mid-July. Gable arrived just before 10 A.M. for the press conference at Carver-Hawkeye. A photographer from the Iowa City paper took his picture entering the building. Gable rode the elevator to the third floor and walked into a room crowded with the media and their cables and cameras and microphones. Kathy, wearing black culottes and a black sleeveless top, sat with her daughters in a line of folding chairs at the side of the room. At a long table draped in front and back with black, Gable sat flanked by Bowlsby and Zalesky. In the funereal decor and ambience, the three confirmed what had already been in the papers: Gable out, Zalesky in, until further notice.

Gable, hobbling noticeably, looked ashen and uncomfortable. He moved stiffly and hesitantly across the keyboard of his decision, playing the requisite notes of why he was leaving and thanking everyone and supporting Zalesky. Bowlsby remarked that he was sitting next to greatness, and that for personal and professional reasons he didn't want to lose Gable. Bowlsby's voice tightened with decorum. Of course, he said, under NCAA rules, Gable—filling the newly created position of assistant to the director for sports operations—must "keep an arm's length relationship" with the wrestling coaches and team, although it was expected that he would work with the Hawkeye Wrestling Club.

A little while later, Gable said, "Wrestling has been a way of life with me, day in and day out. I won't get too far away from it. I might walk through the wrestling room once a week. I could go every day if I wanted. But just walk through. Make sure it's still there."

And for a moment, his words seemed to hang and float in the air, visible, like the message on a streamer stretching from the tail of an airplane passing overhead and out of sight.

I might walk through the wrestling room once a week. . . . I could go through every day if I wanted. . . . But just to walk through. . . . Make sure it's still there. . . .

Index